About CROP

CROP, the Comparative Research Programme on Poverty, is a
response from the academic community to the problem of poverty.
The programme was initiated in 1992, and the CROP Secretariat was
officially opened in June 1993 by the director-general of UNESCO,
Dr Federico Mayor.

In recent years, poverty alleviation, reduction or even eradication
and abolition of poverty has moved up the international agenda,
and the CROP network is providing research-based information
to policy-makers and others responsible for poverty reduction.
Researchers from more than a hundred countries have joined the
CROP network, with more than half coming from so-called developing countries and countries in transition.

The major aim of CROP is to produce sound and reliable knowledge that can serve as a basis for poverty reduction. This is done by
bringing together researchers for workshops, co-ordinating research
projects and publications, and offering educational courses for the
international community of policy-makers.

CROP is multi-disciplinary and works as an independent non-
profit organization.

For more information you may contact:

CROP Secretariat, Nygårdsgaten 5
N-5020 Bergen, Norway
tel: +47-5558-9739   fax: +47-5558-9745
e-mail: crop@uib.no
CROP on the Internet: http://www.crop.org

CROP is a programme under the International Social Science
Council (which has also helped finance this publication).

CROP publications

Poverty: Research Projects, Institutes, Persons, Tinka Ewoldt-Leicher and Arnaud F. Marks (eds), Tilburg, Bergen, Amsterdam, 1995, 248 pp.

Urban Poverty: Characteristics, Causes and Consequences, David Satterthwaite (ed.), special issue on Environment and Urbanization, Volume 7, No. 1, April 1995, 283 pp.

Urban Poverty: From Understanding to Action, David Satterthwaite (ed.), special issue on Environment and Urbanization, Volume 7, No. 2, October 1995, 266 pp.

Women and Poverty – The Feminization of Poverty, Ingrid Eide (ed.), The Norwegian National Commission for UNESCO and CROP: Oslo and Bergen, 1995 (published in Norwegian only), 56 pp.

Poverty: A Global Review. Handbook on International Poverty Research, Else Øyen, S. M. Miller, Syed Abdus Samad (eds), Scandinavian University Press and UNESCO: Oslo and Paris, 1996, 620 pp.

Poverty and Participation in Civil Society, Yogesh Atal and Else Øyen (eds), UNESCO and Abhinav Publications: Paris and New Delhi, 1997, 152 pp.

Law, Power and Poverty, Asbjørn Kjønstad and John H. Veit Wilson (eds), CROP Publications: Bergen, 1997, 148 pp.

Poverty and Social Exclusion in the Mediterranean Area, Karima Korayem and Maria Petmesidou (eds), CROP Publications: Bergen, 1998, 286 pp.

Poverty and the Environment, Arild Angelsen and Matti Vainio (eds), CROP Publications: Bergen, 1998, 180 pp.

The International Glossary on Poverty, David Gordon and Paul Spicker (eds), CROP International Studies in Poverty Research, Zed Books: London, 1999, 162 pp.

Poverty and the Law, Asbjørn Kjønstad and Peter Robson (eds), Hart Publishing: Cambridge, 2001, 199 pp.

Poverty Reduction: What Role for the State in Today's Globalized Economy?, Francis Wilson, Nazneen Kanji and Einar Braathen (eds), CROP International Studies in Poverty Research, Zed Books: London, 2001, 372 pp.

The Poverty of Rights – Human Rights and the Eradication of Poverty, Willem van Genugten and Camilo Perez-Bustillo (eds), CROP International Studies in Poverty Research, Zed Books: London, 2001, 209 pp.

Best Practices in Poverty Reduction – An Analytical Framework, Else Øyen et al. (eds), CROP International Studies in Poverty Research, Zed Books: London, 2002, 144 pp.

Law and Poverty: The Legal System and Poverty Reduction, Lucy Williams, Asbjørn Kjønstad and Peter Robson (eds), CROP International Studies in Poverty Research, Zed Books: London, 2003, 303 pp.

ELISA REIS AND MICK MOORE | editors

Elite perceptions of poverty and inequality

CROP
International Studies
in Poverty Research

David Philip
CAPE TOWN

Zed Books
LONDON | NEW YORK

Elite perceptions of poverty and inequality was first published
by Zed Books Ltd, 7 Cynthia Street, London N1 9JF, UK and Room 400,
175 Fifth Avenue, New York, NY 10010, USA in 2005

www.zedbooks.co.uk

CROP International Studies in Poverty Research

Cover designed by Andrew Corbett
Set in Arnhem and Futura Bold by Ewan Smith, London
Printed and bound in the UK by Biddles Ltd, King's Lynn

Distributed in the USA exclusively by Palgrave Macmillan, a division of
St Martin's Press, LLC, 175 Fifth Avenue, New York, NY 10010.

A catalogue record for this book is available from the British Library.
US CIP data are available from the Library of Congress.

ISBN 1 84277 638 x hb
ISBN 1 84277 639 8 pb

Contents

Tables

Acknowledgements

The roots of this book lie in a survey of the values and beliefs of strategic elites in Brazil conducted by the Instituto Universitário de Pesquisas do Rio de Janeiro (IUPERJ) in 1993–94. The research presented here – a comparative international study of elite perceptions of poverty and inequality – was initiated in 1998, and designed by Abram de Swaan, James Manor, Else Øyen and Elisa Reis. Our special thanks go to:

- Financiadora de Estudos e Projetos (FINEP), and Conselho Nacional de Desenvolvimento Científico e Tecnológico (CNPq.), through the Program for Networks of Excellence – PRONEX – grants Nos. 41.96.0868.00 and 663372/1996-8) for financial support for the original Brazilian research and for the extension into an international project.
- The UK Department for International Development, which supported much of the work through research grants to the Institute of Development Studies.
- Else Øyen who, under the aegis of Comparative Research Programme on Poverty (CROP), brought together the original research team, and provided constant stimulus and support.
- Zairo Cheibub, for research support and friendship in critical stages of the Brazilian study.
- Andre Saldanha da Costa, Bruno Vasconcelos Cardoso, Carolina Botelho Marinho, Felix Garcia Lopes Jr, Maryanne Da Costa Galvão, Nalayne Mendonça Pinto, Reinaldo Nicolai Pinto, Rodrigo Carlo Raiher, Sooraya Karoan and Yuri Lapa e Silva – student research trainees (UFRJ), for frequent challenging questions.
- Cristina Fernandes at the Federal University of Rio de Janeiro and Carol Spencer at the Institute of Development Studies for invaluable editorial, administrative and secretarial support.
- The many colleagues and students with whom we shared ideas and criticisms at seminars, workshops and conferences around the globe.

1 | Elites, perceptions and poverties[1]

ELISA REIS AND MICK MOORE

We had a lot of fun producing this book. The field investigations were stimulating in their own right, but all the more exhilarating because we were aware of being the first researchers ever to collect consistent, comparative information on how national elites perceive the character, causes of and remedies to poverty. It was just as invigorating to engage with one another and with numerous academic colleagues while designing the research and presenting results. Since the idea for the project was first explored in the mid-1990s, we have been quizzed and questioned in more conferences, seminars and meetings than we can recall. If there are deficiencies in this work, we cannot attribute them to any failure of our professional colleagues to engage with us. They have forced us to rethink, many times over, three main sets of questions.

The first were methodological: do we really know what we claim to know about elite perceptions of poverty? That question can be answered only by dealing with a range of more precise queries. What do we mean by *elites*? Did we sample them correctly? What do we mean by *perceptions*? How can we be sure that information derived mainly from face-to-face interviews accurately reveals 'true' perceptions? How reliably did we interpret the information that came to us in open-ended interviews? Why did we choose Bangladesh, Brazil, Haiti, the Philippines and South Africa as the sites for this research? Are our data really comparable among countries? Does it mean the same thing to be a member of the national elite in, for example, both Bangladesh and South Africa?

The second set of questions concerned our motivations. Why did we choose to approach the study of poverty in the South by examining how national elites perceive it? Should this not be, at best, a peripheral concern? Worse, are we not in some way devaluing the experiences and the knowledge of the poor themselves by examining them through the eyes of those who are, at least from some perspectives, either the architects or the beneficiaries of their unhappy fate?

The third set of questions follows closely. What are the policy implications of our findings? How might any understanding of how national elites perceive poverty be of potential use to any political actor?

We say little here about these policy questions. They are the subject of our final chapter. Here we explain our motivations in a little more detail, but most of this chapter is devoted to explaining our research methods. We end the chapter with some summary conclusions about how Southern elites in general seem to perceive poverty.

We start by explaining two of our key terms: *elites* and *perceptions*.

Elites

Conceptually, our *national elites* are the very small number of people who control the key material, symbolic and political resources within a country. Operationally, we identify them in institutional terms: they are the people who occupy commanding positions within the set of institutions that are most salient to national political influence and policy-making within a country. Our standard list of national political institutions is: representative political institutions (legislatures, presidencies, cabinets, political parties); the civilian public bureaucracy; the armed forces and police; large companies and business organizations; large landowners' interest organizations; trade unions; the mass media; prominent educational and professional organizations; voluntary associations; and religious institutions. In adopting an institutional approach to identifying political elites, we are closer to C. Wright Mills than to the other classical theorists who have dealt with elites and politics.[2]

This conception and definition of elites raises a number of questions that are treated later in this chapter. We concentrate at this point on giving the reader an initial taste of what our definition means in practice. Whom did we interview? We are able to provide the most detailed information on our Filipino interviewees. Their institutional roles are listed in the annexe to Chapter 3.[3] In addition to a number of chief executives or owners of very large companies and leading figures in powerful NGOs, the list includes, mainly in their current but sometimes in their recent roles: one vice-president (of the Philippines); seven senators, including three holding important offices within the Senate; eight members of the House of Representatives; one chief of staff of the armed forces; one secretary of defence; two secretaries of finance; four other secretaries to government; three mayors or vice-mayors of large cities; one son of a president; one presidential adviser; one archbishop; five university deans or presidents; one chairman of the board and one editor-in-chief of a leading newspaper; one chairman and one governor of the stock exchange; three presidents or vice-presidents of leading business associations; one Supreme Court justice, and one president of the Bar Association.

We have no complete lists of elites for even one country, and have therefore to rely on our own various back-of-the-envelope calculations about their potential numbers. We stress that, when we talk of 'national elites', we are talking only of a very thin sliver from the 'top', in a 'power' sense, of the population of any country. Even when immediate family members are included, the national 'elites', as we conceive them, probably number considerably under half of 1 per cent of any national population.[4]

Perceptions

Our research was about *perceptions* of poverty. We understand perceptions to comprise a mixture of evaluative and non-evaluative understandings of a situation. They are a combination of *cognitions* (non-evaluative understanding); *norms* (internalized ideas about appropriate roles); and *values* (ideals about what might be). We have been searching for the basic – and relatively stable – values and beliefs that constitute elites' assessments of poverty, looking for their answers to the following types of question: What does 'poverty' mean? Why and how does it represent a problem, if at all? Why are some people poor and others wealthy? Who is to blame for what? Who should take the initiative in dealing with poverty? In interpreting the answers to interview questions, we have always allowed for the possibility of incoherence and internal contradiction within what we define as a set of basic values and beliefs about poverty. For example, there should be nothing surprising about the willingness of an interviewee both to attribute poverty in a moralistic fashion to the passivity or indolence of the poor yet also to volunteer a perception that non-poor people are, in their own way, equally lacking in drive or entrepreneurship. We have tried not to impose excessive order and rationality on the 'normal incoherence' of the ways in which people view the world. We have, however, attempted to adhere to a core principle in what often is still, confusingly, termed public *opinion* polling: to separate short-term *opinions*, driven by recent and current events, from more stable, long-term and significant *perceptions*. Opinions about poverty are like the weather: they might change very fast according to short-term events or stimuli. Perceptions, like climates, are more stable.

Motivations

Let us return to the question of why we undertook this study at all, and to the criticism that, by spending time talking to elites about poverty and writing up the results, we have somehow devalued the poor themselves, their experiences and perceptions, or their potential contributions to reducing poverty and inequality. Do the poor not know much more about poverty than people who live in air-conditioned luxury and get their medical treatment in Miami rather than in the slums of Port au Prince? Are the poor themselves not the principal agents in any solutions to poverty, whether

3

individual or collective, political or economic? And are elites not more part of the problem than part of the solution? In sum, why would a group of modestly progressive social science researchers genuinely concerned about poverty in poor countries want to bother with the views of elites?

Part of the answer to this last question is simple intellectual curiosity. Operating in worlds of social science and public policy research in which there was so much concern about poverty – and widespread, reasonable suspicions and allegations that 'elites' were very much to blame for it – we simply wanted some consistent insight into how these elites perceived the issue. Our individual curiosities, shaped by our personal values and experiences, were diverse. Elisa Reis, the initiator of this research, was motivated by concerns that were simultaneously theoretical and empirical. Living in Brazil, where extreme inequality is so noticeable, she often found herself asking basic sociological questions, such as: How is this society possible? What ties together people who experience such disparate life conditions? Does it make sense to refer to a *civil society*, in the singular, where inequalities among groups seem to rule out any commonality of purpose? Are there particular social bonds, normative commitments or pragmatic concerns that make it possible to attain political legitimacy for policy initiatives aimed at redistributing income or resources to the poor? What could one learn about such questions through digging into the political culture of the very powerful and privileged?

Another source of inspiration was John Toye's commentary on anti-poverty discourse in contemporary international development agencies in the light of the history of anti-poverty policy in Britain (Toye 1997, 1999). Over a long period of time, up until at least the mid-twentieth century, British policy had been shaped in part by moral distinctions of relative merit and worthiness among the poor. The *deserving poor* had sometimes been treated reasonably, while the *undeserving*, as defined principally by behaviour and lifestyle, were treated more harshly or punitively. Part of the art of obtaining political support for the expansion of public welfare had been to redefine more poor people as *deserving* on grounds that would resonate with, and be acceptable to, the more comfortable classes. Were analogous distinctions among the poor to be found within the vernacular cultures of contemporary developing countries? What implications did this have for the crafting of anti-poverty policies? Were international statistics on the proportion of national populations living on less than one dollar per person per day the best way to persuade elites and governments to take more seriously the issue of poverty (see Chapter 8)?

A more diffuse motivation was unease about what we saw as an im-balance in the emerging pattern of applied social science research on poverty in poor countries. We framed this research project at a time when increasing efforts were being made to investigate poor people's own perceptions of poverty. Those efforts culminated in the major *Voices of the Poor* project organized by the World Bank, based on group discussions at 279 sites in twenty-three countries (Narayan et al. 2000). The intellectual and practical value of doing research on poor people's perceptions of poverty is beyond question.[5] And it can be very useful to juxtapose some of their findings with our own.[6] But the perceptions of those who are best placed to mobilize and shape public action against poverty – our elites – are no less relevant. Until we framed the research reported here, these issues had been almost entirely ignored.

We were moved to pool these diverse motivations and curiosities into a common and coherent project in large part because we had available a stimulating intellectual framework around which we could organize comparative research: Abram de Swaan's notion of 'social consciousness'. In his seminal book on the origins of welfare policies in western Europe and the United States, de Swaan links the analysis of macro-historical processes to micro-based approach to policy decisions, focusing on the processes that drove national elites to engage in collective action to counter poverty and deprivation (de Swaan 1988). De Swaan argues that a pre-condition for state action was the development of what he termed a *social consciousness* among national elites. In his own words:

Members of the elite possess social consciousness to the degree that:
(1) They are aware of the interdependence among social groups in society – and, most relevantly, of the external effects of poverty upon the elites, which they may perceive either as threats or as opportunities.
(2) They realize that as members of the elite they bear some responsibility for the condition of the poor.
(3) They believe that feasible and efficacious means to improve the lot of the poor exist or might be created. (Chapter 7, this volume)

In Chapter 7, de Swaan summarizes his own original argument and presents his reflections on the implications of the research on developing countries reported in this book. Let us simply note at this point that, when talking of a sense of 'responsibility' on the part of elites, de Swaan was referring not to something experienced or conceived in personal, individualistic terms, but rather to identification with a larger community of interests. Where the three elements of social consciousness coalesced, he argues, collective solutions to social problems became more common and more encompassing, expanding from the parish to the national level. In engaging with us in this study, de Swaan directed us to the following questions.

Would persisting poverty and inequality in less developed countries point to the absence of a social consciousness among the elites? Would Southern elites exhibit the proto-sociological wisdom that earlier led their counterparts in western Europe and the United States to support social policies? How do Southern elites position themselves *vis-à-vis* collective initiatives for social inclusion?

Knowledge and policy

While our research was in various ways driven by policy concerns, we never envisaged that we would be able to answer the question that clearly is uppermost in many people's minds: Do elites *care* about the poor and poverty? We came across many people who believe that they already know the answer: elites really do not care. It is easy to make such assertions appear true by definition: if elites are clearly not making great efforts or sacrifices to reduce poverty, then one can easily use this as 'evidence' that they do not care. But the question of whether they 'really care' is not answerable in any strong sense of the term. The extent to which, at any moment in time, any group of people 'care about' a societal issue – in the sense of giving some real priority to solving it – is a highly contingent matter. It is more a question about politics – the constitution of collective actors, opportunities for and constraints on political action, and alternative policy agendas – than about states of mind.[7] As far as political elites are concerned, the answer is likely to depend in particular on what other issues are on public and policy agendas at that moment.

Most of the time, poverty is what Albert Hirschman (1981) described as a *chosen problem*: i.e. a policy problem that governments or elites can choose to tackle or not, without courting immediate crisis or disaster if they decide to ignore it. Poverty becomes a *pressing problem*, urgently requiring attention and action, if it becomes associated, in the minds of policymakers, with some critical issue – such as disorder, disease, imminent insurrection, economic crisis or electoral threat – that has to be addressed immediately if some disaster is not to follow. As we explore in more detail in Chapter 8, part of the art of focusing the attention of policy-makers on poverty may lie in upgrading it, in their perceptions, from *chosen* to *pressing problem* status. But some kinds of policy problems are *pressing* for fairly basic structural and institutional reasons. These include high inflation – which forces itself on the attention of governments every day in myriad ways – declines in national income, civil war, external military threat, and a wide range of other short- and longer-term crisis situations. At any moment, the policy attention of a particular national elite might be focused on one or more of these more imperative *pressing problems*.

But the extent to which this is the case, and the character of the pressing problems, will vary very much from place to place and time to time.

If over a particular period of time a particular elite does not assign priority to poverty through its actions – as opposed to its interview responses – one can certainly assert that it does not 'care' about poverty. But that conclusion is either a truism or false. It tells us nothing about the circumstances in which that elite might be disposed to initiate, support or tolerate a more active or effective set of anti-poverty policies. We make no general assumptions about either the goodwill of elites or the accuracy of their perceptions about poverty. We do believe, on the basis of historical evidence, that the extent to which they are willing to help direct public resources towards the reduction of poverty varies widely according to circumstances, as does the kind of programmes they might support, and the representations of poverty and the problems of the poor that are used to mobilize support for those programmes. Because elites are by definition powerful, a better understanding of their perceptions might have a policy pay-off for the poor, strengthening and making more effective public action against poverty in developing countries.

What kind of policy pay-off? No one should read these chapters in the expectation that they will find some broad truths about how elites in poor countries in general understand poverty, with some direct and general implications for poverty policy. We are not dealing, for example, in propositions such as: 'elites find education for the poor highly attractive, therefore it will be politically possible to do more for the poor through educational provision than through other channels'. While we do explore the scope for reaching general conclusions of this nature, it will come as no surprise that many of our findings vary widely from one country to another. Might readers then hope to find here country-specific policy prescriptions, such as, for example: 'Filipino elites think fast population growth is the main cause of poverty, therefore they will eagerly support more birth control'; or 'Brazilian elites should be made to understand that rural poverty really is much worse than urban poverty, and that agrarian reform is not the easy solution to poverty that some think it is'? If some readers draw such policy conclusions about particular countries, and if those policies turn out to be both appropriate and feasible, then we shall be very pleased. But that is not what we ever intended or expected in terms of the policy implications of this research.

We hope our research findings will encourage people to think about anti-poverty policy in terms of what is more likely to appeal – or less likely to alarm – elites. We regret that 'technocrats' on the one side and 'activists' on the other have widely neglected the assessment of the political parameters that make viable specific social policies. The former bet on technical skills and the latter on moral determination. Both tend to forget that ongoing perceptions may constitute powerful obstacles to policy effectiveness as well as promising conditions for successful initiatives. Both perspectives reveal little sensitivity to legitimacy issues, and pay little attention to the cultural dimension of public policy. Unlike them, we assume that knowing about the political culture of those who control resources may help us to better understand why and how poverty becomes a pressing policy issue (Chapter 8).

Political culture

Obviously, when we deal with issues such as poverty and inequality, the actual distribution of material resources is of paramount importance. It is, however, justifiable to concentrate on the sphere of ideas and values to investigate how they help sustain or disrupt ongoing patterns of resource allocation.[8] Why do we need cultural approaches to study poverty and inequality? Mainly because poverty, like inequality, is a cultural no less than a material construct. Even though we can for many purposes use objective definitions of poverty, numbers and parameters do not convey the whole story. They help us to compare societies, but they may give us only a limited indication of what people – poor or not – perceive as acceptable social conditions. What is viewed as 'poverty' in one context may be considered very differently elsewhere. Karl Marx was but one in a long string of observers to have noted that even minimal living standards are culturally defined.[9]

We asked members of our elites to express their views both in the abstract as well as in relation to their particular society and their own context. In expressing their views, they convey not only their cognitions about poverty and inequality, but also their values and norms regarding how to cope with such questions. The fact that we explore elite political culture does not imply any faith that, in explaining social outcomes, values, norms or cognitions have priority over either material conditions or institutional configurations. We simply believe that culture is important. Equally, we are well aware that a focus on culture is analytically problematic and sometimes controversial. One frequent objection is that it entails a conservative bias, because cultural phenomena are believed to be 'primordial' and relatively unchangeable. To focus on them, it is sometimes argued, is somehow to sanction the status quo. Such a fatalistic conception of culture can indeed serve as an instrument to preserve a given order. And the stuff of which culture is made – 'habits of the heart' – is extremely resilient. Yet the chance to change these in the long run is dependent on a careful assessment of their meanings and implications. The adequate understanding of prevailing values and norms can be an important component of success- ful institutional reforms and of effective policy changes. We all know of political reforms that had no impact, policy changes that were ineffective, and laws that remained fiction – because they were in no way grounded in prevailing values and beliefs.

It is also important to explain our conception of the relation of values, norms and beliefs to interests. People commonly conflate self-interested behaviour with the pursuit of material goals, and contrast them both to idealistic motivations. We regard the notion of *interest* as encompassing both material and ideal motivation, however. The only logical corollary of the concept is the premise that actors seek to maximize preferences, whatever their nature. We are being perfectly consistent in this book when, in discussing poverty, we combine a focus on culture with an analytical perspective centred on interests. Members of elites may or may not see the poor as a threat to their interests. Idealistic or opportunistic individuals, motivated by altruistic or selfish concerns to try to improve the condition of the poor, may encounter elites more or less inclined to do something about poverty to the extent that they perceive the existing pattern of distribution as more or less threatening to their interests. Goodwill and selfishness should not be perceived as contradictory principles, logically or empirically.

Representing the diversity of inequalities

Why did we choose Bangladesh, Brazil, Haiti, the Philippines and South Africa? To some degree, 'choose' is the wrong word. Starting with few financial resources, we had to make the best of what we had, and take advantage of the expertise, connections, skills and interests of the various team members – and of the opportunities that arose to augment them. At various points, there were plans or expectations for studies in India, Mozambique and Zimbabwe.[10] To the degree that we had a choice, we used it to select a sample of cases that would (a) represent as far as possible the diversity of national situations in the South, and (b) over-represent countries characterized by various forms of inequality. To the extent that it is possible with such a small sample of countries, we substantially achieved both objectives. The issue of the representativeness of our sample in rela- tion to the universe of Southern countries is treated in the next section. Let us start with the representation of types of inequality.

Most extended conversations about socio-economic inequality within the countries of the South involve at least some reference to two paradigm cases: two relatively large, relatively wealthy countries in which income is distributed more unequally than in almost any other place in the world.[11]

Both are sometimes termed *multicultural societies*. Behind this euphemism lies a history of the construction of states, economies and societies through the coercive exploitation of a predominantly black labour force by a European elite in the context of colonialism and specialization in the export of primary (agricultural, forestry or mineral) products. Our first country chapter deals with one of these paradigm cases – Brazil – and the last deals with the other – South Africa. Another of our country cases – Haiti – has similar historical roots: an economy, society and polity originally constructed around colonial export agriculture and the same kind of 'multiculturalism' (i.e. colour-driven ethnic hierarchy and inequality) that characterized Brazil and South Africa. Haiti adds to the diversity of our cases first in a relatively trivial sense: the European ruling power and culture were French rather than Portuguese (Brazil) or Anglo-Dutch (South Africa). The more distinctive contribution of Haiti to our goal of representing a diversity of types of inequality, however, derives from the fact that, most untypical of the South, European colonial rule was terminated through internal revolt as long ago as 1804. This early liberation did not produce a significantly less unequal society. Haiti has experienced such extensive and continuous economic, political and cultural trauma that it is the poorest country in the western hemisphere, and a byword for bad government. One of the incidental outcomes is that we have no reliable statistics on income distribution in Haiti today. If we did have those figures, and the country did not appear to be especially unequal on standard summary measures such as the Gini Index of income inequality, this would not be because Haiti lacks a ruling class that is obscenely rich by the standards of the typical Haitian. It is rather that so many Haitians – nearly the entire population – are so miserably poor that the opulence of the few would not be enough to result in high inequality on the Gini Index.[12] The most important contribution of the Haitian case to our goal of representing diversity in types of inequality lies more in the cultural than in the economic realm. As Omar Thomaz explains in Chapter 5, the various black and mulatto elites that have ruled Haiti since the French were expelled continue to compete among themselves – and to differentiate themselves from others – in large part in terms of their command of the French language and, by extension, by their access to the universalistic world culture to which this language is considered the key. To a greater extent than in our other cases, inequality in Haiti is structured by, and understood in terms of, *cultural* competencies – in the most pretentious and encompassing sense of the term *culture*.

The Philippines case adds to our sample a rather contradictory mixture of two different colonial traditions: the older, Spanish inheritance is hierarchical, Catholic and authoritarian; the more recent American inheritance is more liberal, democratic and egalitarian. In the global context, income inequality in the Philippines is not especially high (Table 1.1). For our purposes, the Philippines represents a relatively unequal society in two different senses. First, it is more unequal in terms of wealth and income distribution than many of its neighbours in South-East Asia and, more markedly, many of the East Asian countries to the north, especially South Korea, Taiwan, Japan and China. Second, the Philippines has often been understood as a stereotypical Latin American country that happens to be located in Asia: a society dominated by a distinct and enduring elite – a small clique of families whose wealth and political power are to an important degree rooted in their large landholdings and in the persistence of clientelist control over the rural poor. That characterization continues to play an important role in the framing of political debate in the Philippines.[13]

Finally, what about Bangladesh? In so far as the Gini Index of income distribution is an adequate indicator of socio-economic inequality, then Bangladesh is the most egalitarian country in our sample (Table 1.1), and is indeed one of the most equal among those very poor countries on which we have data.[14] In that respect, it is typical of the South Asian region, especially of the largest country there, India. Yet Noushin Kalati and James Manor report in Chapter 6 that some members of the South African elite believed India to be a much more unequal society than their own. This perception cannot simply be dismissed as an indication of the ignorance of some sections of the (white) South African elite. There is a widespread perception that, in India and South Asia generally, the practice of inequality has been elevated into an art form that permeates all aspects of daily life. Exaggerated as this image may be, it is based on an important core of truth. Deeply embedded notions of finely graded hierarchy do shape interpersonal interactions in South Asia to a significant degree. Tones of voice, vocabulary and body language vary in tiny but highly patterned ways according to who is relating to whom. What might appear to the outsider as small differences in status often seem to translate into clear hierarchical subordination. These rituals of hierarchical interaction are more muted in Muslim Bangladesh than in most of India. Bangladeshi Muslims have only a vestigial caste system, and no tradition of untouchability. For the purposes of this volume, however, Bangladesh represents a region of the world where inequality is low according to standard statistical indicators, but rather higher when it is understood in terms of the values, assumptions and practices embodied in daily interpersonal interactions.

Overall, we have a fair representation of different types and degrees of social inequality in our small sample. But inequality is only one of many dimensions on which we might seek to represent variation among the countries of the South. How well have we done on the issue of representativeness more broadly?

Representing the diversity of the South

Table 1.1 is central to this section. It contains a great deal of comparative summary data about our five countries. And the way those data are patterned explains the order in which our country cases appear: Brazil, Philippines, Bangladesh, Haiti and South Africa. Examine the numbers by rows, starting with the first row on average incomes per head, and concentrating on those figures that relate most directly to economic structure. Brazil is not only a wealthy country but, compared to the others that follow it in our listing, it also: is highly unequal; is urbanized; is industrialized; has a relatively sparse population in relation to its surface area; has a government that appropriates an unusually high proportion of GDP through taxation and is generally relatively effective;[15] and receives very little development aid. Next, the Philippines is essentially an intermediate case on all these variables. It is Bangladesh and Haiti which provide the real contrast with Brazil: low incomes; relatively equal income distribution (for Bangladesh – we do not know about Haiti); rural, agrarian economies; high population densities (exceptionally so for Bangladesh); and governments that raise only small proportions of GDP through taxes, and are substantially dependent on aid donors for their financial resources. Imagine that our chapters are arranged, according to average income levels in the respective countries, on a U-shaped curve on a graph. Brazil stands on the top left-hand point of the curve. The Philippines is halfway down. Bangladesh and Haiti are near the bottom. We then end, on an upward sweep, with South Africa – another relatively rich, unequal, urbanized, industrialized country with a sparse population that receives little aid.

From the perspective of economic structure, we have a fair representation of the countries of the South. As mentioned in the previous section, we also managed to capture a large number of distinct colonial-cum-European historical influences: Portuguese in Brazil; Spanish and American in the Philippines; British in Bangladesh; French in Haiti; and Anglo-Dutch in South Africa. It is very difficult to represent the diversity of polities in the South through five cases, but here too we have a wide range. The Haitian state may not have failed as completely as, for example, Somalia, but it is close: Haiti has at times in recent years lacked a government, and, when there is a government formally in power, there is not much of a state apparatus it can call on to get anything done. Recently, much public authority in Haiti has been wielded by shifting combinations of: the Catholic Church;

TABLE 1.1 Basic statistics on the countries studied, late 1990s

	Brazil	Philippines	Bangladesh	Haiti	South Africa
Incomes					
GNP per capita (purchasing power parity, current international $), 1998	6,500	3,700	1,400	1,400	8,300
Average GDP growth rate, 1980–98 (% annual)	2.5	2.3	4.6	–0.2	1.8
Gini index of income inequality, 1993–98	60	46	33	No data	59
Population					
Total population (millions), 1998	166	75	126	8	41
Population density (people per square kilometre), 1998	20	252	965	277	34
Population growth rate (% annual), 1998	1.6	2.2	1.6	2.0	1.8
Urban population (as % of total), 1998	80	57	23	34	53
Index of metropolitan concentration (% of the combined population of the four largest cities who live in the single largest city)	49	82	64	No data	36
Government revenue					
Central government revenue as % of GDP*	27	19	8	11	26
Aid as % of GNP, 1998	0.1	0.9	2.8	10.5	0.4
Occupational patterns					
Employees in agriculture as % of the economically active population**	25	38	70	63	13
Employees in industry as % of the economically active population**	18	16	12	9	28
Employees in services as % of the economically active population**	57	46	14	25	59
Quality of life					
Life expectancy at birth, in years, 1998	67	69	59	54	63
% of population with access to safe water, 1990–96	72	83	84	28	70
Literacy rate, adult total (% of people aged fifteen and above)***	83	93	35	40	83
% of children of primary school age enrolled in school***	90	100	64	22	100

Source: 2000 World Development Indicators CD-ROM, World Bank

Data for different years: * Bangladesh 1989; Brazil 1994; Haiti 1987; India 1998; Philippines 1997; South Africa 1998   ** Bangladesh 1990; Brazil 1995; Haiti 1988; India 1980; Philippines 1997; South Africa 1990   *** Bangladesh 1990; Brazil 1994; Haiti 1990; India 1994; Philippines 1991; South Africa 1994

American peacekeeping troops; foreign development NGOs; personalistic political parties; and the various quasi-public, quasi-private local armed forces that have succeeded the notorious Tontons Macoutes of the Duvalier dictatorship. It is eloquent testimony of the lack of an effective state in Haiti that only one child in five is even enrolled in primary school – a third of the Bangladesh rate (Table 1.1). The governments of our other study countries exercise more authority but, typical of many polities in the South, they do not always have a monopoly over organized armed force. Some rural areas of the Philippines are still under the control of separatist guerrillas, and, in some urban localities in Brazil, gangs organized around crime and narcotics sometimes exercise a kind of public authority. The government in Dhaka controls most of Bangladesh, but has limited influence over local elites in many areas, and finds it hard to stop thugs associated with the ruling party from preying on the population through extortion rackets of various kinds.

In 2004, Haiti did not really have a government in the accepted sense of the term. The governments of the other four of our countries had been elected, although in most of them, with Brazil the main exception, democracy often seemed fragile. In that respect the group is fairly typical of developing countries. Given that none of them had an elected government twenty-five years earlier, we have perhaps over-represented the 1980s and 1990s wave of democratization in the South.

In what other respects have we failed to represent the diversity of the South in our choice of countries? We have mostly chosen countries with medium to large populations, and thus under-represented both the very large countries and the small. Related to this, we have no case from black Africa. We have rather over-represented both Christian countries in general, and Catholic countries in particular.[16] We have no Buddhist or Hindu nations, and Bangladesh is among the most secular of those contemporary states where the population is mainly Islamic. None of our countries enjoys enormous wealth from oil or mineral resources, or the high levels of oppressive rule, corruption and conflict that often accompany such a dubious blessing (Esanov et al. 2001; Global Witness 2004; Ross 2003; Sala-I-Martin and Subramanian 2003). We could go on. Overall, our countries are probably as representative of the diversity of (the more unequal parts of) the South as one is able to achieve with a number as low as five.

Comparing perceptions

To what extent did we collect sets of national data on elite perceptions which were sufficiently standardized that, when we talk of differences between Brazil and the Philippines, or South Africa and Haiti, we really are comparing like with like? Before claiming that we solved the problem, let us explain the issues over which we puzzled, and the solutions we arrived at – in a long series of meetings of different combinations of team members as opportunities arose, including two authors' workshops held in Rio de Janeiro in July 2001 and in Amsterdam in January 2002.

If logic is taken to extremes, the political definition of elites that underpins this work leads to a methodological puzzle that is infinitely regressive. We chose elites from among the people holding top positions within what we believe to be the most important set of institutions in a national polity. In our case, we defined this standard set of institutions such that we were selecting from eleven categories: politicians in power, politicians in opposition, people working in the media, educators and professionals, union leaders, business executives, leaders of voluntary associations, civil servants, military and police officers, prosperous farmers, and religious leaders. This procedure raises two questions. First, how do we know that these are actually the most important institutions in a political sense? Second, how do we determine the importance of these institutions relative to one another, such that one can choose a national elite sample that truly represents the distribution of power in each particular polity? In principle, military personnel should be represented in each national sample to the degree that the military is powerful in each case. The same should hold for the judiciary, the mass media, etc. The logical solution is to engage first in very deep, comparative studies of the various polities, to see where and how power truly is distributed. The practical constraints on that course of action are evident. But there is also a powerful conceptual obstacle: political scientists still do not agree on a common single concept of power or a common analytical framework for the empirical study of power.[17] Two political scientists, looking at the same initial data, might come up with different conclusions. They might also differ about how far notions of 'elites' are helpful in analysing power.

It is evident that there is no elegant or fully satisfactory solution to these conceptual and practical problems. Let us explain what we did:

1 We started from the assumption that contemporary nation-states – and especially the non-failed states that we have studied – share certain common institutional features by virtue of the fact that they are formed and reproduced in interaction with one another in a global system of states. That assumption, alongside a set of judgements about the typical socio-economic features of most contemporary poor and middle-income countries, justifies our starting with our standard set of eleven institutions when selecting elite samples.

15

2 In practice, we relied heavily on expert country knowledge in making practical decisions about the representation of different sectors. Three of our five country teams comprised or included nationals. None of the teams was researching countries with which it was not familiar.

3 It was after the original standard set of eleven institutions was agreed that we included among our cases two countries, Bangladesh and the Philippines, where indigenous development NGOs are unusually numerous, large and influential. The samples were adjusted in a pragmatic way.

4 In degrees that varied from one country to another, it was not always possible clearly to assign one respondent to one sector. In many cases the same individuals occupied leading positions in more than one sector. Leading lawyers might be politicians, or recently retired generals might be prominent in business.

5 When it came to selecting individuals for interview, the procedure varied to some degree from one country to another. The procedure adopted in Brazil is in principle the most neat and transparent. Data were collected in two stages: an initial formal survey of a large and randomly selected population; and a later set of more in-depth interviews, with more purposive choice of types of respondents. In the other countries, more pragmatic considerations came into play. We could not entirely avoid selecting respondents to some degree according to personal links. It is standard wisdom in elite interviewing that it can be difficult to get interviewees to agree to be interviewed, to honour appointments, or to give the amount of time that researchers feel they need (Goldstein 2002). Personal links and recommendations can greatly alleviate those constraints.[18]

6 We agonized over a wide range of issues about research methods – sampling, interviewing, interpretation, coding – that will be familiar to people doing this kind of research. Since we were responsible for no innovations, made the 'normal' compromises, and have not, as far as we can judge, made any very evident mistakes, it seems kinder to all of us to omit any extended discussion of these issues, and simply refer approvingly to a few recent papers dealing explicitly with methods for interviewing political elites (Aberbach and Rockman 2002; Berry 2002; Goldstein 2002; Rivera et al. 2002).

7 We decided that, given the heterogeneity of our countries and their elites, the use of a standard survey questionnaire would risk sacrificing insight and substantive comparability for the sake of formal comparability. We used long semi-structured in-depth interviews that were crafted to suit each context, but guided by a standard set of general questions.

In the interview situation we largely let the respondents talk freely and move the conversation to points that they thought relevant. But elites are at least as prone as other people to wander well off the point, often into personal reminiscences. We tried to move them back into the terrain that most interested us.

8 We combed through the interview notes and coded the responses to the extent that we could. For the Bangladesh, Brazil and Philippines cases, we felt sufficiently confident about the reliability of this process that we have presented some quantitative data in tabular form.

9 We supplemented our core interview data with a wide range of other information about our countries – historical, contextual and statistical.

All things considered, we believe that our methods and data sources are sufficiently homogenous to make legitimate those cross-country comparisons that we do offer. If we were able to start again, with the experience that we have accumulated – and a research budget large enough to allow us to follow our scientific instincts – would we follow the same procedure? Probably not. We would try to ensure a little more standardization in our questions. But we would not be so unrealistic as to attempt to ignore the specific circumstances that inspired each of us to work in a particular way.

What did we find?

What, in general, did we find? In addition to the material in Chapters 2 to 6 about elite perceptions of poverty in five individual countries, what can we say about elite perceptions of poverty in the South? If our answers had to be backed by solid numbers and a sense of near-certainty, then perhaps we could not say very much. We do, however, have some plausible and stimulating insights into a hitherto unexplored subject:

1 Most of the time, our elites understood 'poverty' in much the same terms that we – and, presumably, most of our readers – understand it. Descriptively, poverty was comprehended primarily in terms of material deficits. Normatively, it was undesirable: no one made the case that poverty is a positive or an ennobling experience. That might appear to be a statement of the breathtakingly obvious until we look at the few exceptions: those members of the Haitian elite who defined poverty partly or principally in cultural terms, as the experience of exclusion from those universalistic, scientific cultures to which command of the French language alone (in Haiti) gave access. Few though they are, these exceptions provide a useful warning against the assumption that what appear to be standard terms are understood similarly throughout the world.

2 Our elites virtually all 'imagined' poverty, in the sense that their understandings of it were constructed primarily from indirect sources rather
than from any prolonged and direct personal experiences. This is at
one level obvious: intellectual and existential experiences generally
are distinct. It is significant here because many of the perceptions of
poverty conveyed to us were in some way or another 'unreal' – so highly
abstract, idealized or generalized, or so at variance with the facts, that
we are tempted to label them 'misperceptions'. Few of our respondents
could talk with conviction and fluency about different types of poverty or
poor people, or different routes in and out of poverty. Such inability is
perhaps not surprising. It approaches 'misperception' when, as was true
in at least four of our cases, rural poverty was consistently downgraded
as being less intense or painful than its urban counterpart, despite
statistics of various kinds that suggested the opposite.[19] Most strikingly
in the South African case, white members of the elite tended grossly to
underestimate the extent of rural poverty. In Brazil, where only a fifth of
the population live in rural areas, one could scarcely classify as realistic
the expectations of significant numbers of respondents that land reform
could actually move large numbers of poor people out from the cities
and into the countryside.

3 While virtually all respondents discussed poverty as if it were a problem,
it was difficult for them to identify very pressing or compelling reasons
for concern. The classic threats posed by poverty to elites were generally
perceived to be rather weak. More than any other, it was the presumed
link from poverty to crime which impinged most on the minds of our
interviewees. But even this was rather variable, and most in evidence
in Brazil and South Africa. Bangladeshi elites are very concerned about
crime, but do not see a strong connection with poverty. The crime that
concerns them is orchestrated and tolerated, and often perpetrated
more by urban gangsters and politically connected thugs than by 'the
poor'. Especially since the collapse of the Soviet bloc, the danger of
organized class-based revolution has disappeared from most of the
world; the elites we interviewed were little concerned by this possibility. The nature of modern military technology is such that the poor are
generally not needed in large numbers to fight inter-state wars. Cash
to purchase arms, a strong national economy and a relatively small but
educated and trained cadre of professionals are the immediate sources
of military strength. No interviewee suggested any link between poverty
and national military strength. The weakness or absence of perceptions
that poverty induces crime, revolution or military vulnerability is not
intrinsically puzzling: there are apparent 'objective' explanations. There

is some element of mystery, however, about why elites do not appear concerned that they are at risk from diseases transmitted from the poor. This issue was never spontaneously mentioned during our interviews. One can certainly rationalize this in terms of the partial 'conquest' of most infectious and contagious diseases; the fact that elites in poor countries are vulnerable primarily to the lifestyle diseases of the rich; and their access to expensive private curative medical care. Yet on objective grounds elites should perhaps be concerned. The World Health Organization is concerned that old communicable diseases such as TB and malaria are re-emerging, some in virulent drug-resistant forms. New communicable health threats such as Ebola and HIV/AIDS are also receiving increased publicity. Whatever the reason, the contrast with nineteenth-century Europe is stark (Chapters 7 and 8).

4 Equally, there was no very strong sense that to tolerate persisting poverty is to allow some valuable human resources to go to waste. There was no vocal fraction of any national elite arguing that, were they to be given education, training and healthcare, the (malnourished, uneducated) poor would quickly become assets to the national economy, as workers and consumers. In so far as there were exceptions, they were mainly from South Africa.

5 There was limited support for any notion of introducing a 'welfare state' providing broad-spectrum support for the mass of the population on a relatively universalistic basis. Perspectives on this idea were variable. In Brazil, which has long experience of a substantial degree of welfarism directed mainly at the formal-sector (middle-income) population, elite respondents exhibited a great deal of support 'in principle' for most components of a welfare state. They rejected them mainly on pragmatic grounds of cost. By contrast, Bangladeshi elites, whose government will not find the financial resources to fund any significant degree of welfarism for many years to come, were more likely to reject the idea on principle – as something that belonged to the rich countries, did not work even there, and was inappropriate for Asia. Most of the time, our respondents put their faith in some combination of what we normally term 'trickle-down' (from growth in the national economy) or, less frequently, targeted programmes directed at the genuinely poor.

6 To the extent that our elites appeared to be in agreement over anything positive or proactive, it was that more education was the best way to reduce poverty. The Filipino elites, living in a country that many people already view as over-educated, were the least enthusiastic. But the popularity and legitimacy of the education route stand out in all case studies. Behind that unity lies a diversity of perceptions and motivations for

linking education with the reduction of poverty. The evidence from our case study and other surveys is that Brazilian elites, to a greater extent than more typical Brazilians, value education because it represents equality of opportunity – a fundamental norm in Brazilian political culture. In other cases, education is supported on more instrumental grounds: that it can raise or change the consciousness of people still hampered by 'traditional' ways of thinking; promote entrepreneurship; or provide specific vocational and technical skills. As we remarked above, it was not very common for respondents to suggest strong causal links between education for the poor, the quality of the labour force, and rates of national economic growth.

7   In all the cases we studied the elites viewed the state as the agency primarily responsible for reducing poverty. Only in Bangladesh was there a serious competitor in the minds of the elites: development NGOs. Only in Bangladesh are there very large NGOs running development programmes that reach so many clients, regionally or nationally, that their organizational apparatus can be compared meaningfully with the bureaucratic apparatus of the state. Yet Bangladeshi NGOs are the objects of suspicion as well as admiration. True, they are viewed much more favourably by elites than are NGOs in Brazil. In Brazil, we could find little support for – or tolerance of – the idea that NGOs might relieve the state of some of its responsibilities in relation to poverty. Even in the highly unusual conditions prevailing in Bangladesh, the elites still look to the state, in a normative sense, as the agent primarily responsible for reducing poverty.

8   It is one thing to believe that the state should be responsible for anti-poverty activities, and quite a different thing to believe that it is likely to be successful in this aim. Our respondents were generally deeply sceptical about the capabilities of their governments – to the extent that they appeared often not to appreciate the real progress that had been made in reducing poverty and disease, or expanding access to education. Only the South African elites associated with the African National Congress stood out for their unfashionable faith in the ability of a state, backed by a committed political party, to make major inroads into poverty.

Organization of the book

The five national case studies in Chapters 2 to 6 illustrate both the substance of the generalizations we have sketched out above and – of more interest to many readers – the extent to which elite perceptions are shaped by specific national histories. In Chapter 7, Abram de Swaan examines how far the analytic framework that he developed to help explain the rise of welfare states in western Europe and the United States – specifically the concept of *social consciousness* – is useful for the study of the contemporary South. His conclusion is that the framework is helpful in posing the right questions, but does not provide any neat template into which we can fit answers. Conditions in the contemporary South are both very diverse and very different from those prevailing when welfare states were introduced in western Europe and the United States.

Mick Moore and Naomi Hossain also draw on broad comparisons between 'historical Europe' and the contemporary South in their concluding chapter on the policy implications of this research. They emphasize in particular the extent to which the concept of poverty might be both socially constructed and plastic, and could perhaps be reconstructed by 'friends of the poor' in the South to encourage national elites to be more sympathetic and empathetic towards 'their' own poor. This sounds like cultural engineering on a grand scale. It is consistent with the tone in which we opened this chapter that we should end the book with a proposal for public action that is controversial from several perspectives, but, we believe, more practical and less outrageous than it at first appears.

Notes

1 We are grateful in particular to Gerard Clarke and Naomi Hossain for useful comments on an earlier draft of this chapter.

2 For a good summary of this literature, see Parry (1969).

3 We are unable to provide comparable information for the other countries because we gave our respondents assurances of anonymity, and even listing their roles would put this assurance at risk. In the Philippines, Gerard Clarke and Marites Sison managed to negotiate much more transparency.

4 In discussing, comparing and interpreting our results, it became clear that there were some interesting differences between our elites in terms of two kinds of variables that might affect the extent to which they share common perceptions. The first variable is homogeneity/heterogeneity: there were wide differences in the extent to which members of a national elite shared the same language, religion, ethnicity or regional origin, had been educated in the same kinds of schools, or had spent their life in the same, or similar, cities or environments. The second variable is interconnectivity: the chances that any random member of the elite will tend to have direct personal interaction with any other. Variations in connectivity are shaped by at least four sets of factors. The first is the size of the national elite. Members of smaller elites will interact more. The second is the degree to which the elite was educated in the same small number of schools. Will they all know – or be able to 'place' – each other from school or college days? The third is the extent to which individuals or families either specialize in what we have called 'sectors' or engage in a range of them, e.g. the extent to which lawyers (or their sisters and brothers)

also engage in politics, the military engage in business, large landlords also run industries, or senior religious figures are recruited from other elite segments. The fourth is the pattern of urbanization. For example, the national institutions of Bangladesh are highly centralized in Dhaka. As Naomi Hossain and Mick Moore explain in Chapter 4, the contemporary Bangladeshi elite 'live, work and play' in a few localities of that one city. They really do stand a high chance of meeting one another in someone's drawing room. Bangladesh is a good example of a country where the elite is both relatively homogeneous and relatively interconnected. Haiti is another. South Africa is a complete contrast. Its elite is divided by, among other things, ethnicity, language (Afrikaans and English, as well as Xhosa, Zulu and other African languages), religion, educational experiences, economic sector, and the fact that it is distributed over several large cities, especially Cape Town, Johannesburg, Natal and Pretoria. The chances that one random member of the South African elite would encounter a random other member in someone's drawing room – or office or board room – are not very high. Higley and Lengyel (2000) present a similar framework for categorizing contemporary post-socialist European elites.

5 There are, however, a number of questions about the validity and usefulness of the information derived from studies such as *Voices of the Poor*. More attention needs to be paid to consistency and replicability in data collection and analysis; to the design of comparisons aimed at explaining variations in responses in different sites and situations; and to the potential biases induced by the hopes or expectations of (very poor) respondents that researchers and interviewers might bring assistance from outside (Moore et al. 1998).

6 It is, for example, striking that while, in the *Voices of the Poor* study, poor people identified as major concerns their physical insecurity and vulnerability to violence and harassment by criminals or agents of the state (Narayan et al. 2000: ch. 8), very few of our elite respondents in five countries gave much hint that they viewed poverty in these terms.

7 For explanations of how the configuration of political institutions affects how perceptions and interests are translated into patterns of political action, see Skocpol (1992: 41–60) and Houtzager (2003: 13–18).

8 For recent discussions of the roles of ideas in politics, see Berman (2001) and Lieberman (2002).

9 'A house may be large or small; as long as the surrounding houses are equally small it satisfies all social demands for a dwelling. But let a palace arise beside the little house, and it shrinks from a little house to a hut. The little house shows now that its owner has only very slight or no demands to make; and however high it may shoot up in the course of civilisation, if the neighbouring palace grows to an equal or even great extent, the occupant of the relatively small house will feel more and more uncomfortable, dissatisfied and cramped within its four walls' (Marx 1849/1968: 85).

10 For some of the history of this project, see de Swaan et al. (2000).

11 Data on income inequality in poor countries are not generally very reliable, and inequality itself can be measured in several different ways. There is no need for us to engage deeply with these issues here. The *World Development Report 2000/2001* lists only four countries in which the Gini Index of

income (or consumption) inequality was, according to the most recent data, at the same level as South Africa (59.3) or above: Brazil, Central African Republic, Guatemala and Sierra Leone (World Bank 2000: Table 5).

12 It would be better to use a measure more targeted at the pattern of income inequality that seems to characterize Haiti – for example, the ratio of the incomes of the richest 5 per cent of the population to the incomes of the poorest 50 per cent.

13 In fact, the role of landownership in the construction of the Filipino elite has been consistently exaggerated, and the significance of generalized 'bossism' – localized monopolies of combined economic and political power – somewhat understated (Sidel 1999).

14 In 1999, Bangladesh ranked 168 out of 206 (non-tiny) countries in the world in terms of average income per head (where number one was the richest). At that point, the standard measure of income (or consumption) inequality, the Gini Index, was estimated at 33.6 for Bangladesh. If we take the poorest fifty-seven countries (those ranked from 150 to 206), we have recent estimates of the Gini Index for thirty-two of them. Of those, inequality was higher – and often much higher – than Bangladesh in twenty-five cases. It was lower in only six cases – and in three of those the estimated Gini Index was so close to the Bangladesh figure – 33.1, 33.2 and 33.3 – that it was well within the range of measurement error (World Bank 2000: Tables 1 and 5).

15 In fact, the ratio of taxation to GDP is much higher in Brazil than the figure given in Table 1.1 because, very unusually, Brazilian sub-national (provincial) governments raise a great deal of taxation in their own right.

16 If one takes the view that the prevalence of voodoo makes Haiti only half Catholic, then we have two and a half Catholic countries out of five.

17 The most fundamental difference lies between (a) the 'despotic' conception of power (the influence of one actor over others, with the emphasis on the self-interested use of power by dominant actors); and (b) the 'infrastructural' conception of power as a resource used to shape the action of a range of agents to achieve collective goals.

18 The researchers did not interview people they knew personally, but used personal relationships to make connections.

19 There is nothing new in the claim that elites in the South are 'urban-biased' in perception and action. See, for example, Lipton (1977).

References

Aberbach, J. D. and B. A. Rockman (2002) 'Conducting and Coding Elite Interviews', *PS*, December, pp. 673–6

Berman, S. (2001) 'Review Article: Ideas, Norms and Culture in Political Analysis', *Comparative Politics*, 33 (2): 231–50

Berry, J. M. (2002) 'Validity and Reliability Issues in Elite Interviewing', *PS*, December, pp. 679–82

de Swaan, A. (1988) *In Care of the State. Health Care, Education and Welfare in Europe and the USA in the Modern Era*, London: Polity de Swaan, A., J. Manor, E. Øyen and E. Reis (2000) 'Elite Perceptions of the Poor: Reflections on a Comparative Research Project', *Current Sociology*, 48 (1): 43–56

Esanov, A., M. Raiser and W. Buiter (2001) 'Nature's Blessing or Nature's Curse: The Political Economy of Transition in Resource-based Economies', Working Paper no. 65, London: European Bank for Reconstruction and Development

Global Witness (2004) *Time for Transparency. Coming Clean on Oil, Mining and Gas Revenues*, Washington, DC: Global Witness

Goldstein, K. (2002) 'Getting in the Door: Sampling and Completing Elite Interviews', *PS*, December, pp. 669–72

Higley, J. and G. Lengyel (2000) 'Introduction: Elite Configurations after State Socialism', in J. Higley and G. Lengyel (eds), *Elites after State Socialism: Theories and Analysis*, Lanham, MD, and Oxford: Rowman and Littlefield

Hirschman, A. O. (1981) 'Policymaking and Policy Analysis in Latin America – a Return Journey', in A. O. Hirschman (ed.), *Essays in Trespassing. Economics to Politics and Beyond*, Cambridge, London and New York: Cambridge University Press

Houtzager, P. P. (2003) 'From Polycentrism to the Polity', in P. P. Houtzager and M. Moore (eds), *Changing Paths: International Development and the New Politics of Inclusion*, Ann Arbor: University of Michigan Press

Lieberman, R. C. (2002) 'Ideas, Institutions, and Political Order: Explaining Political Change', *American Political Science Review*, 96 (4): 697–712

Lipton, M. (1977) *Why Poor People Stay Poor. Urban Bias in World Development*, London: Temple Smith

Marx, K. (1849/1968) 'Wage Labour and Capital', in K. Marx and F. Engels, *Selected Works in One Volume*, London: Lawrence and Wishart

Moore, M., M. Choudhary and N. Singh (1998) 'How Can *We* Know What *They* Want? Understanding Local Perceptions of Poverty and Ill-being in Asia', IDS Working Paper no. 80, Brighton: Institute of Development Studies

Narayan, D., R. Chambers, M. K. Shah and P. Petesch (2000) *Voices of the Poor. Crying Out for Change*, Washington, DC: Oxford University Press for the World Bank

Parry, G. (1969) *Political Elites*, London: Allen and Unwin

Rivera, S. W., P. M. Kozyreva and E. G. Sarovskii (2002) 'Interviewing Political Elites: Lessons from Russia', *PS*, December, pp. 683–8

Ross, M. L. (2003) 'Oil, Drugs and Diamonds: How Do Natural Resources Vary in Their Impact on Civil War?', in K. Ballantine and J. Sherman (eds), *The Political Economy of Armed Conflict: Beyond Greed and Grievance*, New York: International Peace Academy

Sala-I-Martin, X. and A. Subramanian (2003) 'Addressing the Natural Resource Curse: An Illustration from Nigeria', Working Paper no. WP/03/139, Washington, DC: IMF

Sidel, J. T. (1999), *Capital, Coercion, and Crime. Bossism in the Philippines*, Stanford, CA: Stanford University Press

Skocpol, T. (1992) *Protecting Soldiers and Mothers. The Political Origins of Social Policy in the United States*, Cambridge, MA, and London: The Belknap Press of Harvard University Press

Toye, J. (1997) 'Nationalizing the Antipoverty Agenda', in L. Emmerij (ed.), *Economic and Social Development into the XXI Century*, Washington, DC: Inter-American Development Bank

— (1999) 'Nationalising the Anti-Poverty Agenda', *IDS Bulletin*, 30 (2): 6–12

World Bank (2000) *World Development Report 2000/2001: Attacking Poverty*, New York: Oxford University Press

2 | Perceptions of poverty and inequality among Brazilian elites

ELISA REIS

The idea that Brazil ranks among the most unequal countries in the world has become something of a truism in Brazil itself. The fact is widely commented on in the media and seems to generate considerable embarrassment and a sense of humiliation. To add to the embarrassment, specialists have shown convincingly that the country cannot technically be classified as poor. That is to say, although the proportion of poor people matches that of countries with acute poverty problems, per capita income places Brazil at an intermediate position in the world stratification system. For this reason, the poverty question in Brazil has become irrevocably associated with the inequality issue. But most Brazilians believe that some sort of original sin or birth defect made the country this way. The nation's colonial ancestry and/or the historical experience of slavery are traditionally held responsible for persistent inequality.

Do those who control the country's resources and shape national-level decisions also share this type of fatalism? Or do national elites see societal actors as responsible agents able to shape the ways in which national income is distributed? Taking into consideration the fact that poverty and inequality are so intertwined in Brazil, and that the idea of inequality necessarily evokes notions of distributive justice, it is particularly relevant to examine elite political culture to see what values, beliefs and ideas shape their perception of the country's social situation. Is poverty a real policy issue for Brazilian elites? How do they perceive the magnitude of poverty? What are their profiles of 'the poor'? What do they think should and could be done about the problem? Which actors are principally held responsible for maintaining the status quo or changing the plight of the poor? This chapter summarizes the answers I have found after several years of investigating these issues with different research strategies.

Section 2 comprises a brief summary of the most relevant historical dimensions of Brazil's social structure and poverty problem. In Section 3, I sketch out the character of the Brazilian elite, and comment on the criteria used to select the elite samples used in the two surveys on which this chapter is based. In succeeding sections, I present and comment on the results of this research. Section 4 summarizes the views about poverty that are shared by most Brazilian elites, while Section 5 deals with some of the more significant intra-elite differences, especially regional variations. In Section 6, I make some comparative observations about Brazilian and other national elites examined in this book. Section 7 contains some concluding comments and speculation about contemporary changes in elite perceptions of poverty in Brazil.

Brazilian social structure in historical perspective

Brazil's recorded history is closely linked to the expansion of world commerce of the early modern era. The Portuguese, the first Europeans to arrive in Brazil, landed in 1500 while searching for an alternative route to India. They encountered scattered native tribes that they managed to subordinate by force or persuasion. Despite being occasionally challenged by competitors, Portugal's colonial rule lasted until 1822 when the representative of the Portuguese crown declared Brazil an independent country. Originally, the colonizers mainly worked at extractive economic activities, exploiting the forests for lumber and trying to encourage the natives to assist them in the task (Furtado 1963; Prado 1969). From the seventeenth century onwards, they turned to mining activities and to large-scale agriculture. Since they encountered difficulties in disciplining the natives, they not only absorbed larger numbers of Portuguese settlers, but also engaged in extensive importation of slaves and bonded labour from Africa, especially to produce sugar cane, cotton and tobacco in the north-east. This workforce later went on to extract gold and diamonds in the centre, and finally, in the nineteenth century, to work on the coffee plantations of the centre south. The extreme south experienced a different pattern of colonization, based mainly upon European migrants of Italian, German and Spanish origin. European migrants also became the main source of labour in the coffee plantations after the abolition of slavery in 1888 (Prado 1969; Hall 1969).

In line with this economic profile, the social structure of colonial Brazil combined two inegalitarian traits that brought it close to a caste system: (a) slavery; and (b) proto-serfdom in the north-eastern and other scattered areas of early colonial occupation where debt peonage and generalized patron–client networks were the norm. The southern colonization project was the exception, to a certain extent paralleling the North American experience of free settlements, though it did not acquire an equivalent political and cultural importance.

Instead of opting for the republicanism that inspired independence movements throughout the Americas, from 1822 to 1888 independent Brazil practised constitutional monarchy with an imperial flavour. There were two emperors, both members of the Portuguese dynasty. This element of continuity has been widely mentioned as both cause and consequence of long-lasting features of the polity, notably (a) the remarkable preservation of the territorial integrity of formerly Portuguese Brazil, in contrast to the fragmentation of Spanish Latin America into separate countries; and (b) a propensity for compromise solutions (Carvalho 1980).

In 1889, a military coup put an end to the empire, opening the way for the oligarchic republic, which lasted until 1930. During this period, the hegemony of the major landowners was unquestioned and the centrality of patron–client networks uncontested. It was also at this juncture that the first attempts at industrialization took place, often on the initiative of the same landowning elite. The oligarchic republic also saw the birth of an active labour movement, headed by urban workers of European extraction. Organized labour was brought under state control in the new power alliance consolidated after the 1930 revolution, which made possible a conservative modernization process (Reis 1982; Schwartzman 1982; Velho 1976).

The combination of an internal and an international crisis in 1930 made it possible for Vargas, a *caudillo* from the extreme south, to overthrow the ruling oligarchy. He enforced new political compromises, which made it possible for him to impose dictatorial rule for fifteen years and even to return later as elected president. Under his rule, the country experienced fast modernization from above. Known as the 'father to the poor', Vargas was responsible for the expansion of social rights to urban workers under a populist system that kept the masses under the government's control, while respecting the old patron–client networks in the countryside (Castro Gomes 1979; Fausto 1970; Santos 1979).

Populism was to last far longer than Vargas himself. Industrialization proceeded apace and the influx of newcomers to cities gave a new boost to populism and increased the scope for demagoguery. Continuing economic growth allowed significant social mobility. Despite widespread poverty and inequality, there was hope and even a realistic expectation of social betterment for all. In the early 1960s, the populist political model became outmoded, as growing popular autonomy pointed to the quick erosion of tutelary control from above (Ianni 1968; Weffort 1978). To a great extent, this explains the military takeover of 1964, which ushered in a period of dictatorship lasting until 1985.

Economic growth without political mobilization was the aim – and the achievement – of the armed forces for approximately the first half of their rule. Thereafter, an economic slowdown and decreasing legitimacy made it clear that the costs of repression were becoming too high. Once again, a conciliatory strategy was the chosen solution: the army negotiated a slow, peaceful and gradual transition to democracy. Indeed, Brazil experienced one of the longest democratization processes among the many that have occurred in the recent past in Latin America (Martins 1986; Stepan 1989).

The call for enhanced citizenship in the democratizing era inspired hope for a reduction of poverty in Brazil. The idea of a huge *social debt* that needed to be paid became a catchword of the politics of the day. The new constitution, enacted in 1988, sought to ensure wider social rights on a universal basis. Unfortunately, constitutional zeal was not enough to ensure effective implementation of social rights. Some progress has been made, but poverty and destitution are still widespread. Indeed, the rate exceeds that of countries with a far less impressive economic performance, and the level of inequality has persistently remained close to the top of world charts.

How much awareness is there about poverty and inequality in Brazil? Is the notion of an outstanding social debt truly deep seated? Judging from the discourse of the elites, there is widespread discussion and awareness of the magnitude of both problems. Nearly everyone interviewed in depth quoted statistics and rates that tallied fairly closely with official indices. Furthermore, most of those interviewed were well aware of Brazil's ranking in comparison with other Third World countries, and many drew attention to the fact that several social indicators rank the country below poorer societies. The same evidence appears in articles written by members of the elite in leading newspapers.[1] But, before going into the perceptions of the elites, let us take a brief look at some facts about Brazil's social structure.

Contemporary Brazil cannot be considered a poor country. GDP per capita grew persistently from the 1950s onwards, and at the close of the century the country was clearly 'middle income' on a world scale. With a GDP per capita of around US$3,000, Brazil ranks today as the ninth largest economy in the world (Ipeadata n.d.). If we look at the distribution of this national income, however, the picture changes. Although poverty has declined in recent decades, this transition has been very slow and a large proportion of the population is still living in poverty (Henriques 2000). Moreover, inequality is extremely high and has remained remarkably stable in the recent past.

Using data from the National Household Surveys, Paes de Barros and his associates have shown that, over the last two decades, between 40 and 45 per cent of the total Brazilian population can be considered poor to the extent that their income does not meet basic needs (Barros et al. 2000). In absolute numbers, these figures refer to around 41 million people in 1977 and 53 million in 1999 (Ipeadata n.d.). Furthermore, if we take into account the different living conditions within the world of the poor we can observe quite significant variations. Thus, of the 53 million poor people in Brazil at the turn of the twentieth century, around 23 million, or around 17 per cent of the total population, live in abject poverty (ibid.).

While most of the poor live in urban areas, poverty is more severe in the countryside. It is also more acute among blacks than whites, affects female-headed households more than their male counterparts, and hits the north-east more than the central or southern regions. The inequality one finds reproduced in every municipality is as significant, however, as gender, regional or rural–urban differences. At the local level, we find the same dramatic distance between the upper and lower social strata, be it measured in terms of income, wealth or access to public goods and services. In short, inequality per se constitutes a serious social and economic problem for Brazilian society, leading Barros and Mendonça to conclude that ' ... the extreme degree of distributional inequality in Brazil represents the main determining factor of poverty' (Barros and Mendonça 1999: 10).

The inequality of Brazilian society can be illustrated by reference to common standard measures. The Gini Index for income distribution stuck at around 0.6 throughout the second half of the twentieth century. When we look at the extremes of distribution, the picture becomes even more dramatic. Taking into consideration only the 1990s, we observe that the top 1 per cent collected 13 to 15 per cent of the country's income, while the top 10 per cent obtained between 45 and 49 per cent. Correspondingly, the poorest 20 per cent received around 2 per cent, and the poorest 50 per cent a mere 12 per cent (Ipeadata n.d.).

How can we explain acute, persistent and pervasive inequality? One could resort to the secular monopoly that the elite holds over all kinds of resources, political, economic and social. This is what Brazilians do most of the time to explain how and why inequalities persist. Academic and lay publications, official and counter-cultural discourses alike, all call attention to deep history: the Iberian influence, the *latifundia* tenure pattern, and slavery. These three 'colonial pillars' are assumed to underpin poverty and inequality in Brazil. It is striking that people seldom question how this legacy has persisted for so long, and why. While we have made many more or less successful attempts to explain social changes in Brazil, little effort has been dedicated to investigating why and how inequality has been so persistent.

No one would deny the importance of the colonial cultural and institutional legacy. Important research has called our attention to the patrimonial political structures inherited from Portugal (Faoro 1958; Schwartzman 1977, 1982; Schmitter 1971), and to the corporatist (and conservative) values shaping the nation's culture (Morse 1988; Wiarda 1981; Stepan

1978). Equally important are the analyses that call attention to the fact that Brazil was the last country in the New World to abolish slavery. The path to abolition in 1888 was gradual, shaped by a process of political negotiation that was controlled by the slave owners themselves. Gradualism, and later on the state-subsidized substitution of European migrants for former black slaves, blighted the socio-economic prospects of labourers to the extent that they granted an abundant labour supply (Reis 1982; Reis and Reis 1988). Further, the prevailing land tenure system conferred almost unlimited social, political and economic power upon large landholders until very late in the nation's history (Velho 1976; Reis 1982).

Yet none of these historical legacies, separately or jointly, explains why inequality remains deep and persistent up to the present. Landowner-ship has long ceased to provide control of any basic economic resource. Slave labour has been illegal for over a century. Many institutional reforms have been undertaken, but the past is typically understood as the cause of the deep stain of persistent inequality on contemporary culture. Such beliefs themselves constitute cultural phenomena to be investigated, but what matters to us here is that the inertia of history is not an adequate explanation for the continuity of social phenomena. The combined effect of structural constraints, interests in dispute and circumscribed choices affects both change and continuity. The fact that Brazilian society has remained so unequal, and that inequality contributes to the persistence of poverty, cannot be credited to genetic factors alone. Decisions and pre-varication, actions and inaction, shaped the mechanisms of change and continuity from which historical processes are made.

If we enquire into the perceptions of powerful actors, we can throw some light on their direct or indirect preferences, and that in turn helps us to understand the puzzle of continuity. By *perceptions*, I mean cognitions and values – and not opinions, which are more volatile expressions informing motivation, compliance and non-compliance. Thus, to look for elite percep-tions about poverty is to search for the cognitive and normative views those at the top hold about the poverty problem in Brazil. It is evident that we need more than the likelihood of elite support if effective public action is to be taken against poverty and inequality. But the fact that an understanding of elite perceptions will not alone solve the problem would be a poor excuse not to pursue this ethical, theoretical and practical concern. An expanded understanding of the views and preferences of specific players may provide clues to the motivational ground of solidarity, as well as insights into the motives that lead these players to take action for or against change. Looking at the elite perceptions of poverty and inequality, we may begin to understand how the Brazilian colonial inheritance has been preserved, less

31

through inertia or natural reproduction than as an ideological justification for inaction and the evasion of social responsibility.

Looking at the elite

The Brazilian study started with an elite survey that subsequently became a kind of pilot venture from which the international comparative project developed. In that preliminary study, I worked with a sample of 320 members of the elite representing four different sectors: top bureaucrats, politicians, business leaders and union leaders. The sample of bureaucrats was drawn from people occupying positions in the federal administration immediately below cabinet ministers. Politicians were selected from the members of the National Congress. Representatives of the business elite were selected from a list of top names responsible for the country's 500 largest firms. Finally, the union leaders were picked from an authoritative list of unions provided by the Brazilian Institute of Geography and Statistics. Within each of these groupings, actual interviewees were selected at random.[2] The criterion used to select the population sample was institutional: people were chosen because they occupied top institutional positions. It was the formal roles they played which mattered, not their individual personal characteristics. Statistical analysis of the results of this *initial survey* permits me to make some generalizations about the views of Brazilian elites. All tables in this chapter are based on data obtained from this initial survey.

The decision to undertake an international comparative study on elite perceptions took place after this initial survey was completed. The *second survey* in Brazil was focused more on in-depth interviews using semi-structured questionnaires. The emphasis shifted to the search for new insights into the ways in which elites conceive of poverty. Instead of the fourfold classification of elites, I now used the same more diverse set of categories employed by authors of other chapters: politicians, prominent media actors, intellectuals and professionals, union leaders, business executives, leaders of voluntary associations, top civil servants, military and police officers, big landowners and religious leaders (de Swaan et al. 2000). The same principle of institutional pre-eminence that had been employed to choose the potential sample population in the initial survey was adopted for the second round. Now, however, unlike in the initial sample, the institutions were not randomly selected: they were picked because we considered them to be relevant and illustrative. In total eighty interviews were conducted, half in the adjacent states of Rio de Janeiro and São Paulo in the centre-south, and half in the states of Bahia and Ceará in the north-east. The selection of two regions usually taken as dual poles in the country was an attempt to take into account possible variations in the perception of elites dispersed over such a large territorial base as Brazil. Would the economic, social, political and cultural peculiarities of the two regions affect the way those at the top conceived of poverty and inequality? As will be seen later, while on many issues elites in both regions tend to hold similar views, there are also interesting regional variations, particularly in respect to the ways they see the relationships between market and state.

In practice, the second Brazilian survey also functioned as a check on the results of the initial survey. Hearing what those interviewed had to say, instead of assessing their agreements and disagreements, could perhaps confirm previous results, specify findings and clarify meanings. The two sets of results point in the same direction but provide different insights. The answers from the initial survey were confirmed by the in-depth interviews, but the latter also added some subtleties.

Though Brazilian society has often been described as very elitist, social scientists give us little help in establishing who the nation's elites are. Where do they come from? How are they recruited? What are their particular characteristics? Unfortunately there are few studies on the subject, and those there are were mainly conducted in the 1960s, and only on the entrepreneurial elite (Queiroz 1965; Queiroz et al. 1962). While these studies, and a few individual biographies, provide relevant insights, they do not allow us to make generalizations on social background, recruitment and socialization processes, intra-elite networks, etc. We know that there is a huge gap between the elite and the large majority of the population in terms of income and other indicators of well-being. For our purposes, however, we cannot treat elites as synonymous with the upper social strata (the social elite), as the two do not necessarily coincide in terms of role performance. Many of those who enjoy high socio-economic status are not part of the elite as defined here. And a small minority of the elite as we define it do not have high social and economic status.

Even though it is not possible to use existing knowledge to characterize Brazilian elites in detail, it is certainly possible to provide some background information about them. In terms of social origins, most are upwardly mobile. This reflects the substantial mobility found generally in Brazil. As a new society, and as a result of fast structural transformation, Brazil has opened up a considerable number of new positions to its population. While it is true that the majority of the mobile are concentrated at the bottom layers of society, there has also been space for considerable upward movement in the middle and higher levels of the social hierarchy owing to rapid urbanization and industrialization (Pastore 1989; Pastore and Valle e Silva 2000; Scalon 1999). Many of the elite representatives in my sample of in-depth interviews are of middle-class origin. There is also a small but telling number of persons who started from a lower social status. They tend to be concentrated among the elderly of the group. The lower the age of an upwardly mobile member of the elite, the more likely it is that he or she belongs to the political or union sector. Party and union politics have become the typical channel for new entries into elite positions.

It is particularly among members of the economic elite that we seem to find less social mobility – a possible indication that the transformations of the economic structure are no longer readily associated with a net expansion of high social positions. Predictably, the gender composition of the elite is highly biased. The bias is so intense, however, that it deserves some attention. The initial survey sample did not include a single woman. The deliberate choice of institutional role incumbents, which oriented the in-depth interviews, did produce a few women interviewees. Interestingly, they were highly concentrated in the political and the techno-bureaucratic elites, and, within the latter, they were largely confined to institutions dedicated to social welfare activities.

All things considered, Brazilian elites seem to be remarkably homogeneous. Although they include many newcomers of middle-class origin, members have similar educational backgrounds, are white, and speak the same language. Despite their secularized outlook, a common Catholic upbringing is the norm. The large majority is of urban origin, highly educated, male, of Brazilian-born parents and grandparents. The exceptional cases of foreign-born or first-generation Brazilian elites are restricted to the religious and cultural sectors. It is also rare for people of low-class origin to reach top institutional positions. As previously observed, the exceptions tend to be found in party and union politics.

Does the fact that members of the elite are similar mean that they tend to think alike about poverty?

Elite perceptions of poverty and inequality: consensus

My point of departure is the observation that the Brazilian elite is highly sensitized to the poverty issue. Both the initial survey and the in-depth interviews leave no shadow of doubt that members of the elite list poverty and/or the absence of social rights as being among the country's major problems. The information in the tables illustrates that the Brazilian elite sees close connections between the country's problems and social issues arising from poverty.

As the data in Table 2.1 show, nearly half the respondents affirm that the major obstacles to democracy are social rather than economic or, strictly speaking, political. Thus, the two most often selected answers

TABLE 2.1 Main obstacles to democracy in Brazil: percentage of interviewees citing different obstacles

Low educational level of the population	24
High levels of poverty and social inequality	23
Lack of party political tradition	16
Corporatism of groups and sectors of society	10
Incompetence of power incumbents	6
Lack of popular political organization	6
Selfishness of the elites	5
Political clientelism	4
Too much power in the hands of the political executive	3
High inflation rate	1
Impoverishment of the middle class	1
Prolonged economic recession	1
Threat of military intervention	0
Total	100
Number of interviews	316

were the population's lack of education and poverty/inequality. Other frequent choices included Brazil's lack of party tradition and the 'corporatist' defence of interests and privileges, two responses that together comprised around one quarter of all choices made by those interviewed. Can we conclude that those who identified these two latter issues as the most important obstacles to democracy were also essentially focusing on political explanations? This conclusion seems right as far as the question of party tradition goes, but the same cannot be said about those who pointed to corporatism as the culprit. Corporatism is so much a part of Brazil's cultural tradition that it has become more associated with morality than with structures of representation. References to corporatism are usually allusions to some form of restrictive social morality, which is compared adversely with some notion of attachment to the general will or interest. In the contemporary Brazilian political lexicon, 'corporatism' is tantamount to 'selfishness'. Corporatism is perceived to indicate a lack of social commitment. Thus, all things considered, Brazilian elites tend to associate a consolidated democracy with commitment to social rights.

Table 2.2 shows that the elites also expressed a concern with the social dimension when the question referred to 'national problems' in general rather than to democratic stability in particular. They were asked: 'In your view, what are the two most important problems facing the country today? Name them in what you consider to be their order of importance.' Only the first problem mentioned is taken into account in Table 2.2. The pattern of

TABLE 2.2 Brazil's most important problems: percentage of interviewees citing different problems

Problem	Total sample	Politi-cians	Bureau-crats	Business-men	Labour union leaders
Inflation	17.5	22.6	14.0	25.3	8.8
Education and health	15.9	13.2	23.3	16.8	8.8
Poverty	14.3	15.1	11.6	8.4	23.8
Governability	11.5	11.3	11.6	17.9	3.8
Income distribution	8.3	3.8	11.6	5.3	11.3
Other political issues	8.3	3.8	7.0	13.7	6.3
Other economic issues	5.4	1.9	6.0	3.2	8.9
Corruption	4.8	9.4	3.5	1.1	7.5
Recession and unemployment	4.1	9.4	2.3	2.1	5.0
Behaviour of the elites	3.5	0	1.2	5.3	6.3
Foreign dependence	3.2	3.8	2.3	0	7.5
Moral crisis	2.2	3.8	3.5	1.1	1.3
Other social issues	1.0	1.9	1.2	0	1.3
Total	100	100	100	100	100
Number of interviews	314	53	86	95	80

responses in Table 2.2 differs to some extent from that in Table 2.1, despite similarities regarding the importance of socio-economic problems. More interesting, however, are the variations between elite sectors. For example, at the time the survey was conducted the inflation problem ranked number one overall but did not appear to be a major concern for union leaders or even for bureaucrats. Responses on the importance of the poverty problem were almost the inverse: about a quarter of the union leaders asserted that this problem was paramount, whereas only a small minority of the business leaders expressed the same opinion. The emphasis on educational and health problems, ranked in second place, to a certain extent parallels the high ranking of the education issue in Table 2.1. Again, it is less important in the eyes of union leaders, who tend to rank poverty, income distribution and other economic issues as more significant.

Displaying sensitivity to the size or relevance of a problem does not necessarily mean that it will be placed at the top of the country's policy agenda. The respondents were also asked to rank a given list of policy objectives in terms of priority. Table 2.3 summarizes their answers.

Once again, the educational issue appears in first place. Nearly a quarter of the respondents identified the socio-economic objective of increasing the nation's educational levels as the priority target for the immediate future. Other responses in Table 2.3 that deserve attention are the dissimilari-

Goal	Total sample	Politi- cians	Bureau- crats	Business- men	Labour union leaders
Increase educational levels	23.0	14.8	24.7	29.8	18.5
Reduce size of state	18.2	22.2	13.5	33.0	3.7
Eliminate poverty and reduce inequality	17.6	25.9	19.1	9.6	19.8
Increase popular participation in political decisions	16.4	5.6	14.6	5.3	38.3
Preserve the democratic regime	11.3	20.4	7.9	8.5	12.3
Guarantee economic growth	9.7	7.3	14.6	10.6	4.9
Integrate the economy into the international market	2.2	1.9	2.2	3.2	1.2
Keep order	0.9	1.9	2.2	0	0
Further integrate the country into Mercosur	0.3	0	1.1	0	0
Protect the environment	0.3	0	0	0	1.2
Total	100	100	100	100	100
Number of interviews	318	54	89	94	81

ties between elite sectors. The second-most important goal, downsizing the state, received greatest mention from business leaders, followed by politicians and bureaucrats, in that order. Barely any union leaders chose it as a major goal. On the other hand, while a large number of politicians, union leaders and bureaucrats say the priority should be fighting poverty and reducing inequality, for the business elites such issues are apparently of far less concern. Last but not least, popular participation beyond the polls was not valued highly, except by union leaders.

Focusing now on the problem of poverty – one that has received much public attention and is a constant in government discourse – elite members were asked, by means of a fixed-choice question, what they consider to be the main causes of poverty in Brazil. As indicated in Table 2.4, political and attitudinal explanations rank very high. We can see that objective economic factors were not highlighted as the cause of poverty. Only among business leaders did the recession take on special importance, while insufficient economic growth mattered greatly only to these same businessmen and to bureaucrats. The causes of widespread poverty that were named most often were the state's failure to fulfil its social functions and a lack of political will. Across elite sectors, there seems to be a strong belief in some voluntaristic explanation for Brazil's persisting poverty.

Brazilian elites

TABLE 2.4 Main causes of poverty: percentage of interviewees citing different causes

Cause	Total sample	Politi-cians	Bureau-crats	Business-men	Labour union leaders
The state does not fulfil its social functions	26.0	25.5	25.0	32.2	20.7
Lack of political will to fight poverty	19.6	23.5	18.2	20.0	18.3
Elites lack social sensitivity	13.5	11.8	23.9	10.0	7.3
Insufficient economic development	13.2	9.8	17.0	18.9	4.9
The protracted recession	9.0	7.8	3.4	15.6	8.5
The fatal logic of the capitalist system	8.7	7.8	4.5	0	23.2
Monopolization of opportunities	7.7	9.8	6.8	3.3	12.2
The need for income con-centration for economic development	1.3	3.9	0	0	2.4
Lack of effort on the part of the poor	1.0	0	1.1	0	2.4
Total	100	100	100	100	100
Number of interviews	311	51	88	90	82

TABLE 2.5 Main means of reducing poverty: percentage of interviewees citing different initiatives

Initiative	Total sample	Politi-cians	Bureau-crats	Business-men	Labour union leaders
Promote agrarian reform	31.1	35.3	32.6	6.8	53.8
Increase the efficiency of public social services	16.4	21.6	17.4	21.6	6.3
Control population growth	13.4	7.8	14.0	26.1	2.5
Deregulate the economy	10.2	5.9	4.7	26.1	1.3
Increase progressiveness of income tax	9.5	11.8	12.8	9.1	5.0
Increase social expenditures	8.5	9.8	10.5	5.7	8.8
Implement profit-sharing schemes for labour	8.2	5.9	5.8	3.4	17.5
Tax wealth	2.6	2.0	2.3	1.1	5.0
Total	100	100	100	100	100
Number of interviews	305	51	86	88	80

TABLE 2.6 Viability and desirability of particular social policies: percentage of interviewees citing particular policies as viable and/or desirable

Policy	Viable and desirable	Desirable but not viable	Viable but not desirable	Neither viable nor desirable	Total
Free and universal basic education	85.5	11.0	3.2	0.3	100
Popular housing programmes	80.3	13.3	3.2	3.2	100
Free and universal access to health services	56.9	36.7	3.2	3.2	100
Early retirement*	52.6	15.9	11.4	20.1	100
Unemployment insurance	48.5	39.2	6.5	5.8	100
Food distribution programmes	35.6	24.8	21.8	17.8	100
Free university education	35.1	37.4	8.5	19.0	100
Minimum income for everyone above age 25	27.8	39.2	26.1	30.4	100
Old-age pension regardless of previous contribution	9.4	24.7	3.9	62.0	100

* Refers to early retirement under federal laws that permit women and men to retire after 30 and 35 years of service, respectively, regardless of age

Respondents were also asked to choose, from a given list, what they felt would be the most important initiative for reducing social inequality. The data summarized in Table 2.5 reveal sharp differences between business leaders and other sectors of the elite. As can be observed, agrarian reform, which overall was the most popular means cited to reduce inequality, was unpopular among the business elites. On the other hand, the two initiatives that business leaders declared best suited to promoting social equality, namely population control and economic deregulation, did not receive much attention from other elites. Increased efficiency in providing social services was also picked frequently by everyone, except labour elites. Lastly, while one might expect business leaders to be sceptical about the beneficial aspects of more progressive taxation and expanded social expenditures, it is somehow surprising that politicians, bureaucrats and particularly union leaders appeared to feel equally dubious.

I also enquired about the desirability and viability of particular social policies. The idea was to invite the interviewees to relate the normative and evaluative dimensions of specific policy initiatives. Looking at Table 2.6, we observe that from a purely normative perspective (first and second columns) 60 per cent or more of the elites affirmed the desirability of every

TABLE 2.7 Why social policies do not meet their objectives: percentage of interviewees citing different reasons

Reason	Total sample	Politi- cians	Bureau- crats	Business- men	Labour union leaders
Bad planning or implemen- tation	29.3	34.6	33.7	33.7	16.0
Lack of political will, or low priority	18.8	19.2	19.1	14.1	23.5
Political and/or personal use of these policies	12.7	7.7	4.5	15.2	22.2
Corruption	8.6	9.6	10.1	6.5	8.6
Characteristics of the elite*	5.4	5.8	5.6	2.2	8.6
Paternalistic and/or palliative nature of policies	5.7	7.7	5.6	6.5	3.7
State concentrates on other activities**	5.4	3.8	4.5	7.6	4.9
Lack of resources***	4.5	3.8	6.7	4.3	2.5
Lack of participation by civil society	3.8	0	5.6	4.3	3.7
Structural economic problems	2.2	5.8	1.1	1.1	2.5
Greater private sector partici- pation in implementation	1.3	1.9	0	3.3	0
Others	2.2	0	3.4	1.1	3.7
Total	100	100	100	100	100
Number of interviews	314	52	89	92	81

* Selfishness, short-sightedness, authoritarianism, etc. ** i.e. the state is too big and also too active in direct economic activity, thereby diverting human and capital resources from social areas *** This answer implied no critique of the activities of the state but rather pointed to a scarcity of funds for implementation of social policy

social policy except the last – contribution-free old-age pensions. Moreover, the proportion of those who classified the policies in question as both desirable and viable is always quite high, implying that the elites must have some measure of confidence in the potential of these social policies. What explanations did our respondents give for their typical perception that in practice social policies fail to meet their objectives? Table 2.7 summarizes the answers obtained for this open-ended question.

Most of the elites explained the failure of social policies principally in terms of mismanagement or attitudinal issues, rather than objective structural constraints. It is intriguing that bad planning and policy mis-management were ranked first among the reasons for failure, particularly when these responses come from the bureaucratic elite in charge of policy

TABLE 2.8 Worst consequences of poverty in large cities: percentage of interviewees citing different consequences

Consequence	Total sample	Politi-cians	Bureau-crats	Business-men	Labour union leaders
Violence, crime, insecurity	51.6	64.1	49.4	44.8	55.9
Dehumanization, social apartheid	10.2	7.7	6.2	13.8	11.8
Risk of social conflict or social chaos	8.4	7.7	9.9	11.0	2.9
Declining quality of life	5.5	2.6	8.6	6.9	1.5
Social misery	5.1	5.1	3.7	2.3	10.3
Unemployment	4.4	5.1	1.2	4.6	7.4
Vicious circle of poverty	4.0	2.6	6.2	5.7	0
Obstacles to development	2.9	0	3.7	3.4	2.9
Housing problem (slums)	2.2	0	3.7	0	4.4
Threat to democratic stability	1.5	2.6	2.5	1.1	0
Encourages political oppor-tunism	1.1	0	1.2	1.1	1.5
Others	3.3	2.6	3.7	4.6	1.5
Total	100	100	100	100	100
Number of interviews	275	39	81	87	68

planning and implementation. It is equally intriguing that politicians and top bureaucrats in particular listed lack of political will among the most important factors behind policy failure.

Initially, the data we have been discussing seem to paint a rather contra-dictory picture. Our elites seemingly felt that issues of poverty and inequal-ity were of great relevance to Brazilian development in their own right, and were in addition among the most important obstacles to democracy. Further, several policies aimed at fighting poverty and providing some form of social protection were classified as both desirable and viable. Yet, at the same time, a large proportion of the elite claimed that social policies fail owing to a lack of political will, opportunistic misuse of social programmes, and a lack of social conscience. I would argue, however, that no contradic-tion exists. It is to be expected that, from the perspective of these kinds of politically strategic elites, the role played by will, decision-making and policy management should be deemed paramount. Going even farther, I suggest that the very predominance of 'voluntaristic' rather than 'structural' explanations of public policy indicates that my respondents recognized the extreme concentration of social, economic and political resources in Brazil.

Brazilian elites

In other words, being conscious of the gravity of poverty problems, and also of the acute social inequalities prevailing in the country, members of the elite are also deeply aware of their own power and privileges. Equally, these data suggest our elites believe that they are in a privileged position to alter the status quo. That then raises the question of what incentives they might have to introduce change. They are most certainly aware of the risks posed by excessive poverty and inequality. Thus, for example, when asked to name the worst consequence of poverty in large cities, a significant majority mentioned violence, crime and insecurity (Table 2.8). Brazil's strategic elites see the urban poor as a 'dangerous class'. There is nothing to indicate, however, what factors might explain their concomitant lack of collective will to attack social problems. Based on this survey, we can only speculate as to what might make the elites sensitive to the acute social problems Brazil faces, yet unable or unwilling to make a concerted effort to change the situation.

So let us speculate a bit. Based on a pattern that emerged in Table 2.8, I suggest that it may often be hard to move from the individual to the collective level. Many members of the elite placed emphasis on the individual negative consequences of poverty, such as crime and lack of security, whereas a far smaller proportion pointed to its collective negative consequences (i.e. social conflict or social chaos). This may reflect the individualized or fragmented social identity of both elites and masses (Reis 1998). Whatever the case, further investigation is necessary if we are to clarify this apparent dissociation between social awareness and social responsibility among the elites.

From the survey data the salience of poverty issues appears mostly as a relative question: those who answered the questionnaire ranked such issues in relation to others they were confronted with. In the in-depth interviews, elites were invited to comment on issues that they considered to be the most important for the country, whatever their nature. This free choice of issues revealed a similar pattern of response, even though at this stage my elite sample included eleven sectors and not just the four that comprised the survey research. Nearly every one of those interviewed mentioned poverty and inequality as being among the major concerns. It is interesting to observe that most people referred to both poverty and inequality. Often they would refer to these two problems as if they were synonymous. And, when asked to indicate which was more important, most had trouble in distinguishing between the two. As they often said, 'poverty and inequality are head and tail of one and the same problem'.

Among those who did manage to distinguish between poverty and inequality, there is a tendency to perceive the latter as being more problematic, more serious or more perverse. Many of those interviewed emphasize that, all things considered, inequality 'causes' poverty. Others indicate that, while poverty can be dignified, inequality is always associated with indignity, breeds violence, or has other adverse consequences. These responses, however, do not indicate adherence to any sort of radical egalitarianism or even to a milder doctrine such as equality in initial socio-economic conditions. What is perceived as reproachable or dangerous is too wide a gap between the poor and the non-poor.

The in-depth interviews suggest a remarkable consensus among the elites about the causes of poverty and inequality. Actually their views were typical of the Brazilian population: poverty and inequality are immediately attributed to Brazil's origins. As explained in the first section, our social evils are constantly blamed on the Portuguese colonial inheritance and slavery, almost as an original sin. Nearly all those interviewed resorted to these arguments at one point or another. Some stressed cultural rather than political or economic dimensions of this history, but at heart the arguments are the same: contemporary social evils are inherited, and not of our own creation. Iberian values are blamed, for example, for Brazil's deficit in community initiatives or lack of a competitive drive. Actually, this basic belief seems to act as the foundation myth for Brazilian society and as such constitutes an important part of the national culture. To seek the specific view of the elite we must go farther, searching for the ways in which they deal with the myth of the nation's birthmark.

How great a problem is poverty? I did not ask this question in the initial survey, but did so in the in-depth interviews. Politicians, senior officials and cultural elites usually answered in terms of the official statistics. Those who did not seem to be so well acquainted with the statistics still saw poverty as a top-priority problem, and often used as their indicators urban decay, the incidence of beggars, rates of violence and criminality. These are the factors most often associated with poverty. Although a few gave priority to the consequences of the problem for the poor themselves, there is a tendency to emphasize negative consequences of poverty for the non-poor.

It is mainly when discussing the size of the poverty problem that elite members reveal the greatest sensitivity to its consequences. The typical response would indicate that the problem is a major issue because its consequences spill over into society as a whole. How? First, by affecting the quality of life of both the poor and the non-poor; and second, by affecting adversely the quality of the labour force. The latter is perceived as simultaneously hampering the prospects for economic growth and the life opportunities of the poor. As already suggested by the initial survey data, Brazilian elites portray the poor as 'dangerous people'. This revelation is nearly always followed by spontaneous statements absolving the poor from the responsibility for frightening the non-poor, such as: 'it is not their fault, they are victims themselves of structural constraints, of unjust conditions'. Other typical comments echo the words voiced in one of the interviews: 'Violence is the worst consequence of poverty. A poor person lacking a job, income, housing, etc. will have to look somewhere for money ... where can that person find alternatives other than in robbery, drug dealing and the like?'

From what has been said thus far, the findings suggest that at least some of the components of social consciousness of poverty seem to exist among the Brazilian elite: they give great prominence to the problem which they see as being among the major issues confronting the country. Moreover, they perceive it as something that affects society as a whole. We may conclude that one of the components of de Swaan's concept of 'social consciousness' is clearly present: the elite is aware of the problem of poverty and perceives it as one generating negative externalities. What can we conclude about the other two components of the concept: some notion of responsibility for the problem and identification of feasible action to overcome the status quo? Here again the initial survey and the unstructured interviews point in the same direction.

The elite believe that something should and could be done to combat poverty. Thus, the survey research indicated that elites considered several hypothetical anti-poverty measures as both desirable and viable (Table 2.6). The in-depth interviews point in the same direction. Nearly all those consulted point out that it is possible to do something to alter the present situation. Furthermore, there is also a widespread consensus that action should not be left to the poor themselves. The poor are perceived as a 'threat' to the well-to-do and to society at large, but the reason is that they themselves are the victims of major social forces. Most members of the elite reject suggestions that the poor are lazy or responsible for their own fate. Rather, those who experience deprivation are pictured as victims of perverse structures, political inaction and inadequate policies.

Who should be responsible for taking action against poverty? Across sectors and regions, priority is definitely assigned to the state. Even those who emphasize the need for societal and state initiatives make it clear that the primary responsibility lies with the 'state' or with 'the government' – terms often used interchangeably. For the analyst, though, the source of perplexity has to be: who, in the elite's view, constitutes the state or the government? Like people from other social strata, elites always depict the state as 'they'. Even among those who occupy public political or administrative positions, it is usual for the state to be referred to as 'the other'. This seems to seriously compromise the chances that elites might assume social responsibility for poverty. The fact that they assign blame for overcoming poverty and inequality to an agency held to be beyond their control implies that they exempt themselves from the task.

The manner in which elites conceive of social partnership in welfare initiatives is also worthy of note. The majority of those interviewed tend to look with reservation upon private philanthropy and the involvement of NGOs in social policy. Either because they distrust the efficacy and efficiency of the non-governmental players or because they fear the state might pass its legitimate responsibilities on to others, the majority within the elite is sceptical of the third sector. More research will be required to delve further into the motives that lead the elite to prefer public authority to community initiatives. Perhaps it will be even more important to identify the implications of this preference in the shaping of a social consciousness among elite sectors. At this juncture, though, I merely want to draw attention to the fact that this attitude towards voluntary involvement in social policy is a distinguishing characteristic among the Brazilian elites. There are obvious exceptions here, but they are mainly concentrated among particular niches of the business elite committed to philanthropy. Many people state very explicitly their suspicions about 'private bodies performing public tasks', making statements on the following lines: 'Who actually benefits from these NGOs? NGOs are opportunistic; it is different when the communities themselves take the initiative. NGOs are NGOs and the state is the state. The former should limit themselves to monitoring the government's social policies and be discouraged from getting themselves directly involved.'

In short, the suspicion one finds within the elite with respect to non-governmental players suggests that to most of them the state remains exclusively responsible for the plight of the poor. When provoked, interviewees would often make 'politically correct' statements about the desirability of partnerships between the state and civil society, but their subsequent analyses and normative judgements suggested that in most cases this was mere rhetoric.

The evidence in Table 2.5 suggests that our respondents favoured government action to counteract poverty. All except the business elite give top priority to agrarian reform. And everybody thought that the state should provide better public services and goods. The in-depth interviews reveal the same priorities, but enable us further to explore their meaning. Policy preferences are not just instrumental judgements about relative efficacy and efficiency. Justifying their preference for one initiative or another, respondents revealed their implicit normative concepts of responsibility, justice and equality. For example, it was clear that the strong commitment to education was grounded in the ideal of equality of opportunity. In their view, the state should actively promote equal educational opportunities so that the poor could improve their condition and even reduce the distance that separates them from the better off.

When expressing their opinions about affirmative action, respondents made their preference for equality of opportunity even more explicit. At the same time, they openly rejected equality of outcomes or conditions. As they often put it, the latter would represent official discrimination against non-minorities and a denial of 'true' (universal) equality. Actually, the condemnation of affirmative action constitutes one of the strongest areas of consensus among Brazilian elites. Although everybody admitted that blacks and women suffer discrimination, with very few exceptions they expressed strong objections to quota systems in education or in the labour market. These objections are mostly voiced in terms of the defence of principles of equality of opportunity. People from a wide variety of political persuasions shared a preference for liberal, universalistic measures. As one interviewee said: 'To establish quotas is to give discrimination a blueprint, thereby making discrimination official. What has to be done is to open up opportunities for all and let both equalities and inequalities develop freely. Everything that is compulsory sounds even derogatory towards the ones supposedly protected.'

Less ideological objections to affirmative action were voiced far less frequently. A few people claimed, however, that affirmative action hampers the productive sector by forcing it to use less qualified, poorly trained labour. As one of them put it: 'affirmative action is a form of state demagoguery at the expense of the business sector'.

Analysing the interviews even further, we can grasp the connection between these views and the predominant interpretation of the elite's moral responsibility in relation to poverty and inequality. As I explained above, many interviewees believed that the state should provide good educational opportunities for all. The poor would then be able to use these opportunities to obtain the qualifications which, when used in the labour market, would help them to climb the social ladder. Should the wealthy make some sacrifice to help make good educational opportunities possible? A large proportion of the elite perceived that they already made a fair (or more than fair) contribution. To increase their tax burden would be unjust and perhaps even detrimental to economic growth. They blame state incompetence, or lack of political will, for the failure of the existing education system to provide the right opportunities. Many respondents had no doubt that the amount of resources devoted to social policies is already sufficient. They believed that the problem lay in a shortage of good management. Some were eloquent in blaming the government: 'To increase taxes is craziness! We already pay too much. Instead of penalizing production, the state ought to promote administrative efficiency and to punish the mismanagement of public funds.'

This preference for enhanced educational opportunities for all seems to be partially justified by the long-term social mobility trends in the country. From the 1950s until recently, changes in economic structure and the expansion of educational opportunities allowed for significant upward mobility with scarcely any downward mobility at all (Pastore and Valle e Silva 2000). This helps justify the belief that the opening up of opportunities is more efficient as a strategy than any kind of redistribution. There are also more explicit indications, however, that, while our respondents voiced support for a wide range of social policies, the underlying commitment was implicitly weak. Elites themselves were unwilling to bear the costs. Costs should be borne by 'the state' or some other parties. And some proposals were unrealistic, suggesting that in large part they served a rhetorical purpose. One can illustrate all these points from my in-depth explorations of the fact that the initial survey showed widespread elite support for agrarian reform.

It was widely suggested that, if the state were to redistribute land, the poor would be better off and other sections of society would benefit because there would be fewer poor people putting pressure on public services in large urban centres. Two aspects of this argument require critical attention. First, this was not seen as a measure that would impose any cost on the people advocating it. The initial costs would be covered by the state, and support for land reform typically came from elite sectors that have no stake in rural land, especially public officials, intellectuals, professionals and others for whom private property is not the major asset. Conversely, private entrepreneurs typically mounted a strong defence of the principle of respect for private property. Speaking of elite supporters of agrarian reforms, a banker said: ' ... tell these people that the landless movement will now claim urban property and they will immediately withdraw support for the cause'. Second, there was a distinct sense of unreality about the land reform programme that was typically envisioned: the movement of the urban poor back to the countryside. It is not credible that this could be effected on a sufficient scale actually to reduce urban populations and the pressure on urban resources, and therefore generate the benefits for the more wealthy urban populations which my respondents referred to. Further, the idea was often underpinned by an idealization of rural life and by ignoring the fact that a large portion of the urban poor has actually no rural experience at all. Both this exaltation of rural life and a self-interested

47

search for restoration of urban centres seem to inspire the judgement of one of my interviewees: ' ... the poor in the countryside are much happier than the rich in the large city, besieged by threats to their property and physical integrity'.

Note finally that land distribution was seen essentially as a social policy initiative rather than a component of a 'pro-poor' economic strategy. Many respondents explicitly indicated that the goal was to give the poor a useful occupation and not to maximize economic efficiency. Here in particular the views of our respondents differ radically from those of Bangladeshi elites, who would rarely countenance any distribution of material assets or opportunities to the poor unless this could be justified in terms of 'productivity' (Chapter 4). Members of the Bangladeshi elite have a strong sense of affinity with the poor but, unlike Brazilian elites, do not consider that they owe any 'social debt' to them.

Elite perceptions of poverty and inequality: variation

Overall, there was a substantial degree of homogeneity in elite perceptions of poverty. We could sensibly talk of a 'common elite culture'. The variations are often correlated with other characteristics in a fairly predictable way. These include: political party affiliation; 'sector' – the basis of several variations discussed above; and region, occupation and gender, which are treated in this section.

The hypothesis that there would be significant regional variations shaped the original research design, through the focus on a potential contrast between the centre-south and the north-east. It soon became clear that, while members of the elite were well connected among themselves across regions and sectors, direct personal networks were more visible in the north-east than in the centre-south. The explanation is probably demographic: members of the elite are more numerous in the centre-south, and therefore less likely to be connected to another person in the same survey sample. This suggests that the north-eastern elites are better placed to act collectively than their counterparts in Rio de Janeiro or São Paulo.

Some regional variations in responses to questions can be explained in terms of the peculiarities of particular contexts. One difference was, however, clear from the interviews and especially interesting. While the elites in the north-east, and particularly in Ceará state, tended to see economic liberalism in quite positive terms, in the centre-south one could detect some sort of nostalgia for the developmental state. Naturally, this regional divide was not absolute. Yet the pattern is clear. Elites in the two less affluent north-eastern states viewed the withdrawal of the state from direct involvement in production activities in very positive terms. They praised the opening up of the economy to the outside world even more, although domestic regional protectionism was strongly defended as 'still necessary'. In turn, interviewees from the centre-south – and more in São Paulo than in Rio de Janeiro – often regretted the disappearance of what they refer to as a 'national economic project', namely state protection of domestic producers through reserved markets, subsidies and incentives for joint ventures between domestic and foreign capital.

The fact that the centre-south finds reason to complain about neo-liberal policies while the north-east elites tend to be content with them can be explained in terms of Brazil's historic process of industrialization. While it is true that in both regions we find sectors and groups that benefit from the opportunities brought about by the shift to neo-liberalism, the losers are far more visible in the more industrialized regions. Thus, even outside the ranks of industrial sectors, several respondents were sensitive to the decline of leading firms in the metropolitan areas of Rio de Janeiro and São Paulo. Many openly blamed the retreat of the state for the flow of capital away from industry and commerce in the region, not to mention the decay in urban infrastructure. The cry of many of those interviewed in the centre-south that 'the state has abandoned a national project' is heard even among supporters of the (Cardoso) government responsible for the changes in economic policy. Moreover, some added persisting or aggravated poverty to the deficit ledger. In their view, the opportunities to take people out of poverty would have been far greater if the state had continued to champion economic growth. As one interviewee put it: 'Nowadays we lack clear orientation on economic policy. In this new reality, marked by open markets, we lack state guidance. ... We are very vulnerable because day by day we see the domestic productive sector lose ground to international business. People lose jobs, companies lose consumers ... without state guidance the whole society becomes highly vulnerable.'

While our north-eastern respondents generally blamed the state for persisting poverty, they seem to see social exclusion mainly as the failure of governmental social policies rather than a consequence of poor economic performance. These regionally divergent perceptions might just be transient, but they suggest that support for specific change in welfare policies will probably differ along regional lines.

Other differences in perceptions were related to functional specialization and generally conformed to predictions. The role that an individual plays naturally influences his or her view. For example, those in top bureaucratic and technocratic positions, as well as politicians in government, tended to approach the poverty problem through the perspective of the technical and economic constraints the country faces. These constraints were seen as obstacles to a more efficient campaign to eradicate poverty and inequality, and removing them as an essential preliminary to more effective social policies. Conversely, politicians in opposition tended to blame poverty on government mismanagement, lack of political will or blatant disinterest. Top leaders in the labour sector were also critical of government for not fighting social exclusion and for maintaining unjust distribution patterns. They differ from professional politicians in opposition because they perceive themselves as some sort of 'union government'. They stress the divisiveness of interests within labour as one of the major obstacles to progressive politics that could promote the whole working class. As one labour leader puts it: 'It is only when you arrive at the top of the scale that you realize how short-sighted, selfish and egotistical union politics is. Every union wants to advance their own specific, narrow interests. They simply cannot perceive that their specific concerns may hamper the interests of the labour class as a whole.' Again, aware of problems of government, this same labour leader goes on to point to the trap of the 'iron law': 'An important part of my problem is dealing with those who become union leaders and end up developing interests of their own. They become professionals, losing all contact with their former occupation, striving to secure their continuity as labour representatives because that has become their current occupation.'

Finally, gender differences deserve some comment. Although there were very few women in top institutional positions, I did interview a small group of women in both regions, mainly occupying political or public administrative roles. They all shared some peculiarities that, for lack of a better term, I shall call a 'feminine style' of conveying values, beliefs and perceptions. They tended to talk in ways that gave prominence to expressive views over technical opinions. Even when firmly arguing for universal policy initiatives, they often related to such measures in terms of particular cases. I also noticed a tendency for female respondents to volunteer information from their own personal experiences.[3]

Brazilian elites in comparative perspective

The views of other national elites reported in later chapters help to sharpen our understanding of the images that Brazilian elites have of poverty and inequality. For example, the tendency for Brazilian elites to blame the state for the persistence of poverty and inequality – and load upon it full responsibility for solving the problem – becomes more significant in comparative context. Even if everywhere elites attributed to the state responsibility for combating poverty, the extent to which other actors were expected to share in this task varied significantly from country to country. In Bangladesh, respondents believed that civil society in general, and NGOs in particular, did or should play a major role. Even our Filipino respondents, who were relatively focused on state responsibility, were less emphatic in their stance than the Brazilians. In none of the other countries that feature in this book are the elites so adamant in assigning to the state responsibility to act over poverty and blame for failure. In Brazil, even when a member of the elite is active in government, he or she often blames the state as an abstract body for every action or inaction perceived as bearing the responsibility for perverse patterns of distribution of income and opportunity.

It is quite consistent that Brazilian elites should have been reserved or suspicious about the involvement of NGOs and philanthropic institutions in social policy activities. South African elites were sceptical in the same way. The strong reservations of Haitian elites about NGOs in part have a different basis. They do not fear that NGOs might be ineffective against poverty or may be used as an excuse for state inaction. They seem more concerned that NGO personnel earn very high salaries and compete with the local elites for status, power and prestige.

I have already noted that Brazilian elites tend to conflate concerns about poverty and about inequality. This becomes particularly noticeable when we confront their images of who is poor with those expressed by elites in Bangladesh. The latter see poverty as straightforward absolute deprivation, and rarely conflate it with inequality. None of the other national elites studied puts as much stress on inequality as do Brazilians. Not even in South Africa, which competes with Brazil for the top position on social inequality on objective measures, do we observe such an acute perception of poverty as relative deprivation.

Concluding comments

What have we learned about the ways in which Brazilian elites perceive poverty and inequality? Did they tell us something new or unexpected? What use could possibly be made of the information they volunteered on their perception of poverty and inequality, and about their normative preferences for tackling these issues? How can such perceptions affect social policy?

Brazilian elites have a strong preference for policies that would minimize direct redistribution. The taxation of wealth and affirmative action for minorities were almost unanimously condemned in the in-depth interviews; the results of the initial survey point in the same direction. Does the fact that such ideas elicit a less vociferous response from elites in the other countries suggest that a liberal ideology is stronger here? If so,

51

how does this fit with the preference given to state rather than societal initiatives against poverty? The explicit defence of equality of opportunity, combined with a preference for governmental action, is perhaps consistent in a society that, for many years, lived with the idea of a development project championed by the state. Some authors have pointed out the elective affinity of this growth strategy with the patriarchal structure inherited from Portugal: a modernization matrix of authoritarian bent, combined with the Iberian corporatist tradition. Rather than turning again to the search for historical roots, I prefer to enquire about the implications of recent institutional changes for social policy. Will the democratization processes experienced over the past fifteen years foster the conditions for significant change in public policies affecting inequality? Even knowing that democracy does not necessarily correlate with equality, it is appropriate to ask what will be the impact of increased electoral competition on the social consciousness of the elite.

Brazilian elites voice a clear concern about social problems. They say that poverty, social misery, lack of education, the concentration of income, and other forms of inequality should rank high as national priorities. Overcoming such problems is stated to be important for laying the groundwork for democratic consolidation, as well as for attaining the nation's most important goals. There is apparent sensitivity to the nation's acute problems of social incorporation. Moreover, there are clear indications that members of the elite feel personally affected or threatened by existing poverty levels. The issue is very important in their view and calls for action. That component of social consciousness is unmistakably present.

We may also conclude that Brazilian elites believe there are feasible policies for tackling the poverty problem. The majority of those interviewed identify a series of ameliorative programmes as both desirable and viable. There is a widely shared belief in education as the most efficient corrective to poverty and extreme inequality. In fact, both the initial survey and the in-depth interviews leave no doubt that elites trust in the classic ingredients of social citizenship as the best corrective to poverty and inequality. They believe in the possibility of expanding health provision, housing and other welfare measures. What seems to be lacking for the full development of a social consciousness, however, is a sense of co-responsibility for action. The elites place the responsibility for public action on the state, and seek private means to protect themselves against the negative consequences of poverty. In their view, they should be freed from the constant threat of violence, urban decay and other negative consequences of poverty by the active involvement of the state. The fact that so many of the elite opt to protect themselves privately by hiring bodyguards, equipping cars and homes with special security, etc., is perceived as a way of compensating for an inefficient state that fails to fulfil this obligation in the same way that it fails to protect the poor.

This feeling of alienation that members of the elite feel towards the state – even when, as politicians or bureaucrats, they are important state players – accounts for the deficient social consciousness of the Brazilian elites. It is this missing component which leads them to fall short of collectivized initiatives and to opt for private defence strategies. Herein lies the main difference between these elites and those in Europe who entrusted the state with responsibility for action in the past. When the elites analysed by de Swaan (1988) in Europe and the United States opted for collective solutions to poverty, they perceived the welfare state as their own creation. They tried private individual and collective schemes first, and then moved to public policy because they realized it would strike a better solution in terms of costs and benefits.

Brazil, and other countries of the South, went through a very different process of state-building from western Europe. Having gone through a period of colonial rule, they inherited the nation-state form as a ready-made solution. What in Europe emerged gradually as a fusion of state and nation was adopted in the South as a formal solution. The combination of solidarity and authority that made up the real nation-state in the South was an amalgamation of distinct components often leading to conflicting legitimacy principles. Each of these societies experienced distinctive combinations of state and nation traditions over different time scales. Yet all of them still face the challenge of expanding citizenship, both horizontally and vertically.

In the particular case of Brazil, one wonders how progress in making classic civic, political and social rights effective will alter the normative foundations of distribution patterns. It is true that democratic forms of government do not necessarily correlate with less poverty or less inequality (Reis and Cheibub 1993). It is also true that the hopes for a more just society brought by the democratizing experiences that recently took place in societies in the South are quickly vanishing. Among the cases presented in this book, Brazil, South Africa and the Philippines clearly attest to underlying disillusion with regard to the social record of democratization. Despite that, there is no doubt that the way competing social interests act in a democratic environment differs significantly from the way they act under authoritarian regimes.

Such differences, I propose, may open up new opportunities for change. The increase in competition for power may contribute to strengthen the pressure from below and force the non-poor to change their perceptions.

Moreover, increased intra-elite competition for power opens the way for active leadership to force anti-poverty measures on to the agenda. One wonders whether such new opportunities will contribute to the development of a social consciousness among the elites. In Brazil, will the acute sensitivity to the negative externalities of poverty and inequality gradually lead to perceptions of social responsibility among those who are increasingly bound by democratic institutions?

Naive as it may seem to trust in liberal democracy to fight poverty, if one places it in context some reasons for optimism may surface. In a lecture entitled 'Is Rising Inequality Inevitable?', Tony Atkinson has convincingly suggested a negative answer to his own question. As he indicates, despite the predicaments of market forces, there is a considerable margin of freedom of choice and action in the realm of politics. Calling attention to the effect of social norms on income differentials, he questions the narrow assumptions made by many economists that income differentials are determined by blind market forces. Looking at evidence for OECD countries, he insists that there is space left for policy decision-making and leadership even when a global technocratic consensus seems to reign (Atkinson 1999).

It is true that the structural and institutional transformations of the Brazilian economy in the recent past seem to point in the opposite direction. The faith in open markets weakens the very idea of social responsibility and of a national community of interests. Once the mystique of a national community weakens, what can provide a proper normative ground for concerted interest negotiations in parliaments, and other public arenas? I would contend that the importance of anti-poverty policies in the governmental agenda would be more affected by power competition than by fixed normative preferences. Power competition itself may have an impact in altering distributive norms. In other words, the incomplete social consciousness we observe among the Brazilian elites may expand as a consequence of intra-elite competition for power. The feeling of personal responsibility – the component lacking for a strong social consciousness – may arise out of a more disputed political power. As de Tocqueville knew, decisive as *moeurs et coeurs* appear to be in shaping behaviour, the most effective way to interfere with them is through the constraint of institutions.

Notes

1 My sample of newspaper columns signed by elite members covered five years of eight large daily periodicals published in four metropolitan Brazilian cities: for São Paulo, *O Estado de São Paulo* and *Folha de São Paulo*; for Rio de Janeiro, *O Globo* and *Jornal do Brasil*; for Salvador, the capital of the state of Bahia in the north-east, *A Tarde* and *Correio da Bahia*; and for Fortaleza, the capital of Ceara, also in the north-east, *O Povo* and *Diario do Nordeste*.

2 For a detailed description of the survey study, see Lima and Cheibub (1994).

3 For a comprehensive study of women elites, see Vianello and Moore (2000).

References

Atkinson, A. B. (1999) 'Is Rising Inequality Inevitable? A Critique of the Transatlantic Consensus', Wider Annual Lectures 3, UNU/WIDER

Barros, R. P. de and R. Mendonça (1999) 'Uma Caracterização das Condições de Pobreza e Desigualdade no Brasil', Rio de Janeiro: IPEA, Diretoria de Estudos e Políticas Sociais, September

Barros, R. P. de, R. Henriques and R. Mendonça (2000) 'Desigualdade e Pobreza no Brasil: Retrato de uma Estabilidade Inaceitável', *Revista Brasileira de Ciências Sociais*, 15 (42): 123–42

Carvalho, J. M. (1980) *A Construçao da Ordem: A Elite Política Imperial*, Rio de Janeiro: Campus

Castro Gomes, A. M. (1979) *Burguesia e Trabalho. Politica e Legislaçao Social no Brasil, 1917–1937*, Rio de Janeiro: Campus

de Swaan, A. (1988) *In Care of the State; Health Care, Education and Welfare in Europe and in the USA in the Modern Era*, Cambridge/New York: Polity Press/Oxford University Press

de Swaan, A., J. Manor, E. Oyen and E. Reis (2000) 'Elite Perceptions of Poverty: Reflections for a Comparative Research Project', *Current Sociology*, 48 (1): 43–56

Faoro, R. (1958) *Os Donos do Poder, Formação do Patronato Político Brasileiro*, Porto Alegre: Globo

Fausto, B. (1970) *A Revoluçao de 1930: Historiografia e Historia*, São Paulo: Brasiliense

Furtado, C. (1963) *The Economic Growth of Brazil*, Berkeley: University of California Press

Hall, M. (1969) *The Origins of Mass Immigration in Brazil, 1871–1914*, PhD dissertation, Columbia University

Henriques, R. (ed.) (2000) *Desigualdade e Pobreza no Brasil*, Rio de Janeiro: IPEA

Ianni, O. (1968) *O Colapso do Populismo no Brasil*, Rio de Janeiro: Civilizaçao Brasileira

Ipeadata (n.d.) Database of the Instituto de Pesquisa Economica Aplicada: <www.ipcadata.gov.br>

Lima, M. R. S. de and Z. B. Cheibub (1994) 'Elites Estrategicas e Dilemas do Desenvolvimento', Rio de Janeiro: IUPERJ

Martins, L. (1986) 'The Liberalization of Authoritarian Rule in Brazil', in G. O'Donnell, P. Schimtter and L. Whitehead (eds), *Transitions from Authoritarian Rule: Latin America*, Baltimore, MD: Johns Hopkins University Press

Morse, R. (1988) *O Espelho de Próspero. Cultura e Idéias nas Américas*, São Paulo: Companhia das Letras

Pastore, J. (1989) 'Inequality and Social Mobility: Ten Years Later', in Bacha and Klein (eds), *Social Change in Brazil, 1945–1985. The Incomplete Transition*, Albuquerque: University of New Mexico Press

Pastore, J. and N. do Valle e Silva (2000) *Mobilidade Social no Brasil*, São Paulo: Makron Books

Prado, C., Jr (1969) *The Colonial Background of Modern Brazil*, Berkeley: University of California Press

Queiroz, M. V. de (1965) 'Os grupos multibilionários', *Revista do Instituto de Ciências Sociais*, 2 (1)

Queiroz, M. V. de, L. Martins and J. A. Pessoa de Queiroz (1962) 'Os Grupos Econômicos no Brasil', *Revista do Instituto de Ciências Sociais*, 1 (2)

Reis, Elisa (1982) 'Elites Agrárias, State-building e Autoritarismo', *Processos e Escolhas, Estudos de Sociologia Politica, Dados, Revista de Ciências Sociais*, 25 (3): 331–48

— (1998) 'Banfield's Amoral Famililism Revisited', in Alexander (ed.), *Real Civil Societies*, London: Sage, pp. 21–39

Reis, E. and Z. Cheibub (1993) 'Mercado, Cidadania e Consolidação Democrática', *Dados, Revista de Ciências Sociais*, 36 (2): 233–60

Reis, E. and E. Reis (1988) 'As Elites Agrárias e a Abolição da Escravidão no Brasil', *Dados, Revista de Ciências Sociais*, 31 (3): 309–41

Santos, W. G. (1979) *Cidadania e Justica: a Politica Social na Ordem Brasileira*, Rio de Janeiro: Campus

Scalon, M. C. (1999) *Mobilidade Social no Brasil: Padroes e Tendencias*, Rio de Janeiro: Revan/IUPERJ

Schmitter, P. (1971) *Interest Conflict and Political Change in Brazil*, Stanford, CA: Stanford University Press

Schwartzman, S. (1977) 'Back to Weber: Corporatism and Patrimonialism in the Seventies', in J. Malloy (ed.), *Authoritarianism and Corporatism in Latin America*, Pittsburgh, PA: Pittsburgh University Press

— (1982) *Bases do Autoritarismo Brasileiro*, Rio de Janeiro: Campus

Stepan, A. (1978) *The State and Society, Peru in Comparative Perspective*, Princeton, NJ: Princeton University Press

— (ed.) (1989) *Democratizing Brazil: Problems of Transition and Consolidation*, Oxford: Oxford University Press

Velho, O. G. (1976) *Capitalismo Autoritario e Campesinato*, São Paulo: DIFEL

Vianello, M. and G. Moore (eds) (2000) *Gendering Elites, Economic and Political Leadership in 27 Industrialized Societies*, Basingstoke: Macmillan Press

Weffort, F. (1978) *O Populismo na Politica Brasileira*, Rio de Janeiro: Paz e Terra

Wiarda, H. (1981) *Corporatism and National Development in Latin America*, Boulder, CO: Westview Press

3 | Voices from the top of the pile: elite perceptions of poverty and the poor in the Philippines

GERARD CLARKE AND MARITES SISON[1]

The Philippines is a middle-income country with a level of income inequality that is only moderate on a global scale but high by Asian standards. The richest 20 per cent of the population received more than half of total income in 1994 (World Bank 1996: 4).[2] Within East and South Asia, only Malaysia and Thailand have higher levels of income inequality. The Philippines income distribution figures are similar to those found in Latin America, a region with which it shares a similar colonial history. One shared legacy, commonly attributed to European colonial rule and to American policy in the twentieth century, is of enduring elite power, influence and status, often rooted in landownership, international trade in commodities and control of the levers of political power at local and national level.

For much of the 1980s and 1990s, it was widely believed in the Philippines that an elite of as little as 400 families controlled both the economy and the political process. Although it was often difficult precisely to define this elite, it was blamed for most of the country's ills. According to Benedict Anderson, the Filipino elite of the late 1980s constituted a 'national oligarchy', composed of the 'wealthiest and most powerful dynasties', and the Philippines was a *cacique* democracy, dominated by landed political bosses (Anderson 1988). In recent years, academics such as Pinches (1996, 1999), Sidel (1999) and Hedman and Sidel (2000) have questioned the relevance of the *cacique* democracy model. In the Philippines itself, many acknowledge that the 'national oligarchy' has been weakened and that membership of the national elite has broadened. Nevertheless, in popular discourse poverty is still widely attributed to elite domination of the polity and economy. Consequently, poverty and inequality are seen as intimately connected.

In this chapter, we argue that members of the Filipino elite subscribe to a popular discourse of elitism, a discourse which both asserts and challenges the social, political and economic hegemony of a distinct class and status elite. They attribute poverty to a range of political phenomena, including the inequitable distribution of resources, the prevalence of corruption and the persistence of 'traditional' (semi-feudal or oligarchic) politics. They blame 'the elite' for these problems yet disassociate themselves from this elite, much as elites do in the other countries that appear in this volume. Our respondents feel that rural poverty is less significant than its urban equivalent, that Filipinos need not and do not die of hunger, and that the Philippine state is among the world's most corrupt.

Elites, however, are distinct from other groups that subscribe to this popular discourse of elitism. In contrast to other social groups, the Filipino elite is psychologically insulated from the negative effects of poverty, both in their personal and professional lives. This insulation stems from a significant social distance between the elite and the poor, arising not only from class, income and status differentials but also from linguistic, ethnic, educational and spatial factors. The Filipino elite are predominantly English-speaking Chinese or European mestizos who live in the wealthier districts of Metro Manila and other major cities. Many have been educated overseas. Their perceptions of the interdependence of rich and poor stem from the patron–client ties that bind them to the poor rather than a shared sense of citizenship or nationalism. Given the privileged political, economic and social position that the elite occupies, these perceptions have significant implications for public policy. The study of elite perceptions of poverty provides valuable insights into the social construction and dynamics of poverty, and provides clues as to the kind of political project needed to tackle it.

Research methods

In this chapter, we analyse information on perceptions of poverty and the poor in the Philippines obtained through interviews with eighty members of the Filipino elite. Sixty-five interviews were conducted in the capital, Manila, and fifteen in the second city of the Philippines, Davao. Interviews were carried out between May and October 1999, one year into the presidency of Joseph Estrada. During this period, poverty featured prominently in political discourse. Estrada was elected in May 1998 with the support of both urban and rural poor, and was forced to resign in January 2001. Anti-poverty issues were prominent on his agenda and in the media. Note also that the interviews were carried out two years after the beginning of the East Asian economic and financial crisis that engulfed the country from September 1997.

In conducting our research, we employed a broad definition of 'elite' and a flexible sampling protocol. Verba and his associates (1987: 58–9) argue that there is no accepted definition of a sample frame for elites. Even if there were, they continue, 'one might not wish to draw a random sample from it', especially where researchers seek to examine consensus and disagreement among significant political groups (ibid.). Our interviews were carried out with the aid of a semi-structured questionnaire.[3] The respondents occupied prominent positions in institutions that help to frame policy and discourse with respect to poverty and inequality: representative elective bodies, the bureaucracy, the armed forces, the private sector, the media, academia, the Catholic Church, and civil society organizations, including business associations, professional bodies and non-governmental organizations.[4] They included senior politicians, prominent businessmen and -women, senior military officials (both serving and former), religious leaders, and other prominent members of the intelligentsia, including academics, journalists, philanthropists and NGO leaders, and socialites.[5] Our institutional definition of the term 'elite' does not rely solely on occupational or wealth categories and encompasses a wider range of social groups and actors than in some previous surveys of 'elites' conducted in the Philippines.[6] Many of our interviewees, for instance, are elite because of their family connections as well as their occupations, while others belong to a distinct status elite because of a series of alternating posts in the public and private sectors (e.g. businessmen who have served as ambassadors overseas). Interviews with prominent people such as cabinet members or senior businessmen/women are difficult to obtain. Not only is strict random sampling of questionable justification (see above), it is also difficult to implement. We identified interviewees in part on the basis of our personal contacts. Nevertheless, we are confident that our sample is broadly representative of the Philippine elite.

This elite is in some respects relatively homogeneous. It is very urban.[7] It is very much English-speaking and well educated. The interviews were conducted exclusively or predominantly in English, mainly according to the preferences of interviewees. Although respondents were not explicitly questioned about their ethnic identities or religious affiliations, we know that the sample represents the Christian Filipino majority. It includes at least eight Chinese-Filipinos, but no Muslim leaders. On the basis of previous career, a secondary occupation or positions held, at least twenty-five of our interviewees could be assigned to more than one elite institutional category.[8] Familial ties also contribute to the relative homogeneity of the elite: at least six of our interviewees are related to, or immediate cognates of, one other interviewee.[9]

In other respects, however, our sample represents a diverse elite.[10] It includes ten people who, in our estimate, have significant rural property interests or who are members of the Philippines' traditional political families or clans. Most of the businessmen or -women interviewed, however, do not have significant interests in agriculture or related activities (e.g.

mining, logging), although most have interests in urban property or real estate. Many of these are antagonistic to the old landed elite. Our sample also includes philanthropic, civic or NGO leaders, including political activists formerly associated with the underground left.

Elitism and the national oligarchy

Poverty in the Philippines is often traced to social inequalities and to the traditional power of a distinct national elite or oligarchy, centred on landownership, financial resources, access to state patronage, and influence over elected politicians. The enduring power of a distinct 'national oligarchy' derives in part from the importance of the family as a social institution in Philippine culture. As in other parts of the world, the nuclear and extended family represents one of the most important social institutions. In addition, however, Filipinos extend the notion of 'family' through affinity ties that bind to family groupings people who do not share blood ties. This extended notion of the family has historically been an important means by which people acquire *padrinos* (patrons) who can help them in later life, and equally a means by which those same *padrinos* extend their influence and command the loyalty of wider networks of people beyond their blood relations. The social roles and characteristics of the family have remained remarkably resilient over time, and they still permeate business life and politics. As Hutchcroft notes in his study of banking in the early 1990s: 'The basic building blocks of the Philippines business community are extended family conglomerates, and amongst the surest way for such groups to secure credit is through ownership (or partial ownership) of a commercial bank ... [As a result] most ... private banks ... are family dominated' (Hutchcroft 1998: 9–10).

With economic development and concomitant social change, the average size of the nuclear family is declining, yet the family remains a significant social institution. It exerts a forceful hold over its members and is still sufficiently powerful to reduce the strength of other, more broadly defined social institutions. Diokno notes that: 'arenas of family (private) interest and public (national) good are highly demarcated ... hardly any connection is made between family interest and the larger common good ... This is ... the "underside" of Filipino familism ... [the] seeming inability of the Filipino to care for the "anonymous stranger"' (Diokno 1999: 140–1).[11]

The family has also played a central role in the recent history of the Philippines and in the emergence of a distinctive political economy in which a landed family-centred elite is a significant element. According to Anderson, the origins of the landed family-centred elite lie in the pattern of landownership and control established under Spanish, and later American, colonial rule. In the late sixteenth century, Philip II of Spain parcelled land out among the Catholic orders that settled in the Philippines. From the late eighteenth century, these orders built up the first great haciendas, pioneering the development of commercial agriculture. In the second half of the nineteenth century, Chinese migrants came in large numbers, providing the capital needed to further stimulate the commercialization of agriculture (Wickberg 1965). Many became hacenderos in their own right and members of a nascent national elite (Anderson 1988). During the period of American rule (1899–1946), a solid and visible 'national oligarchy' cohered and crystallized, first through the distribution of church lands to private landowners and second through the establishment of a US-style bicameral legislature (ibid.). 'The new representational system', Anderson argues, 'proved perfectly adapted to the ambitions and social geography of the *mestizo nouveau riche*' (ibid.: 201). Between 1954 and 1972, 'the heyday of *cacique* democracy' (ibid.: 207–8), the national oligarchy dominated the political system and consolidated their economic position through privileged access to US markets for agricultural commodities and diversification into industry and services behind tariff walls in an era of import-substituting industrialization.

According to John Sidel, the origins of the national oligarchy lie less in the landownership patterns established during the era of Spanish colonial rule than in the control of elected political office in the period of American rule. Case studies of local elites, Sidel argues, 'reveal that the accumulation of large landholdings often followed from, rather than preceded, the assumption of political power' (Sidel 1999: 11). According to Sidel, the emergence of a twentieth-century national oligarchy dates to the pre-colonial period and the emergence of leadership patterns that relied on coercion and violence to build and maintain political followings ('local strongman' power). These leadership patterns were institutionalized during the Spanish era, through municipal elections and revenue farms that facilitated local monopolies in coercion and taxation. 'American colonial rule', Sidel writes, 'expanded private control over the local coercive and extractive agencies of the state "upward" by subordinating the national state apparatus to provincial and national-level elected officials' (ibid.: 16). 'Bosses' – networks of local strongmen who rely on coercion and violence to command political office and economic resources, and to legitimize that command – represent, in Sidel's view, the key to the process of state formation, and the emergence of national and local oligarchies in the twentieth-century Philippines.

The basis of the national oligarchy changed during the fourteen-year dictatorship of Ferdinand Marcos (1972–86), becoming less centred on land

and even more centred on state patronage and financial muscle (Hedman and Sidel 2000). Marcos tried to establish himself as a supreme *cacique* by displacing the elite, confiscating their economic assets and shutting down the institutions through which they maintained political hegemony. In its place, he established around him a network of cronies who provided political support and who prospered fantastically on the economic rents accompanying privileged access to the ruling circle. The fall of the Marcos dictatorship, in particular the restoration of US-style electoral democracy in 1987, including not only a bicameral legislature but also a surfeit of locally elected positions, facilitated the partial restoration of *cacique* democracy and the dominance of the national oligarchy.

Today, traditional clan dominance of politics is gradually waning. Of 214 members of the House of Representatives elected in May 2001, for instance, an estimated 50 per cent are members of established family-based political clans, compared to 73 per cent of those elected in 1992 and 82 per cent in 1987 (Datinguinoo and Olarte 2001; Guiterrez 1994: 4–5). These researchers show that, in elections since 1986, a new generation of young politicians without ties to the traditional political clans has gradually emerged. The passage of the Election Modernization Law in 1997 helped to weaken the established political clans, although since then a number of draft bills seeking to further the process have been blocked (Datinguinoo and Olarte 2001). Outside Congress, a vibrant civil society has emerged over the last two decades, providing non-governmental organizations and their leaders with a powerful political voice. The restoration of a free press in 1986 has also enhanced the prominence of professionals such as journalists and academics, and of activists formerly associated with the underground left.

Economic growth and social change are also eroding the power of the country's traditional landed elite. With liberalization, deregulation and the growth of new industries and sectors, the elite economic positions have been opened to new entrants. As Pinches (1996, 1999) argues, a 'new rich' emerged in the Philippines in the years from 1986. They comprise high-earning salaried professionals and the owners of small and medium enterprises, many of them subcontractors or franchise holders. The 'new rich' wield considerable market clout, as consumers and as company executives, and political clout, as opinion leaders and as a significant electoral constituency. More generally, the middle class has grown in size and become more socially differentiated, and serves as a stronger countervailing force to the traditional elite than in previous decades. Many Chinese-Filipino businessmen and -women have also pulled themselves above the 'glass ceiling' that traditionally prevented members of the bourgeoisie from entering a higher social segment, and have achieved membership of the corporate elite.

In general terms, therefore, the Filipino elite shares important characteristics with the Brazilian elite, in so far as it was shaped by Iberian influences such as Catholicism, large agricultural estates and family-based networks. Like Brazil, the Philippines has also experienced significant capitalist transformation and concomitant social change since the collapse of authoritarianism in the mid-1980s. In addition, however, the Filipino elite was shaped by Chinese migration and by American colonial rule, factors that distinguish it from Brazil and other countries in this volume and which influence the perceptions of poverty and the poor examined in the following sections.

Poverty as a problem

There's a lot of opportunities in the countryside, you will never die. My own perception is you'll never die in those areas because there is enough resources. You plant *camote*, you plant cassava, you can live. You can plant bananas, you will live. There are a lot of resources there if people only work, be industrious. They don't have to come to Manila. (Quote 1: political appointee in government service)

There are some politicians who wish there were more poor people. The poor are the bailiwick because ... if you are a moneyed politician, it's better to have poor people because you can buy them. Give them P200, P300 in the elections and they will vote for you.[12] (Quote 2: politician)

Chronic poverty, the flip side of this privilege and elitism, remains significant in the Philippines. An estimated 28 per cent of the population survived on less than US$1 a day in 1994 (UNDP 1998: 146–7). The number of poor people as a percentage of the total population has been declining over time. In 1985, 44 per cent of the population lived below the official poverty line (UNDP 1997: 32). By 1997, this had fallen to 32 per cent before rising to 35 per cent in 1998 as a result of the East Asian economic and financial crisis.[13] Poverty continued to rise in 1999, when our research was carried out, especially in urban areas where industrial activity was affected by the East Asian financial and economic crisis, but soon began to fall again. According to the 2000 Family Income and Expenditure Survey (FIES), 34 per cent of the population lived below the poverty line, including 20 per cent of the urban, and 47 per cent of the rural population.[14] Overall, low economic growth and population growth over the last twenty years have meant that per capita income in the Philippines has still not returned to the level of 1982 (World Bank 2000b).[15]

Filipinos see a close relationship between poverty and inequality and blame poverty primarily on 'the elite'. Surveys of social inequality in the

63

Philippines carried out in 1992 and 1999 as part of the International Social Survey Programme (ISSP)[16] suggest that conflicts between rich and poor represent the most important perceived cleavage or fault line in Philippine society.[17] According to both surveys, Filipinos feel that income differences between people are too great. Respondents also agree that inequality exists because it benefits the rich and powerful and because ordinary people do not organize and mobilize to change the situation.[18] These responses indicate that poverty and inequality are widely perceived in the Philippines as political problems. Ironically, people feel that income inequality is conducive to economic prosperity to the same extent that they believe that income differentials are too high.[19] This suggests that while Filipinos broadly dislike inequality and the perceived elitism from which it derives, they are not sufficiently concerned, organized or linked to other political forces to challenge this situation. Inequality, it appears at first sight, is deeply and stably embedded in Philippine social norms and discourse and in economic and political structures. Yet, in reality, Philippine twentieth-century history was characterized by a series of rural-based insurgencies, including the *Sakdalista* revolt of the 1930s, the *Huk* rebellion in the 1950s, and from the end of the 1960s a long-term insurgency led by the New People's Army and its political master, the Communist Party of the Philippines. The Philippine state has also proved increasingly effective since 1992 in tackling poverty and inequality (see further below). Poverty and inequality are not as stably embedded in people's minds as the survey results suggest.

Survey data also suggest that well-off Filipinos are concerned about poverty and inequality. According to the 1992 survey, people in urban areas and from higher socio-economic classes feel disproportionately that income differences in the Philippines are too large. Such people also disagree disproportionately with the suggestion that large income disparities are necessary for the economic prosperity of the country (Guerrero 1993: 13). This suggests that well-off people, including the urban middle class, are more critical of poverty and inequality, by virtue of their education and their relative personal prosperity. The rural poor, the survey suggests, are more inured to the embedded inequalities that perpetuate their plight, despite the history of rural political activism.

Interviews with members of the Filipino elite, however, help to unpack these assertions and reveal a more complicated and ambiguous picture. Some members of the elite care about the plight of the poor but historical, cultural, spatial and ethnic factors, as well as their class and status positions, heavily influence their social consciousness. Many members of the Filipino elite, for instance, have particular views about the nature

64

and extent of poverty, views that directly influence their social conscious-ness. This social consciousness in turn influences the social dynamics of poverty. Among our sample, less than a quarter of interviewees felt that poverty represents the biggest problem facing the country, although two-thirds felt it was either a big problem or the biggest. A small minority felt that poverty was not a big or a significant problem, and in some cases politicians and businessmen acknowledged the benefits they derive from poverty (see Quote 2).[20]

Joseph 'Erap' Estrada was in many respects the epitome of this phe-nomenon. In general elections held on 11 May 1998, Estrada was elected president, the ninth to hold the office since independence in 1946. With 40 per cent of the vote in a seven-way contest, Estrada's victory represented a landslide, with almost double the 23 per cent achieved by Fidel Ramos in 1992 in a similar seven-way contest. Estrada's popularity stemmed in part from his close rapport with the Philippine *masa* (masses), especially Manila's urban poor, and from a populist commitment to fight poverty and reform the Philippines' elitist system of democracy. On 20 January 2001, however, Estrada was removed from office by a controversial decision of the Supreme Court, following impeachment by the House of Representa-tives on charges of corruption. Yet far from being an anomaly, Estrada's corrupt behaviour reflects important characteristics of legislative politics in the Philippines. According to Eaton (2001: 114), citing Carey and Shugart's (1995) ranking of electoral preferences, members of the lower House of Representatives in the Philippines face some of the most extensive par-ticularistic demands of any democracy. This encourages clientelism and corrupt political exchanges. Legislators meet these demands by exerting significant influence over the disbursement of funds by government depart-ments, using clauses that they insert in legislative bills.

In the Philippines, as in other cases discussed in this volume, many members of the elite are deeply sceptical about the extent of poverty in rural areas. Many argue that abundant natural resources in the Philippines help to mitigate the effects of poverty in rural areas and that poor people have no reason to be hungry. Often this belief stems from a concern with urban poverty, and with migration from rural to urban areas (see Quote 1). A number of interviewees repeated the mantra that people do not, or need not, die of hunger in the Philippines. Hunger-related deaths are, however, a significant reality in rural areas. In 1982/83, hundreds died of malnutrition and related illnesses on the sugar-producing island of Negros following the collapse of international sugar prices, while in late 1997 and early 1998 up to one hundred people died of hunger on the southern island of Mindanao, mostly from eating poisonous tubers collected in the aftermath of the East Asian crisis. None of our interviewees, including those interviewed in Mindanao, mentioned these deaths. As a result, many interviewees felt that rural poverty was a less significant problem than its urban equivalent.[21]

Members of the Filipino elite see the poor, especially the rural poor, in relatively undifferentiated terms. They see the poor as a relatively homogeneous group, i.e. those who lack money or who are unable to meet their basic needs, an economic group rather than a series of groups with important social attributes. Few interviewees, for instance, differentiated between the different social groups within which the poor feature prominently – for example, urban squatters, landless farmers or particular indigenous peoples.[22] Few mentioned the ethnic dimensions of poverty and few distinguished between different categories of the rural poor (e.g. landless labourers, subsistence farmers or small-scale fishermen/women).[23] Only one alluded to *Tagalog*, *Visayan* or other vernacular terms that differentiate between categories of poor people, although such terms are well established in popular political and social discourse.

Many interviewees, however, were articulate in pointing to relatively new faces of poverty, amid the economic hardship triggered by the East Asian crisis. In both Manila and Davao, many people had noticed the increasing numbers of migrants, and the attendant problems of squatters and street children. As one interviewee explained, 'It's only recently that you actually see families living in the street ... pushcart families ... that's a relatively new [phenomenon].' 'Every time you drive out into the streets [now],' another noted, 'you see children begging, risking their lives in the traffic to earn one peso, two pesos.' Respondents noted other trends in Metro Manila: men selling *sampaguita* (a sweet-smelling flower), an occupation previously dominated by women and young girls; or parents languishing in jail for consuming or selling drugs, a problem previously confined to young men. In a social sense, therefore, members of the elite are sensitive to the urban and novel dimensions of poverty rather than to the more deep-seated and enduring features of rural poverty that they are more inclined to take for granted and less inclined to question or challenge.

The root causes of poverty

... before, those who had land had economic power. Now it has transferred from land to banks ... over financial mechanisms, control over the media, control over political processes ... If you look at the composition of our current Congress ... some [members] represent very narrow interests – multinationals, big corporations, the traditional landed elite or families. (Quote 3: member of the House of Representatives)

Almost a third of our resources are lost to graft and corruption. The Philippines is considered the third-most graft-ridden, most corrupt country in the world ... where roads are being built at a cost of ninety million pesos per kilometre when it should only be four million. (Quote 4: member of the House of Representatives)

The causes of poverty in the Philippines run far deeper than the East Asian crisis, and members of the Filipino elite have strong views about them. In the minds of our interviewees, poverty in the Philippines is primarily a *political* problem, caused by the inequitable distribution of resources, the prevalence of corruption and the persistence of 'traditional' (semi-feudal or oligarchic) politics. In addition, interviewees criticize the lack of government commitment to reducing poverty, the impact of the Marcos dictatorship and the political weakness of the middle class. Elites in the second city, Davao, blame neglect of the island of Mindanao by 'imperial' Manila. These perceptions echo a broader discourse about the root causes of poverty and inequality shared by most social groups in the Philippines, and confirm data from the 1992 and 1999 ISSP Social Inequality surveys reported above in which respondents attribute poverty and inequality to political variables.

These perceptions, however, and the discourses about elite power which they help underpin, are not entirely consistent with the 'facts', as revealed through recent research. According to Hedman and Sidel (2000: 68, 78), for instance, oligarchic politics centres on control over money and state resources rather than land, and on access to political brokers and fixers in the Senate and House rather than direct occupation of elected positions. Perceptions of poverty (see Quote 4) are similarly problematic. The Philippines was listed joint 55th of 85 countries and joint 65th of 91 countries surveyed in 1998 and 2001 respectively for the Corruption Perceptions Index (CPI) compiled by Transparency International.[24] Corruption is a significant problem in the Philippines but by no means as significant as some members of the elite imagine.

Our respondents blame 'the elite' for these political problems yet many of them, including politicians, businessmen/women and religious leaders, distinguish and disassociate themselves from this elite. A number of interviewees who have moved between political office and the private sector since 1986, for instance, referred to themselves as middle class when by any objective measure they belong to a distinct class and status elite. These responses contrast with those obtained in Haiti, for instance, where respondents were much more willing to acknowledge their 'elite' identity (Chapter 5). They are consistent with data from the 1992 and 1999 ISSP

TABLE 3.1 Explanations of the causes of poverty offered by interviewees (N=57)

Causes, in order of priority	First	Second	Third
Political including the inequitable distribution of resources, the prevalence of graft and corruption, the persistence of 'traditional' (semi-feudal or oligarchic) politics, lack of government commitment to reducing poverty, the impact of the Marcos dictatorship, the political weakness of the middle class and 'imperial' Manila's neglect of Mindanao	27	15	2
Economic including a lack of employment opportunities, inadequate incomes, low rates of agricultural productivity, low savings rates and the effects of globalization	13	5	0
Cultural including overpopulation, the influence of the Catholic Church, the colonial mentality of leaders and the laziness of the poor	13	3	0
Social low levels of educational attainment	2	1	0
Historical Spanish and/or American colonialism	2	1	0

NB: The question 'What are the root causes of poverty in the Philippines?' was put to 33 interviewees. The questions 'What are your views on poverty in the Philippines?' and/or 'Why is poverty [in the Philippines] so persistent?' were put to a further 31 interviewees, of whom 24 gave answers that could be classified for the purposes of Table 3.1. These questions did not appear in the semi-structured questionnaire. The horizontal axis records respondents' first three answers, where more than one was provided.

Social Inequality surveys, where respondents disproportionately identified themselves as middle or working/lower class.[25] Many of our respondents also sought to criticize other elite groups and to deny the culpability of their own group. Businessmen and -women, for instance, criticized government corruption or the Catholic Church's attitude to family planning; politicians criticized the power of the economic and social elite and their reluctance to pay taxes; religious leaders criticized venal politicians and economic elites. This is consistent with the findings of Verba and associates (1987: 264) in their study of elites and inequality in Sweden, the USA and Japan: elite respondents – and especially those from the most established groups – consistently denied their own influence.

Imagining the poor

The poor are not really nice people. They're ignorant, they're distrustful, they're the biggest snobs one can find, they are ungrateful ... And they're *balasubas* [rogues] ... *Matumal* [slow] and then they take advantage ... They feel they've a right; they have a mendicancy attitude ... That's their attitude and it prevents them from raising themselves up. (Quote 5: prominent businessman).[26]

John Gokongwei was not a rich man. He didn't have a rich father. So was Lucio Tan. He was unemployed [early in his business career]. So was Henry Sy. These are some of the richest people today. What will you say? 'My father is poor, so I cannot go to a good school'? But look at all these *taipans*, they went to the [worst] schools. Some of them didn't even graduate. So who's supposed to take responsibility for what they are? [It's] so easy to blame others. When something's wrong with us, it's others. (Quote 6: prominent Chinese-Filipino businessman)

You just look at the way your maids treat you. If they break a dish, they will hide it in the garden. If you ask for it, they will say, 'I don't know where it is.' And if the neighbour [offers] her five pesos more, she will leave [to work for the neighbour] and say, 'My mother is sick.' She'll never tell you: 'I need more money. I need a raise.' Isn't that the way they behave? (Quote 7: socialite)

How can you impose responsibilities on the poor, when they cannot find a job? For example, we chastise these squatters who ... are now living on top of the garbage pile of Payatas[27] and other such dumping sites. Do you think they want to live in that stinking garbage? Simply because, within the reach of their hopelessness, they say '*eto lang ang pagkatataon ko*' ['This is my only chance']. (Quote 8: former presidential candidate)

Fifty-four per cent of our interviewees felt it was possible to distinguish between a deserving and an undeserving poor,[28] while 58 per cent felt that the poor bore some responsibility for their own poverty.[29] There was a wide range of views on the morality of the poor. Some were quite harsh (e.g. Quote 5). Overall, compared to most other country cases in this volume, the Filipino elite were not very sympathetic to their poor. One reason for this was that Filipinos of Chinese origin, who accounted for 10 per cent of our sample, tended to hold especially harsh views of the poor. The Chinese-Filipino elite,[30] especially businesspeople, feel they share a strong work ethic with Chinese communities elsewhere in the region which distinguishes them from the mainstream Filipino majority, including the poor. The Chinese-Filipino elite feel they were born into poverty but worked hard to gain their pre-eminent position in the Philippine economy. The poor, they often feel, should emulate their example (e.g. Quote 6). This willingness of one ethnic group to condemn another contrasts strongly with South Africa, where racial and ethnic distinctions are more politically sensitive. In South Africa, elites censor themselves when questioned about the cultural or attitudinal dimensions of poverty, but in the Philippines the economic prominence of Chinese-Filipinos is much less politically sensitive (in contrast to the neighbouring countries of Malaysia and Indonesia) and Chinese-Filipinos do not feel under similar constraints.

Filipino elites not of Chinese origin, however, also ascribe negative traits to the (undifferentiated) poor. Such interviewees often felt, for instance, that the poor are weighed down by a sense of despondency and fatalism embodied in the common *Tagalog* expression *Bahala Na* (roughly translated, 'Come what may'). This view of the poor – and indeed of Filipinos in general – is deeply ingrained in Philippine culture. A character in one of the touchstones of Philippine literature, Jose Rizal's *Noli Me Tangere* (Touch Me Not), written at the end of the nineteenth century, bewails the 'indolence of the Filipino'. Since the overwhelming majority of our interviewees have domestic helpers, these helpers bore much of the brunt of the elite's antipathy to the poor (e.g. Quote 7).

There is in the attitudes of the Filipino elite a distinct duality in the way they view the poor. On the one hand, interviewees condemn the poor as lazy, opportunistic and fatalistic, yet simultaneously the same interviewees balance that harshness with sympathetic accounts of the predicament in which the poor find themselves. Filipino elites mirror their Bangladeshi peers, for instance, in their sometimes sympathetic accounts of the poor (Chapter 4). In the Philippines, however, elites feel a greater sense of social distance from the poor and are consequently more prepared to criticize them. This distinguishes them not only from their Bangladeshi peers, but also from their peers in South Africa who hold negative views of the poor, in part because of their distance from them, but who are reluctant to voice overtly critical opinions of the poor, because of the racial or ethnic implications (Chapter 6).

Looking in the mirror: the elite on the elite

I know many rich people who are very concerned. I know also those who don't care ... I know a fellow, for instance, he gives away P30 million [roughly US$0.8m or £0.5m] a year ... He likes to build structures, he builds training centres and schools... He's naughty, he has many sins. In fact he tells me he does it because maybe God will look the other way. And he asks, '[name deleted], you think God will forgive me?' I said, 'I'm sure He'll forgive you. But don't talk to me, talk to a priest.' (Quote 9: prominent businessman)

We have the Chinese, we have those of Spanish ancestry, those that are American ... all of them happen to be elite ... They don't seem to have a ... nationalistic ... temperament ... like other countries [which] seem to have a common culture. (Quote 10: prominent businesswoman)

Singapore might be rich in human resources but it doesn't have any natural resources, the Middle East is rich in natural resources but it doesn't have any human resources. The Philippines is so blessed that we have both so we Filipinos should really feel very bad that despite being so blessed, being so endowed, we are so far behind because we are not making use of these resources. (Quote 11: prominent businesswoman)

I've seen some children of the elite who have become socially conscious despite the fact that they live in Forbes Park or Dasmariñas [residential districts in downtown Manila]. I think their experience while they were university students [before and after the fall of Marcos] is going to really affect them. There's no turning back for them. It will be a lifelong impact. (Quote 12: leading academic)

In contrast to their views on the attitudes of the poor, our interviewees were far more ambivalent about their own attitudes and their own treatment of the poor. When asked the question 'Do the well-off care about the plight of the poor?' the majority of respondents refused to provide unequivocal answers, more so than for any other question.[31] Most respondents suggested that some people cared but that others didn't, while other respondents argued that the members of the elite who cared did too little, or acted primarily out of self-interest (e.g. Quote 9). In general, interviewees were far more willing and able to draw distinctions about the attitudes or behaviour of different components of the elite than they were able confidently to draw distinctions among different elements of the poor.

Many of our interviewees were well aware that a developed social consciousness is not generalized within or across sub-elite groups in the Philippines. In explanation, some argue that philanthropic traditions, and the values underpinning them, are still comparatively recent in the Philippines. Many acknowledge the work of prominent philanthropic foundations such as Philippine Business for Social Progress (PBSP) but feel their numbers and resources are insufficient to have a significant impact on poverty. Others felt that the cultural diversity of the Philippines has historically prevented the development of a Filipino notion of social consciousness to which all elite groups can subscribe (e.g. Quote 10). These views suggest a direct relationship between the elite's relatively weak sense of national identity and their perceptions of poverty. Unlike much of South-East Asia and the developing world, the Philippines achieved its independence peacefully, without recourse to deep nationalist and anti-colonial political mobilization or violence. The absence of a victorious nationalist movement with a multi-class appeal and significant stock of popular legitimacy undermined the forging of a national agenda and the resultant sense of nationalism. The Katipunan, the nationalist movement that assumed power in 1898, is viewed with some national pride. The centennial of the 1898 revolution was celebrated with vigour in 1998. Yet the subsequent defeat of the Katipunan by the Americans in a brutal counter-insurgency campaign, followed by colonization by the Japanese during the Second World War, has left deep scars on the national psyche. A number of respondents, for instance, suggested they felt ashamed that the Philippines had fallen behind relative to other countries (e.g. Quote 11). This contrasts with Bangladesh, for instance, where a successful nationalist struggle for independence helps underpin a common sense of national identity, which links rich and poor.

Related to this weak sense of nationalism or national identity is the close relationship between the Philippines (and Filipino elites) and the United States. One reason why elites have not taken poverty more seriously may be the historical link with the USA. Hutchcroft (1998: 245), for instance, argues that ' ... client relations with the United States seem to have insulated Philippine elites from any real sense of intrastate competition – competition that has often been the historic starting point for serious state-building projects. Until recently, the availability of external resources has greatly curbed any need for reform.' Close links to the USA also provide Filipino elites with the option of migrating to the USA or elsewhere, eroding the sense of national identity and commitment. Hedman and Sidel (2000), however, describe the emergence of a new popular nationalism in the media and arts[32] and some of our interviewees pointed to parallel changes

in elite attitudes, especially the emergence of a nascent social consciousness, heralded by the democratization of the state and the atmosphere of
reform which it induced (see Quote 12). Others note similar trends: the
proliferation of corporate and philanthropic foundations, the rising prominence of non-governmental organizations, the increasing atmosphere of
national self-confidence following the economic growth of much of the
1990s, and the coalition of disparate interests supporting the (Estrada)
government's agenda.

Ties that bind: links between the elite and the poor

I'm not poor but I'm not immensely wealthy or anything. All my children
are out of college. But come June, I'm broke because I have to send so many
children to school. Everybody that works for me eventually comes to me and
says, 'We have this one child' or this niece or this nephew. I'm broke. We
might have the cheapest tuition here, [but] I send them to decent schools.
And then around Christmas ... [there are] all the donations I have to give to
charity, from religious to educational. If you take it seriously, it hurts. But of
course giving has to hurt for it to be meaningful. I'm not complaining but
that's how it affects me. And sometimes I even have to hire people I don't
need just to help them. And I think it's everybody, it's not just me. Anybody
who has extra income will be doing this kind of thing unless they're misers
or hard hearted or whatever. No family that I know, no friend that I know,
does not do that. (Quote 13: female philanthropist)

I'm just vice-mayor but you know I have an average of twenty to thirty people
every day in [my] house, in [my] office, asking for support. I have no money
and they need money. Even if it's P100, I'm spending P2,000 a day. It's good
I have other businesses, if not you'll be forced to steal money from the
government to give to the poor ... Once you're a government official, people
think you are a rich person, that you can get money from the government.
That's not true ... My salary is only P21,000 [per month]. (Quote 14: local
politician)

Elite perceptions of the poor and of their own attitudes to the poor are
influenced in significant part by the concrete ties that link them together.
There is a real sense in which the Filipino elite live in an enclave society,[33]
insulated and isolated from the poor and the effects of poverty. They are
concentrated in the Metro Manila area. Here, where an estimated 4 million
of the city's 10 million people are squatters,[34] the rich frequently live in private residential estates surrounded by high walls, sometimes protected by
armed guards. Many of these private estates are close to Pasig and Makati,
the main business districts in the capital. Many rich people commute

between these private estates and the business districts, and live their social and professional lives with minimal physical contact with Manila's urban poverty and decay. Further, the gulf between Metro Manila and the rest of the Philippines is unusually large. Compared to the other countries appearing in this volume, the urban population of the Philippines is very heavily concentrated in the metropolis (Table 1.1). Further, the Philippines is a mountainous archipelago. Many of the poorest provinces are located outside the main island of Luzon, and/or in remote mountainous areas.

Yet there are real ties that bind elite Filipinos to the poor. Unlike in South Africa in particular, elite and poor are predominantly of the same race and the same religion. More importantly, they share a culture shaped by Spanish, and later American, colonial rule, combining patron–client ties with more coercive pressures in a system of social relations deriving from the semi-feudal economy that dominated the nineteenth and early twentieth centuries. In rural and urban areas alike, poor people depend on help and support from the well off and the well off in turn are culturally conditioned to provide it.[35] In a sense, the system provides an important informal safety net on which the poor rely, although by no means the most important one.[36] A sizeable minority of our respondents, for instance, without being asked directly, told us that they provided material support to poor people with whom they had direct contact, including employees, relatives and neighbours (e.g. Quote 13).[37]

Chinese-Filipino interviewees distanced themselves from patron–client relationships, saying they supported formal philanthropic endeavours but did not provide assistance on a 'dole-out' basis (a common Filipino term, equivalent to 'handouts'). Other interviewees implied that they accepted patron–client claims as a means of fulfilling their social obligations to the poor. Politicians, however, including congressmen, mayors and vice-mayors, complained about the obligations this system imposes (e.g. Quote 14). Patron–client ties have protective elements that help the poor but essentially they are exploitative. In the Philippines, 'dole-outs' are an established feature of the political system (especially, but by no means solely, at election time) and an essential means by which the old elite maintains its weakening hegemony. The Filipino elite, however, is by no means a homogenous entity and many are critical of the dole-out system, especially its impact on electoral politics (see further below).

This system of urban patron–clientelism is changing with the proliferation of foundations, and assuming a more institutionalized character. In the Philippines, foundations are established by prominent individuals or families and by corporations, and serve as important vehicles in maintaining their social prestige. The Association of Foundations, for instance, has a membership of 115 philanthropic foundations, many of them linked to prominent elite families (AoF 1997). Among our interviewees, at least seven (or almost 10 per cent) are connected to a family-based foundation.[38] Most interviewees support traditional philanthropic activities (donations to schools, hospitals, churches, etc.), but a number of them support activities such as community organizing or investigative journalism. Other members of the Filipino elite support mass-membership philanthropic organizations. There are over five hundred Rotary Clubs in the Philippines, for instance, with a combined membership of over 16,000 people, and similar organizations such as the Lions Club or the Jaycees (Junior Chambers of Commerce) (De Castro 1997: 221). The proliferation of foundations points to an important trend. Personal charity or philanthropy is based on particularistic values, but the work of these philanthropic organizations is underpinned by a greater commitment to the universalistic values associated with citizenship and state action. Gradually, the nature of the ties that bind the well off to the poor are transmogrifying from the particular to the universal.

Citizenship and the Filipino elite

I used to take jeeps and buses before as a student. I don't think my parents had any fear for me ... Now, my children don't take public transport as a general rule and I still worry about them. I think the problem with poverty is that you can't help but equate criminality with poverty. (Quote 15: female civic leader)

As a businessman, because I am in [the] retail [trade] ... If people have more money, then our sales will go up. Our sales are ... a reflection of [people's] disposable incomes. Outside of food, you don't buy clothing, shoes [etc.] unless you have ... income [to] cover basic requirements [such as] housing, transportation and food. (Quote 16: prominent businessman)

The importance of patron–client ties in creating tangible bonds between the rich and poor, as well as the proliferation of foundations, implies a social consciousness and a degree of social engagement on the part of the elite, including a belief in the interdependent fates of rich and poor alike and an interest in the welfare of all. But this rarely amounts to an ethos of citizenship and a commitment to universal values, the essential underpinnings of pro-poor public policy. When asked about the impact that poverty has on their personal and professional lives, some respondents said they noticed poverty and that it made them feel guilty, while some perceived that their own wealth inspired envy in others. As noted above, a significant minority mentioned the demands that poor people place on them. Very few respondents reported that poverty impacted on their quality of life in other ways. A number mentioned crime (e.g. Quote 15) but few mentioned pollution or an unpleasant urban environment. Nobody mentioned a fear of illness or disease, or a fear of demonstrations or other acts of militancy by the urban poor. In a country that has been racked by a cycle of rural-based insurgency and counter-insurgency throughout the twentieth century, only two respondents mentioned insurgency and the social polarization that sustains it.[39]

Similarly, interviewees felt relatively insulated from the effects of poverty in their professional lives. Few businesspeople were able to articulate a sense in which poverty adversely affected their businesses, for instance, by depriving them of market growth, skilled workers or economic stability. A few businessmen and -women argued that poverty deprives them of the consumer base needed for market growth (e.g. Quote 16) but a greater number alluded to the benefits they derive from poverty, for instance through cheap labour. Filipino businessmen and -women have long proved adept at dealing with the effects of poverty, especially by diversifying beyond their core activities to compensate for the small market sizes stemming from low average disposable incomes. Poverty, and the social polarization to which it leads, has traditionally reduced competition from new market entrants and has enabled businessmen and -women to secure privileged access to scarce resources such as capital.

Other authors have pointed to this weak sense of citizenship, including but by no means limited to members of the elite. 'Filipinos', Diokno argues, 'will help out in an emergency, but might be indifferent to violations of human rights. They bathe daily and value cleanliness in the home but readily throw cigarette butts and other garbage in the street. This dualism highlights the contradiction between self-interest and the good of the community' (Diokno 1999: 144–5). In the case of elite groups, for instance government officials, Diokno continues, perceptions of citizenship are invariably articulated in terms of individual, mostly professional, interests (ibid.: 147). A similar pattern emerged in our study. When asked the question 'How can you help to reduce poverty as a [respondent's profession] and as a citizen?', respondents concentrated almost exclusively on their professional lives. Politicians said they could pass laws that would benefit the poor, businesspeople said they could create jobs and pump-prime economic growth, journalists said they could write stories highlighting the plight of the poor, while NGO leaders said they could continue to work on their behalf. Very few respondents, however, suggested that they could have an impact on poverty in their personal lives. None, for instance, said they could help reduce poverty by voting responsibly or supporting a political party committed to poverty reduction. Political parties in the Philippines are not organized on the basis of coherent political programmes or ideologies and remain largely inactive between election campaigns. People do not see the party-political system as an effective means of enabling individuals to participate in the fight against poverty. Equally, very few respondents suggested they could reduce poverty by donating money to a charity or civic organization. Many, as noted above, have connections to family foundations, but traditions of donating money to professional organizations are not well established and few NGOs or other civic organizations raise money through donations or regular giving schemes. Equally, few people mentioned working for a civic organization on a voluntary basis. In this sense, the elite has a weak sense of citizenship as viewed in Western terms, which stress civic participation. In interviews carried out in late July and August 1999, however, it was evident that a number of interviewees attended, or intended to support, the 20 August demonstration against efforts by the Estrada government to change the 1987 constitution. A nascent sense of citizenship is therefore evident in the commitment to the post-1986 tradition of 'people power', a tradition in which many sections of the elite feel they have actively participated.

Institutional responses to poverty

Not enough of our policy-makers and implementers of these policies believe that this is a serious problem and that it is the business of government. Generally they believe that it is the business of every individual to lift himself up from poverty through his own effort. (Quote 17: former presidential candidate)

My own feeling is the money ... that's supposed to be intended for the public, they go to the politician. I believe twenty per cent to forty per cent [is] pocketed. They want to collect so much tax, yet twenty to thirty per cent of total tax is not even spent on people. They're just pocketed. (Quote 18: prominent businessman)

Why should you pay [taxes to the government]? After all, if you pay the real thing, they'll still come back to you and ask for money from you ... For example, you have to pay P10 million [in taxes]. Why not pay P2-3 million? Then [the politicians] they'll come, you give them some money here and there and they'll all love you. But if you pay the right taxes, nobody is going to see you because you don't want to give to them. So this is a real concern. (Quote 19: prominent businessman)

The Filipino elite are profoundly critical of both the government and the state as institutions, despite almost sixteen years of democratic government at the time of our interviews. They are cynical and pessimistic about the will and capacity of either institution to tackle poverty (e.g. Quote 17). Philippine political culture has traditionally emphasized limited state intervention in the economy and in society – a legacy of American colonial rule and American values. Filipino politicians are often unreceptive to appeals for greater state intervention. In general, however, the Philippine state demonstrates a far greater political will or capacity in the area of poverty reduction than many of our interviewees conceded. For instance, it has a significant capacity to generate revenue from taxation, especially taxes on the well off. Between 1991 and 1995, 29 per cent of government revenue came from taxes on income, profits and capital gains, a large increase on the average of 23 per cent between 1981 and 1990. This is much less than South Africa (51 per cent) but significantly greater than in Brazil (16 per cent) (World Bank 1997: 196–7). Further, the Philippine state commits a significant share of its revenue to the provision of social services. Between 1991 and 1995, for instance, health and education accounted for 20 per cent of government expenditure in the Philippines, compared to 9 per cent in Brazil (ibid.: 198–9).[40]

Yet despite these achievements, our interviewees perceive the government and state primarily as corruption-ridden institutions (e.g. Quote 18). Corruption has long been a significant political problem in the Philippines, due in large part to the power of individual senators and members of the House of Representatives in determining the spending priorities of government ministries (see above). The World Bank estimates that corruption costs the country US$47 million a year and that it has drained $48 billion from government coffers over the twenty years to 1997 (BBC 2000). In the case of wealthy businesspeople, antipathy to government corruption is evident in the underpayment of tax. Businesspeople readily concede that the government needs tax revenues to provide social services and that they stand to benefit from compliance with tax regimes. They feel unable to fully comply with tax demands, however, because of the obligations placed on them by politicians to contribute additional 'taxes' to electoral war chests or to bribe officials of the Bureau of Internal Revenue (BIR) (e.g. Quote 19).

Corruption is one important explanation for the reluctance of businessmen and -women to comply with tax demands, although elite respondents exaggerate its extent. Corruption, however, is not the only important explanation for the reluctance of businesspeople to pay taxes. The behaviour of businesspeople in the Philippines is culturally conditioned. In a country where many hospitals, schools and colleges rely on private rather than state funding, businesspeople are expected to support philanthropic activities from their earnings, again limiting, in their eyes, their ability to meet tax

TABLE 3.2 Answers to the question: 'Apart from government, who can make the greatest contribution to poverty reduction efforts?' (N=67)

Answers, in order of priority	First	Second
Non-governmental organizations (NGOs) (including people's organizations)	23	11
The private sector/businessmen and -women	18	5
The Church	6	9
Society	8	2
The poor themselves	9	2
The education system	1	2
The cooperative sector	2	0

demands. As a result many businesspeople and business organizations actively campaign to keep tax rates on income and capital down and to deter efforts to collect back taxes. The Philippine tax system is still regressive, with a high reliance on taxes on goods and services. It was made more progressive during the early 1990s. In the 1996 Congress, however, with significant support from business groups, the president's Comprehensive Tax Reform Package, intended to close loopholes long exploited by the business community and to institute a more progressive tax system, was defeated (Gutierrez 1997).

Our respondents make distinctions between the government or state as impersonal institutions and the people who run them. In general, they were critical of the record of both the Aquino and Ramos administrations (1986–92 and 1992–98 respectively), though far less critical than of government as a whole, and readily acknowledge certain achievements. President Corazon Aquino is credited with restoring and maintaining democratic institutions despite six coup attempts in as many years, but is criticized for her lack of commitment to agrarian reform. Similarly, Fidel Ramos is praised for reviving economic growth, dismantling monopolies and restoring Filipinos' sense of confidence in their nation. Yet he is also criticized in some circles for promoting industrialization at the expense of agriculture and liberalization at the expense of the poor. Some suggested that his programme of privatization strengthened the economic elite and facilitated a concentration of wealth, or that he failed to erect safety nets to cushion the effects of economic liberalization.

Apart from government, respondents felt that NGOs and people's organizations were best placed to tackle poverty (Table 3.2). NGOs have emerged as a significant actor in the development process since 1986. The Philippines has more NGOs per capita than any other developing country. NGOs have had a significant impact on political discourse and on both government policy and legislation (Clarke 1998), yet elite faith is at odds with the limited financial resources available to NGOs for pro-poor programmes. Faith in NGOs underlines the extent to which the elite believe that poverty in the Philippines is essentially a *political* problem, although it also reflects traditional elite support for philanthropic activity. Equally, however, it reflects a belief among many that poor people must be 'empowered' and that NGOs have a central role to play in facilitating this process. In some respects NGOs have encouraged this attitude among the elite, by emphasizing the discourse of 'empowerment', but many respondents, as a result, believe that the poor must drag *themselves* out of poverty with NGO support, enabling the elite to evade their own responsibility.

Conclusion

In the Philippines, the elite, as we define it in this volume, is no longer dominated by the narrowly based national oligarchy. A range of reforms, including the redistribution of land, the dismantling of cartels and monopolies, and the removal of obstacles to foreign investment, has opened up the economy to new market entrants. Economic growth, especially in urban areas such as Metro Manila, Cebu, Davao and Cagayan de Oro, has led to an expansion of the middle class. In Congress, the stranglehold of the traditional political families, the *caciques*, has weakened. Finally, the proliferation of non-governmental organizations and people's organizations has opened up and transformed civil society, eroding the hegemonic grip of the old elite.

Despite this process of social differentiation and consequent elite expansion, members of the Filipino elite whom we interviewed possess a relatively coherent set of perceptions about poverty and the poor. Of the three elements of social consciousness identified by de Swaan and associates (2000) – awareness of the interdependence of groups; a feeling of responsibility for the condition of the poor; and a belief that feasible and efficacious means exist to reduce poverty – none is fully evident in the perceptions of Filipino elites. A substantial minority of our interviewees did not articulate either a sense of social connectedness to the poor and an awareness of their plight, or a sense of responsibility for the situation of the poor and confidence that the means existed to tackle poverty effectively. The responses varied from group to group. Serving and former military officers, for instance, emerged as the group with the most developed sense of social consciousness, perhaps because soldiers come disproportionately from modest backgrounds and spend long periods in rural areas. Some religious leaders, journalists and activists in the NGO and voluntary community also articulated a strong sense of social consciousness. Most politicians, businesspeople and civil servants, however – the main Establishment elites in closest proximity to the real levers of power – demonstrated a much less complete social consciousness.

The Filipino elite feels a sense of responsibility towards the poor, but this responsibility is met through the provision of assistance on a patron–client basis or through philanthropic activity, rather than a more substantive commitment to redistributive action led by the state, involving, for instance, more elaborate social safety nets financed by higher taxes. The elite look to the state to lead the fight against poverty, yet they are deeply sceptical of the state's capacity to lead this fight – as evidenced, for instance, by exaggerated perceptions of corruption in state institutions. Equally, however, despite their insulation from the practical consequences of poverty, the elite in some respects is sympathetic to the plight of the poor.

Political discourse in the Philippines was dominated by the concerns of democratic consolidation and economic growth following the fall of the Marcos dictatorship in 1986. Following the election of Fidel Ramos in 1992, however, poverty was propelled to the top of the national agenda. 'We regard poverty as another tyranny, oppressing half of our population of 66 million,' Ramos declared in 1995, 'a tyranny against which we must wage the equivalent of a moral war.'[41] The imagery was significant. The Filipino population united in rejoicing at the fall of the Marcos regime, and Ramos sought to tap into this renewed sense of national purpose. Poverty, Ramos suggested, was an even greater tyranny than Marcos. In similar vein, President Gloria Macapagal-Arroyo sought to make the fight against poverty a central national purpose in her inauguration speech in January 2001. 'The first of my core beliefs', she declared, 'pertains to the elimination of poverty. This is our unfinished business from the past. It dates back to the creation of our Republic, whose seeds were sown in the revolution launched in 1896 by the plebeian Andres Bonifacio. It was the unfinished revolution, for to this day, poverty remains our national problem. We need to complete what Andres Bonifacio began.'[42]

Macapagal-Arroyo had little choice but to argue in these terms. Her ascendancy to the presidency was acclaimed by the elite and middle classes but jeered by Manila's urban poor. The previous, brief presidency of Joseph Estrada had revealed the gulf between the poor and non-poor as the most important cleavage in Philippine politics. The new president was forced to move quickly to address it. Whatever the immediate objective, the speech was deeply significant, for it suggested a continuity in the strategy begun during the Ramos years of putting the fight against poverty at the core of the national agenda and of mobilizing a broad multi-class coalition in support.

In a country with a relatively weak national identity, it was implied, the fight against poverty could become the new nationalist struggle. The state, President Macapagal-Arroyo suggested, accepted responsibility in leading the fight against poverty, but it needed the support of all social groups.

There is much cause for optimism here. Poverty levels have been falling slowly but steadily since the mid-1980s and income inequality fell slightly during the 1990s (Balisican 1999: 24). The Philippine state is demonstrating increased competence in the fight against poverty. Yet if the state has made progress in defining its role in the fight against poverty, elites remain far more ambiguous. As noted above, elites articulate some confidence in, and support for, pro-poor public policy. Such support, however, is shrouded in a much larger fog of ambivalence when it comes to the larger plight of the poor and elite responsibility for the situation. Fighting this ambivalence and the disparities from which it stems will be a major challenge for the foreseeable future.

Annexe: list of interviewees

Abad, Florencio 'Butch', member of the House of Representatives

Abalos, Benjamin, mayor of Mandaluyong City (Metro Manila)

Angarra, Gloria, president, Cultural Centre of the Philippines; board member, Metrobank Foundation

Anglingto, Sebastian, chairman, Mindanao Economic Development Council; Philippine Senior Official for BIMP (Brunei, Indonesia, Malaysia, Philippines) – East Asian Growth Area

Ang-See, Teresita, chair, Kaisa Para Sa Kaunlaran (Unity for Progress) (Filipino-Chinese NGO)

Antalan, Rogelio P., mayor, Samal City, Davao del Norte

Aquino, Butz, member of the House of Representatives

Aquino III, Benigno, member of the House of Representatives

Bagahaldo, Aniano G., executive vice-president and chief executive officer, Philippine Exporters Confederation Inc.; vice-president, Employers Federation of the Philippines

Balisican, Arsenio, Professor of Economics, University of the Philippines, Quezon City (prominent specialist on poverty in the Philippines)

Bengzon, Dr Alfredo, president and chief executive officer, Medical City, Makati (private hospital); dean, School of Governance, Ateneo de Manila University

Biazon, Rodolfo G., senator; chairman, Senate Commission on National Defence and Security

Bonguyan, Luis C., vice-mayor, Davao City

Capalla, Bishop Fernando R., Archbishop of Davao City

Caro, Maj. Max, public affairs chief, Philippine army

Casolan, Renaldo, member of the House of Representatives

Claudio, Yolanda, executive director, Philippine Business for Social Progress–Centre for Corporate Citizenship

Constantino-David, Karina, presidential adviser on housing; chair, Housing and Urban Development Council

Coronel, Sheila, executive director, Philippine Centre for Investigative Journalism

Coseteng, Anna Dominique, senator

De Ocampo, Roberto, former finance secretary

De Villa, Renato S., chairman, Independent Insight Inc.; former defence secretary; chief of staff, armed forces of the Philippines

Durize, Jesus, former member of the House of Representatives; former presidential assistant for Mindanao

Ejercito, Joseph Victor, son of President Joseph Ejercito Estrada; national president, Junior Chamber of Commerce of the Philippines

Escador, Col. Emilio, president, Royal Mandaya Hotel, Davao City

Espiritu, Edgardo, finance secretary

Fernan, Marcelo, senator and Senate president (written reply)

Filler, Alfredo L., director, Independent Insight Inc.; former general, armed forces of the Philippines

Florentino-Hofileña, Chay, deputy editor, *Manila Times*

Gaisano, John Y., Jr, president and chief executive officer, JS Gaisano Inc.

Garchitorena, Vicky, president, Ayala Foundation

Garcia-Dizon, Jackie, president, Galleria Hotel, Davao City and Crocodile Farm Resort, Davao del Norte

Gokongwei-Pe, Robina, chair of the board, *Manila Times*

Gonzales, Br Andrew, education, culture and sports secretary

Guerrero-Nakpil, Carmen, writer and journalist; socialite

Honasan, Gregorio 'Gringo', senator

Ilagan-Bian, Joji, president, Joji Iligan Foundation College of Business and Tourism, Davao; executive vice-president, Nikkei Garden Hotel, Cebu; country director (Philippines) BIMP–East ASEAN Business Council

Kalaw, Trina, chairperson, Philippine stock exchange

Libarios, Roan, member of the House of Representatives

Ligot, Brig. Gen. Jacinto, Assistant Division Commander, 4th Infantry Division, armed forces of the Philippines

Llanillo, Llewelyn, president, Philippine Bar Association; partner, Sycip Gatmatian & Llanillo

Lobregat, Celso, member of the House of Representatives

Lotilla, Raphael Perpetuo, under-secretary, National Economic and Development Authority

Luz, Guillermo, president, Makati business club

Macapagal-Arroyo, Gloria, vice-president of the Philippines and Social Work and Development Secretary

Malay, Carolina S., dean, Department of Journalism, University of the Philippines, Quezon City

Mangahas, Malou, editor-in-chief, *Manila Times*

Mercado, Fr Eliseo R., president, Notre Dame University, Cotabato City

Mercado, Orlando S., Defence Secretary

Mitra, Ramon, president, Philippine National Oil Company

Monsod, Solita, chair, School of Economics, University of the Philippines, Quezon City

Morales, Horacio, Agrarian Reform Secretary

Moran-Floriendo, Margarita, TV magazine show host

Muñoz-Palma, Cecilia, chair, Philippine Charity Sweepstakes Office; former president, 1986/7 Constitutional Convention; former Supreme Court justice

Narciso, Dr Antonio, director, Caucus on Poverty Reduction, De La Salle University

Ocampo, Satur, former official spokesperson and chief negotiator, National Democratic Front

Ongpin, Mirabel, chair, Jaime V. Ongpin Foundation

Osmeña, John, senator

Osmeña III, Sergio, senator (written reply)

Pelaez-Marfori, Berry, corporate communications manager, Ayala Land

Perez-Davide, Virgina, chair, Philippine National Volunteer Service Coordinating Agency

Puno, Ronaldo, Interior and Local Government Secretary

Quintos de Jesus, Melinda, executive director, Centre for Media Freedom and Responsibility

Racelis, Dr Mary, president, Community Organizers Multiversity; vice-president, Caucus of Development NGO Networks (CODE-NGO)

Romualdez, Alberto, Health Secretary

Salonga, Jovito, president, Kilosbayan (independent people's organization); former Senate president

Santos, Gloria, president, Davao Orchid Society

Sasin, Anthony B., presidential assistant for regional concerns for Eastern Mindanao; senior vice-president, Anflo Management & Investment Corp.; chair, Filipino Banana Growers and Exporters Association

Simbulan, Roland, Professor of Development Studies, University of the Philippines, Manila

Siy, George, chairman, Richfield Inc.; chairman, Fil-Pacific Apparel Corp.

Socrates, Msgr Villegas, rector, Our Lady of the Peace Parish, Epifanio de los Santos Avenue, Manila

Tambunting, Jesus P., president and chief executive officer, Planters Bank Inc.; chairman, Jesus P. Tambunting Foundation

Tan, Bienvenido, president and chief executive officer, Philippine Tobacco Flue-Curing and Redrying Corporation

Tan, Sr Christine, prominent Catholic Church activist working with Manila's urban poor; former member of the Constitutional Commission, 1986/7

Templo, Emiliano, vice-president, Fil-Invest Inc.

Teodoro, Prof. Luis V., dean, College of Mass Communication, University of the Philippines, Quezon City

Teves, Rey Magno, board secretary, Technical Assistance Centre for the Development of Rural and Urban Poor Communities; former member of the House of Representatives

Tirol, Vic, publisher, *Sulong Pinoy*

Tiu-Laurel, Herman, president, Goto King Inc.

Yuchengco, Vivian, governor, Philippine stock exchange

Notes

1 We are both grateful for research assistance provided by Jessica Mills in Swansea and Lourdes Santiago in Manila; to Jay Kynch in Swansea and Jeannette Ureta of Social Weather Stations Inc. (SWS) in Manila for their help in obtaining and analysing the results of SWS's 1999 survey on social inequality in the Philippines; and to Mick Moore and the other contributors to this volume for helpful comments on earlier drafts of this chapter.

2 This figure had barely changed by the late 1990s. In 1997, the richest 20 per cent of the population commanded 52.3 per cent of national consumption (UNDP 2002: 195).

3 Not all questions from this questionnaire were put to all interviewees. All interviews were tape-recorded with the permission of interviewees and transcribed, although each interviewee was assured that specific views would not be attributed.

4 De Swaan et al. (2000: 46) define elites as 'those persons who occupy the strongest power positions, control the most property and hold the highest prestige'. 'As a rough rule of thumb,' they suggest, 'individuals (and people closely related to them) who belong to the uppermost one tenth of one percent on at least two out of these three dimensions constitute these elites.' As the Philippines had a population of 77 million in 1999 when the research was carried out (World Bank 2000a), the elite represent the wealthiest, most powerful and most influential 77,000 people. We believe our interviewees, with a few possible exceptions, would all fall within this group on at least two of the three dimensions.

5 Based on principal occupation/position, we interviewed 23 businesspeople, 22 politicians, 7 NGO leaders/civic activists, 7 academics, 7 government officials, 4 journalists, 3 religious leaders, 3 socialites, 2 serving military officers, 1 lawyer and 1 political activist associated with the underground left. Politicians hold elective office or serve as members of the cabinet while government officials hold (sub-cabinet) appointed positions, rather than elective office. Politicians interviewed included 6 members of the cabinet, 5 senators and 6 members of the House of Representatives. Of the 80 interviewees, 53 were male and 27 female. Full details of our interviewees are provided in the annexe.

6 A wide-ranging questionnaire-based survey of Philippine political elites

in 1991 by Social Weather Stations, with a sample size of 465, was limited to senators, members of the House of Representatives and senior civil servants (see Romana 1993).

7 For practical reasons, all the interviews were carried out with people who live exclusively or predominantly in cities, including politicians representing rural districts or towns. But we believe this reflects the reality – that the Philippine elite is very urban-centred.

8 For example, politicians who retain significant business interests, former military officials entering politics or former cabinet secretaries returning to the private sector.

9 These relationships consist of one case of siblings and two sets of uncle–nephew relationships. This degree of consanguinity was a random outcome of our selection protocol.

10 Following Verba et al. (1987: 59–60), our sample includes representatives of Establishment, mediating and oppositional elites. Establishment elites structure basic economic conflicts, benefit from the status quo and support tinkering, at best, with the existing distribution of rewards. Oppositional elites are typically disadvantaged within the existing system, support greater change in the status quo and confront Establishment elites (for example, feminists, or members of ethnic minorities). Mediating elites deal less with tangible resources than with ideas and are neither supportive nor fundamentally challenging of the economic status quo.

11 In referring to the 'underside' to Filipino familism, Diokno cites an unpublished manuscript by Fernando Zialcita, also published as Zialcita (1997).

12 At the time of our interviews in 1999, the exchange rate was roughly 38 pesos to the US dollar, or 60 pesos to the pound sterling.

13 Interviews with government officials.

14 Report from the National Statistical Coordination Board to President Gloria Macapagal-Arroyo, 19 July 2001. The national poverty line for 2000 was set at P13,916 (US$347) per month for a family of six, equivalent to roughly US$2 per person per day.

15 The World Bank reference is to per capita income valued in US dollars. The Philippine peso has devalued significantly relative to the dollar since 1982.

16 Both surveys, undertaken by Social Weather Stations Inc., had a sample size of 1,200.

17 In the 1992 survey, conflicts between rich and poor emerged as more significant than those between management and workers, the unemployed and those with jobs, farmers and city people, young people and the old, and the working and middle classes (Guerrero 1993: 5), with 55 per cent of respondents believing that 'very strong' or 'strong' conflicts exist between the poor and rich. In the 1999 survey, that figure increased to 69.3 per cent – our analysis of data in SWS (2000).

18 In 1992, 51 per cent of respondents agreed or strongly agreed with the statement that 'inequality continues because it benefits the rich and the powerful' (compared to 50.4 per cent in 1999), while 57 per cent agreed or strongly agreed with the statement that 'differences in income in the Philip-

pines are too large' (compared to 64.8 per cent in 1999) (Guerrero 1993: 13, 6); and our own analysis of data in SWS (2000).

19 In 1992, 57 per cent of respondents agreed with the statement that 'differences in income in the Philippines are too large', while 17 per cent disagreed or strongly disagreed (65 per cent and 17 per cent in 1999 respectively). In contrast, 57 per cent of respondents also agreed with the statement that 'large differences in income are necessary for the Philippines' prosperity', while 15 per cent disagreed (53 per cent and 24 per cent respectively in 1999) (Guerrero 1993:13); our own analysis of 1999 data in SWS (2000).

20 Of 63 interviewees who were asked the question 'How big a problem is poverty in the Philippines?' (or Mindanao, in the case of interviews in Davao), 14 (22 per cent) said it was the biggest, 28 (44 per cent) said it was a big problem, 8 (13 per cent) said it was a problem, and 5 (8 per cent) suggested that it was not necessarily a problem. The remaining eight answers could not be categorized.

21 Interviewees were not asked to contrast urban and rural poverty, although many did in answer to other questions.

22 We put the question 'Who are the poor in the Philippines' to 58 of our 80 interviewees. Less than 20 per cent distinguished between three or more social groups that helped to make up 'the poor'. A further 20 per cent perceived the poor as those who were unable to meet their basic needs while 20 per cent perceived them as people with insufficient income. Ten per cent of interviewees confined their answers to the urban poor while almost 10 per cent gave no answer.

23 Of the 58 interviewees who were asked the question, 10 listed three or more categories; 9 mentioned the inability to meet basic needs; 8 mentioned insufficient income; 5 confined their answers to the urban poor; and 5 were unable to give an answer. Of the 58, 4 mentioned indigenous peoples and 1 mentioned Muslim *Moros*.

24 In both cases, the Philippines achieved a higher ranking than other South-East Asian nations such as Thailand, Vietnam and Indonesia <www. transparency.org>.

25 In 1992, respondents were asked the question 'In our society, there are groups which tend to be towards the top and groups which tend to be towards the bottom. Below is a [ten-point] scale that runs from top to bottom. Where would you put yourself in this scale?' In response, 2 per cent put themselves in the top group and 1 per cent in the group second from top. Sixty per cent of respondents placed themselves in groups four to six, i.e. in the middle groups (see Guerrero 1993: 16, 18). In 1999, 3 per cent of respondents classified themselves as upper middle class or upper class, the top two of six class categories (our analysis of data in SWS 2000). In both cases, respondents' perceptions are significantly at odds with the real pattern of income distribution in the Philippines, although the survey samples were structured to reflect this.

26 Continuing, the same interviewee added, 'But it's not all their fault; the whole system works against them because there's a lack of resources. They don't have the kind of education that they should have; don't have the connections they should have and therefore no opportunities. They really can't do much by themselves', suggesting a more sympathetic attitude.

27 A dump on the fringes of Metro Manila which supports an estimated 60,000 people. In July 2000, an estimated 125 people died in the dump when a 50-foot mound of rubbish collapsed following heavy rain.

28 Sixty-three interviewees were asked the question 'Is it possible to distinguish between a deserving and an undeserving poor?', of whom 34 said that it was, 20 said that it was not, and 9 did not answer.

29 Fifty-seven interviewees were asked the question 'Do the poor bear any responsibility for their own poverty?', of whom 33 said that they did, 21 said that they did not and 3 were unable to say.

30 Although, as Hedman and Sidel (2000: 68) note, 'Chinese' can be a problematic category in the Philippines given the extent to which the Chinese have assimilated.

31 Thirty-seven interviewees were asked this question, of whom seven said yes and three said no. Twenty-seven respondents provided equivocal or ambivalent answers.

32 Chapter 7.

33 Or 'citadel society', the term used by Kalati and Manor in Chapter 6 with respect to South Africa.

34 Mangahas 2001: 6. This high figure is due in part to migration to Manila in the aftermath of the 1997 regional economic crisis.

35 According to Sidel (1999: 7–9), frameworks that stress the significance of patron–client ties are of limited use in explaining the relationships between poor and well-off people, whether they draw on the idioms of reciprocity, smooth interpersonal relations, and the kinship and fictive kinship bonds stressed in modernization theory or those of social inequality, material scarcity and the failure of kinship, village units and state institutions in the case of historical materialism. Coercive pressures (such as electoral fraud, skulduggery, vote buying and violence) and local power monopolies, Sidel argues, also play a critical role in determining social relations. Sidel is undoubtedly correct, although it is possible to exaggerate the impact of direct coercive pressures and minimize the role of alternative, less coercive but no less insidious means by which the powerful interact with the weak. Sidel's model is sensitive to the behaviour of male elites, but says less about the ways in which the female elite interact with the poor.

36 Overseas employment and the extended family system have been more important as informal safety nets in recent decades.

37 We did not ask interviewees directly if they provided material assistance to poor people with whom they had contact, so it is impossible to establish the percentage of our respondents who did provide such help. Some may have done so without mentioning it to us.

38 The seven either mentioned the foundation themselves or are known by us to be connected to one.

39 The communist insurgency, which waned considerably in the early 1990s, began to revive again from 1998 in the aftermath of the East Asian crisis. The New People's Army was estimated to have 7,000 armed regulars in 1999 (anonymous interviews). In addition, the Moro Islamic Liberation Front and

a more militant group, Abu Sayaf, continue to oppose government forces in Muslim Mindanao.

40 Compared to Brazil, however, the Philippines commits a much smaller share of government expenditure to social security.

41 Speech to the World Summit for Social Development, Copenhagen, 12 March 1995, quoted in World Bank 1996: 1.

42 'Inauguration Speech of President Gloria Macapagal-Arroyo, 20 January 2001', Office of the President.

References

Anderson, B. (1988) 'Cacique Democracy in the Philippines: Origins and Dreams', *New Left Review*, 169, May/June

AoF (1997) *Partnering with Business for Social Development: Annual Report 1997*, Manila: Association of Foundations

Balisican, A. M. (1999) 'What Do We Really Know – or Don't Know – About Economic Inequality and Poverty in the Philippines', in A. Balisican and S. Fujisaki (eds), *Causes of Poverty: Myths, Facts and Policies – a Philippine Case Study*, Diliman: University of the Philippines Press

BBC (2000) 'High Cost of Corruption in the Philippines', BBC News website <http://www.bbc.co.uk/news> 6 December

Carey, J. and M. Shugart (1995) 'Incentives to Cultivate a Personal Vote: A Rank Ordering of Electoral Formulas', *Electoral Studies*, 14

Clarke, G. (1998) *The Politics of NGOs in Southeast Asia: Participation and Protest in the Philippines*, London: Routledge

Datinguinoo, V. and A. Olarte (2001) 'Political Clans Make a Comeback', Philippine Center for Investigative Journalism, Manila, 3–4 December, <www.pcij.org>

De Castro Jr., I. (1997) 'Profit and Social Consciousness in the Business Sector', in M. Coronel-Ferrer (ed.), *Civil Society Making Civil Society*, Diliman: Third World Studies Center, University of the Philippines

de Swaan, A., J. Manor, E. Øyen and E. P. Reis (2000) 'Elite Perceptions of Poverty: Reflections for a Comparative Research Project', *Current Sociology*, 48 (1)

Diokno, M. S. I. (1999) 'The Democratising Function of Citizenship in the Philippines', in A. Davidson and K. Weekley (eds), *Globalisation and Citizenship in Asia-Pacific*, Basingstoke: Macmillan Press

Eaton, K. (2001) 'Political Obstacles to Decentralization: Evidence from Argentina and the Philippines', *Development and Change*, 32

Guerrero, L. L. (1993) 'Social Inequality in the Philippines: The 1992 ISSP Survey', SWS Occasional Paper, May

Gutierrez, E. (1994) *Ties that Bind: A Guide to Business and Other Interests in the Ninth House of Representatives*, Manila: Philippine Center for Investigative Journalism and Institute for Popular Democracy

— (1997) 'The Impact of the Business Sector on the Comprehensive Tax Reform Package' (abstract), in M. I. Wui and G. S. Lopez (eds), *State–Civil*

Society Relations in Policy-making, Diliman: Third World Studies Center, University of the Philippines

Hedman, E. L. E. and J. T. Sidel (2000) *Philippine Politics and Society in the Twentieth Century: Colonial Legacies, Post-colonial Trajectories*, London: Routledge

Hutchcroft, P. (1998) *Booty Capitalism: The Politics of Banking in the Philippines*, Ithaca, NY: Cornell University Press

Mangahas, M. (2001) 'The Transactional Presidency', *i: The Investigative Reporting Magazine*, Manila, April/June

Pinches, M. (1996) 'The Philippines' New Rich: Capitalist Transformation Amidst Economic Gloom', in R. Robison and D. S. G. Goodman (eds), *The New Rich in Asia: Mobile Phones, McDonald's and Middle-class Revolution*, London: Routledge

— (1999) 'Entrepreneurship, Consumption, Ethnicity and National Identity in the Making of the Philippines' New Rich', in M. Pinches (ed.), *Culture and Privilege in Capitalist Asia*, London: Routledge

Romana, E. R. (1993) 'On Survey-Interviews of Filipino Political Elites', SWS Occasional Paper, June

Sidel, J. T. (1999) *Capital, Coercion and Crime: Bossism in the Philippines*, Stanford, CA: Stanford University Press

SWS (2000) *ISSP 1999 Module on Social Inequality III in the Philippines: Data and Documentation*, CD-ROM, Manila: Social Weather Stations Inc.

UNDP (1997) *Philippine Human Development Report 1997*, Manila: United Nations Development Programme

— (1998) *Human Development Report 1998*, United Nations Development Programme, New York and Oxford: Oxford University Press

— (2002) *Human Development Report 2002*, United Nations Development Programme, New York and Oxford: Oxford University Press

Verba, S., with S. Kelma, G. R. Orren, I. Miyake, J. Matakuki, I. Kabashima and D. G. Ferree Jr (1987) *Elites and the Idea of Inequality: A Comparison of Japan, Sweden and the United States*, Cambridge, MA: Harvard University Press

Wickberg, E. (1965) *The Chinese in Philippine Life 1850–1898*, New Haven, CT: Yale University Press

World Bank (1996) *Philippines: A Strategy to Fight Poverty,* Country Operations Division, East Asia and Pacific Region

— (1997) *World Development Report 1997: The State in a Changing World*, New York: World Bank and Oxford University Press

— (2000a) *World Development Report 2000/2001: Attacking Poverty*, New York: World Bank and Oxford University Press

— (2000b) 'The World Bank's Role in the Fight against Poverty in the Philippines', Philippines Country Office, World Bank, April

Zialcita, F. N. (1997) 'Barriers and Bridges to a Democratic Culture', in M. S. I. Diokno (ed.), *Democracy and Citizenship in Filipino Political Culture*, Quezon City: Third World Studies Center, University of the Philippines

4 | So near and yet so far: elites and imagined poverty in Bangladesh

NAOMI HOSSAIN AND MICK MOORE

Bangladesh and its elites

Tension Virtually every story about elites and poverty in Brazil or South Africa takes off from an observation about gross inequalities of incomes and wealth. Although income is more equally distributed in the Philippines, it is often placed in the same category. Bangladesh, like most of South Asia, is, and feels, altogether in a different category. From the perspective of the Bangladeshi poor, the Bangladeshi elite no doubt appear amazingly opulent. But to the international observer, this is not a country of great material contrasts. The dominant first impressions are of mass poverty, and of the physical press of poor people. Population density is exceptionally high. Bangladesh's international image as the embodiment of destitution is reinforced by the absence of elite residential areas into which the poor are allowed only for work purposes. Even in the most elite residential areas of Dhaka, the Bangladeshi capital, the poor are on the streets in large numbers by day; by night, thousands camp out on pavements, in alleyways and on building sites. How do the Bangladeshi elite, embedded in a sub-continental culture known internationally for its strong sense of hierarchy, cope with the pervasive proximity of the poor? There is powerful tension at the core of the dominant elite political culture of South Asia in general, and Bangladesh in particular. Interpersonal relations and conceptions of society are suffused by notions of hierarchy that have a special twist: the expectation that superiors can and will share physical space with inferiors without sharing social space. To a greater extent than in any other region of the world, South Asians are consistently able to ignore the physical presence of people lower in the social hierarchy. The South Asian poor are 'unseen' – not literally, as in the Philippines or South Africa, where they are safely housed miles away from the places where the rich live – but because they are unrecognized. They are never far away. South Asian elites have learned to live with the physical presence of the poor by largely ignoring them. Yet – and herein lies the tension mentioned above – the political discourse that has dominated in South Asia for decades stresses the obligations of public authorities to care for the poor and needy, and to reduce poverty.[1] That obligation is repeated more insistently and consistently than in almost any region of the world, and is manifest not only in discourse but in legions of governmental and public programmes intended to reduce poverty. Moralistic attitudes about shared responsibility towards the poor and unfortunate extend far beyond politicians' rhetoric. They were very evident in our interviews in Bangladesh. Not a single respondent rejected the notion of public responsibility for reducing poverty; differences of views concerned the degree of responsibility, its location and modes of intervention.

This tension – between 'not seeing' the poor while consistently articulating concern at their situation and some kind of commitment to improving it – is not fundamentally puzzling. Belief and value systems do not require logical coherence, and can accommodate a great deal of internal discrepancy. Some mitigation of that tension is implicit in the perceptions of the Bangladeshi elite about poverty that are explored in this chapter: their concern *for* the poor was unmatched by empirical knowledge *about* the poor; and their attitudes in general were 'paternalistic' – i.e. marked by a sense of self-confidence about their own capacity usefully to diagnose and prescribe for poverty, and a belief in the importance of their own benevolence in relation to the poor.

The Bangladeshi elite is *near* the poor in some very important senses. There is relatively little spatial or residential segregation: the elite live right by the poor. Despite the strong vein of hierarchy in interpersonal relations, income distribution is more equal in Bangladesh – and South Asia generally – than in any other part of the poor world.[2] And, as we explain below, the Bangladeshi elite identify strongly with the Bangladeshi poor in sociocultural and historical terms. Most Bangladeshis are perceived to share a common language, a common religion, a common cultural heritage, and a common national identity born out of successive colonial oppressions, violence and hard-won national liberation. As we explain below, the Bangladeshi nation and the elite itself are largely the products of the last thirty years; and the building of both nation and elite is still visibly in process. This shapes the ways in which elites perceive the poor.

Yet in other ways the Bangladeshi elite are *far* from the poor. As we mentioned above, they have little empirical knowledge of them. Imagination plays the dominant role in constructing their understanding. There is very little direct economic interdependence between elite and poor. In particular, the wealth of the elite has been until very recently based mainly on political, bureaucratic, professional and trading enterprise. Very few members of the elite depend on the employment of significant numbers of poor people in agricultural or industrial production. Similarly, the level of political integration of elites and the (rural) poor is low – especially when measured by Indian standards. The main political parties lack any major programmatic or ideological differences, and have strikingly similar policies on poverty. Since the late 1980s all governments, which have at different times included the three largest parties, have without exception pursued policies of economic liberalization (Economist Intelligence Unit 2000; Baxter 1998). Both major parties are dominated at the legislative level by the wealthy, especially businessmen, and at the more local levels by coalitions of elite individuals. Neither party has a significant permanent organization independent of the personal networks of their leaders. They are in constant danger of fragmenting around personalities; politicians change party loyalties with ease. The poor – the mass of the population – have votes, but little opportunity to use them to influence government policy in any strategic way. Finally, there is no sign that the general empathy that the Bangladesh elite exhibit in relation to 'their' poor translates into any perceived urgency to do anything to alleviate poverty.

Elite integration In comparison to the other cases in this volume, the responses of the Bangladeshi elite to our questions about poverty were relatively homogeneous. There was, of course, variety and dispersion, which we illustrate in some of the tables below. But, unlike in the Brazil, Philippines or South African cases, we could not identify relatively distinctive attitudes to poverty with particular subcategories of the elite. Generally speaking, businessmen, bureaucrats, ministers, journalists and generals espoused similar views. This relative consensus is not surprising. It reflects the relatively integrated character of the Bangladeshi elite itself, in respect of ethnicity, language, religion, culture, occupation and residence.[3] In the terms that we employ here, the Bangladeshi elite is both relatively homogeneous and highly *interconnected*.

The contemporary Bangladeshi elite is overwhelmingly Bengali-speaking and mostly Sunni Muslim. This results from recent history, and stands in sharp contrast to the past. In the late colonial period, in East Bengal, Muslims competed for resources and power with the Hindu middle classes (Broomfield 1968; Ahmed 1981). The landlord class was to a significant degree Hindu. After the partition of India in 1947 and the incarnation of contemporary Bangladesh as East Pakistan, coveted positions in the state and industrial assets were concentrated in the hands of the non-Bengali Muslims from West Pakistan (Maniruzzaman 1980; Ghosh 1990; Kochanek 1993). Large numbers of people from the Bengali elite and middle classes were slaughtered in 1970/71 during the fight for independence from West Pakistan. The struggle and the bloodshed provided independent Bangladesh with a powerful sense of a Bangladeshi national identity, centred on soil, language and culture, with Islam playing some role. The character of the elite has changed substantially as a result of these traumas. Indeed, the last thirty years are viewed by some people as *the* period of social formation at the elite level. At the level of identity, previous markers of status – claims to foreign ancestry, speaking Urdu rather than Bengali – have become suspect on nationalist grounds. Differences of religion, ethnicity and caste are now largely insignificant or under-played. At the material level, the economic basis of the elite has become less political, bureaucratic and professional, and more capitalist. Policies of economic liberalization and privatization, allied with the creation of a garment export industry, have provided many opportunities for private enterprise. These opportunities have largely been seized by people with good political connections. The business elite itself has become dominated by Bengali Muslims, where previously it was more diverse (Kochanek 1993, especially pp. 112–16, 172; Sobhan and Sen 1988).

The increasing salience of business in the composition of the elite, however, has not led to the emergence of a very distinct capitalist fraction.[4] The national elite remains a close-knit group. Members are connected in multiple ways through a web of tightly interwoven social relationships, and are likely to know each other personally (see Lewis et al. 1994). Individuals and families straddle different economic and social sectors, and interact a great deal. Any member is likely to have friends, relatives, and friends of friends and relatives who sit in Parliament, own garment firms, direct NGOs, edit newspapers, produce TV programmes, chair state banks, command regiments, control consultancy companies, preside over government departments, and manage aid offices. This web of interconnection is all the tighter because, to a greater extent than in many countries, the Bangladeshi elite live, work and play in one city – Dhaka.[5] While divided at the interpersonal level over who will be nominated for this electorate, awarded that contract or get that job – and highly factionalized and increasingly confrontational at the level of electoral politics – the elite is not divided by any great political or social cleavage. In class terms it is unified and dominant over Bangladeshi society. In answering questions about poverty, members of the elite do not feel driven to pursue some intra-elite conflict by proxy.

Relatively homogeneous in terms of sociocultural identity, the national elite is keen to stress the ways in which it reflects and represents Bangladeshi society generally.[6] Members do not claim that they are distinguished from the rest of society by ethnic origins or superior cultural or ritual status. Although some remnants of caste-like distinctions persist among Muslims, these have long been both officially and popularly rejected as un-

Islamic (Bertocci 1970; Ahmed 1981). Instead, elites emphasize and value a common sociocultural identity, frequently invoking the memory of the bloody and prolonged 1970/71 liberation war as a sacrifice which united Bangladeshis from all social levels.[7] Compared to groups that have ruled the region in the past, and to many contemporary elites in other countries, this elite credibly claims an affinity with the masses. This image of unity derives from the very recent ascent of the elite to their present positions. Few families of the contemporary elite have been urban for more than two generations, and many still have ties, however weak, to their rural areas of origin (Siddiqui et al. 1990). Most are no more than the third generation in their families to have acquired secular or professional education (see Barua 1978; Sen 1986; Sobhan and Sen 1988; Rahman 1991). Their recent roots are in the middle classes of East Bengal – urban professionals and the rich peasantry – rather than the upper echelons of local society during British colonial rule or the Pakistan period (1947–70). With its 'middle-class elite', the new nation-state of Bangladesh was initially classified as an 'intermediate' regime (Sobhan and Ahmad 1988; Bertocci 1982) – a polity dominated by middle-class professionals, small businessmen and wealthy peasants, rather than by landed or large industrial interests.[8]

Diversity We interviewed ninety-five members of the *national elite* – seventy-five based in Dhaka and twenty in the provincial towns of Chittagong, Comilla and Rangpur. They were unquestionably of elite status, selected because they occupied key positions of power or had the capacity to influence national events and discourses. They comprised prominent national politicians, civil servants and military personnel, including some retired people; editors of English- and Bangla-language newspapers and journals; business leaders from a range of industries and associations; directors of large NGOs and prominent NGO activists; leading socialites involved in charity work; student leaders and prominent Islamic figures.[9] Partly because we were not finding much diversity in responses, we decided to extend the survey to one hundred members of what we term the *local elite* in small urban centres in five districts across Bangladesh. We used the same semi-structured questionnaire. Lists were drawn up in each area of the people locally considered to be important and influential. These included large landowners, businessmen, local government representatives, state officials, local intellectuals and religious leaders and some NGO staff. The views of these two sets of elites are presented separately in some of the tables below. In fact, those views are not radically different. This is not entirely surprising, given the recent roots of most of the national elite in rural areas (above), and the fact that some still have kinship ties and land in their home districts. The most striking difference in responses was that local elites were far more willing than national elites to support direct state action to reduce poverty. This may reflect the fact that, compared with members of the national elite, more local elites hold political or bureaucratic positions. They have a more direct stake in the distribution of resources through government channels, and more direct responsibilities for the livelihoods of poor people. We are interested here mainly in the perceptions of the national elite, and use our information on local elites principally to contextualize and enrich that understanding.

There is one source of diversity in views on poverty that is significant but not evident from the arithmetic of our sampling: the attitudes of prominent Islamic figures. Governmental and elite (and middle-class) culture is substantially secular, reflecting a variety of historical influences, including the organizational weakness and marginality of Islamic institutions during British colonial rule, and the fact that the 1970/71 liberation war was fought to free the country from a federation with West Pakistan that was only ever justifiable in terms of a common Islamic identity. The interaction of the historically marginal status of Islamic institutions and increasing engagement with pan-Islamic ideas and organizations have generated radical Islamicist movements and sentiments in many small towns and rural areas. There is a growing tension with the secularism of elite and governmental culture. This has often crystallized around the success of large non-governmental micro-credit organizations – notably the Grameen Bank, BRAC, Proshika, ASA – in providing credit to millions of rural people, most of them women, in ways that require them to come into the public domain. The organizations that provide micro-credit, and the many other development NGOs that thrive in Bangladesh, have undeniably close links to Western aid agencies. The tensions between Islamic organizations and political parties on the one side and development NGOs on the other have occasionally flared into violence. These tensions affected not so much the responses of Islamic leaders to our queries as their willingness to be interviewed at all, or to accept our definition of the relevant questions. Their replies do not significantly shape our overall pattern of responses, largely because few Islamicists are members of the elite, as we defined it.

Elites There was some reluctance among our interviewees to accept that they themselves might be members of the 'elite', in the sense of possessing power or influence. There were usually other individuals or groups who were felt to be more powerful. Alternatively, 'eliteness' was sometimes interpreted more normatively in terms of a responsibility to exercise moral leadership. Respondents could assess other individual members of the elite

– and simultaneously pursue intra-elite quarrels and status contests – by assessing the extent to which they fulfilled this obligation. But the fact that such criteria were used is some indication of the overall strength of the normative commitment of the elite to the nation, and to the project of nation-building.

How do Bangladeshi elites imagine poverty?

Bangladeshi elites are under few illusions about the scale, severity or character of poverty in their country. In their imaginations, there is a massive national problem, identified mainly with low absolute incomes and the chronic inability to meet basic needs, rather than with less tangible concerns about social inequality or vulnerability. Our talk of poverty in the elite 'imagination' is not intended to suggest that they perceive poverty in ways that are radically divorced from reality. It is rather that perceptions of poverty are unlikely to be a simple reflection of reality, even when poverty is in plain view. Elites recognized that a large proportion of the population of Bangladesh is poor: in fact, most judged the problem to be larger than the official estimates.[10] Although in some contexts rural life is idealized as somehow 'better' for the poor, elites also recognized that poverty is primarily a rural problem, linked to dependence on an agrarian base decreasingly capable of providing a living for the vast population. Poverty was rarely characterized as a relative concept, or a matter of being short of money, vulnerable or insecure. The implicit definition is more direct and stark: most members of the elite know that, in their country, poverty is a matter of life-threatening deprivation. Many poor people routinely struggle simply to survive. A newspaper editor described how he was shocked by the differences between the urban poor of Dhaka and Bangkok: 'I had this vision of a slum in Dhaka, and so I went to this slum in Bangkok and many houses had televisions. So it's a whole different level of perception. So our poor are really, *really* poor.'

Urban poverty, being closer and more visible, was generally perceived as a more pressing priority by members of the national elite. It was, however, conceived as being linked to the larger rural problem, since the urban poor were believed to be recent rural migrants, coming to the cities to escape unemployment and landlessness, possibly temporarily. Perhaps partly because of the sense that poverty is rooted in more or less the same causes across the nation, regardless of location, elites proved unable to make distinctions between types of poor people – whether these were practical distinctions between types of poverty, or moral judgements between (for example) the more and less 'deserving' poor. The practical obstacles to distinguishing among different types of poor people are compounded by

TABLE 4.1 Respondents' estimates of the extent of poverty in Bangladesh (per cent)

Proportion of the population estimated to be poor by:	National elites	Local elites
75–100	32	49
50–74	39	27
25–49	1	9
Less than 25	3	6
Other responses	25	9
Total	100	100
No. of respondents*	79	91

* Here, as in some other tables, the total number of responses is less than the total number of interviewees because some either did not respond to the question, or did so in a way that makes it difficult to categorize their response.

a nationalist consciousness that stresses social and ethnic commonality, rendering elites unwilling to pinpoint social or other distinctions within the national community.

Three main themes dominate elites' conceptions and explanations of persistent mass poverty:

- national economic underdevelopment;
- bad governance;
- the attitudes and behaviour of the poor themselves.

National economic underdevelopment As Toye points out, aggregate income poverty statistics which prove that the vast majority of developing country populations are 'poor' imply that the solution to poverty must 'collapse back into the broad strategy for economic development' (Toye 1999: 8). It is not altogether surprising that a vast, intractable problem on the scale of poverty in Bangladesh turns elite attention towards national economic development, rather than to discrete, specific anti-poverty measures. Much of the time, 'poverty' is imagined as national economic underdevelopment – the consequences of the lack of wealth at a national aggregate level. Poverty was viewed as a shared, collective concern of all Bangladeshis rather than a problem restricted to poor people and their capabilities or constraints. Not only was it believed that there are many poor people, but the nation was itself understood to be 'poor'. Members of the elite know Bangladesh's international image as a 'basket case'. This is reinforced by the perception that Bangladesh has little national wealth: land and other resources are insufficient to meet the needs of

TABLE 4.2 National priorities and the causes of poverty compared (data from both national and local elite interviews; multiple responses included; per cent)

Proportion of respondents citing different factors	National priorities	Causes of poverty
Education and health: lack of access to, poor quality of	21	19
Bad governance: lack of political consensus /stability, inefficient administration, corruption, breakdown of law and order	20	20
The economy: over-reliance and under-investment in outdated agriculture, slow pace of industrialization, inadequate infrastructure	16	15
Structural inequalities: unemployment, lack of access to assets (and, in the case of the 'priorities' question, poverty itself)	19	13
Overpopulation	10	10
Attitudinal and motivational problems: fatalism, lack of awareness, the selfishness of the rich, religious fundamentalism, lack of morality	7	12
Environmental problems: land erosion, natural disasters	2	7
Other: legacies of colonialism, donor dependence, the status of women, the burden of demands from the poor (local elites)	3	4
Total	100	100
Total number of responses (individuals provided multiple responses)	563	506

the still overwhelmingly agrarian population; there are few mineral or other natural resources; industry and infrastructure are underdeveloped. While Bangladesh's large offshore natural gas reserves had become public knowledge by the time we conducted our interviews, this had little impact on the perception of Bangladesh as a country lacking natural resources. Our respondents seemed aware that no other large poor country has so many rural people as dependent on agriculture as does Bangladesh.

The image of poverty as a problem of national economic underdevelopment means that there is an important sense in which poverty is seen as a high priority by elites. This is evidenced in the high degree of overlap between (a) the problems elites claim to be the national priorities for government to tackle, and (b) their views on the causes of poverty (see Table 4.2). In (largely) equating poverty reduction with economic growth, the Bangladeshi elite are, of course, fully in tune with recent international orthodoxy about development strategy. Bangladesh was heavily aid dependent for the first two decades of its existence, and currently engages with many official aid donors. Bengal – encompassing both Bangladesh and the adjacent Indian state of West Bengal – has a distinguished intellectual tradition, notably for poetry, literature and economics. Economists of Bengali origin are prominent in development economics worldwide. Many members of the Bangladeshi national elite have close connections with international development organizations and derive much of their understanding of poverty from global academic and policy discourses. They knew about 'poverty lines', 'nutritional indicators', 'basic needs approaches to poverty measurement', 'pro-poor growth' and the 'two-pronged strategy of poverty reduction'. This familiarity with recent international development discourse thus conspires with the high level of absolute material deprivation to generate an understanding of poverty that assigns priority to increasing the national product, and provides limited space for concerns about the distribution of well-being between groups – or for any fancy notions that poverty is different from hunger and lack of clothes and shelter.

Bad governance Bangladesh has sustained a steady rise in per capita national income for two decades, and the incidence of poverty has diminished appreciably. There is still, however, a great deal of impatience and a feeling on the part of members of the elite that more could have been achieved. Because successive governments have generally adhered to what are conventionally viewed as the appropriate pro-growth, market-friendly macroeconomic and sectoral policies, explanations for the failure to make faster progress in reducing poverty cannot easily be attributed to the general direction of economic policy. Bad governance was a popular alternative. Here too our respondents echoed global conventional wisdom. They pointed to the weakness of successive administrations, the politicization of the bureaucracy, economic mismanagement, corruption, political instability, and what is widely presented as the 'lack of political consensus', by which is usually meant the violent and disruptive character of political party competition. Certainly the reliance on confrontational extra-parliamentary activities, such as the ubiquitous *hartal* (strike) used by all major opposition groups, has proven costly and disruptive for business, making Bangladesh even less attractive to foreign investment. But notions of what constitutes 'bad governance' took some unexpected forms: for some respondents, competitive multi-party democracy is itself an obstacle to poverty reduction, as the 'lack of political consensus' is understood to manifest itself in changes in poverty policy with each incoming administration. In fact, the truth is almost the opposite: there has been a high degree of continuity in anti-poverty policy, reflecting the cross-party consensus on this issue (see below).

The behaviour and attitudes of the poor The dominant explanations of poverty (above) were secular and rationalist in tone. They attributed agency and rationality to the poor, and located the causes of poverty in broad historical and socio-economic forces and in the behaviour of other agents, including the elite themselves. These are the types of argument one would encounter in the World Bank or in a social science seminar in any Western university. There was, however, another line of argument, possibly muted because our interviews were understood as some kind of social science. Our interviewees perceived a set of problems relating to the motivations and attitudes of the poor themselves: a lack of 'awareness' or 'consciousness' (*chetona; shocheton*), best glossed as fatalism or passivity. As one former senior civil servant described it: '[A] poor man thinks *Allah amake gorib banaise, amake gorib thakte hobe* [God has made me poor, so that is how I will have to stay] – this is how he accepts it. How do you change that attitude?'

This conviction about the fatalism of the poor appeared in different ways, informing the views of those on the political left, who lamented the inability of the poor to recognize their own exploitation, as well as those on the right, who felt that it prevented the poor from behaving like economically rational actors. Others felt that superstition (*kushongshkar*) prevented the poor from planning their families; and 'the inability to think beyond tomorrow' encouraged them not to invest in the future. These behaviours and attitudes could only be changed, it was generally felt, through mass education, which was the single most favoured development strategy and anti-poverty intervention (see Table 4.2).

Elite representations of the (rural) poor as passive and fatalistic are deeply rooted in South Asian culture. They date at least from British colonialism, and have often been articulated by impatient modernizing national elites. It was no surprise to encounter them. They were, however, relatively rare (see Table 4.2), and some other respondents articulated what is in effect a counter-narrative, expressing strong faith in the capacity of the poor collectively to solve their own problems. Some versions of this counter-narrative were presented by conventionally leftist intellectuals and political and NGO leaders. They drew attention to structural causes of poverty such as 'the exploitative social structure' or the 'dependent' character of the Bangladeshi economy within the international system, and argued for more vigorous state intervention to promote development. Others rejected the entire enterprise of 'development', and viewed state and donor interventions against poverty as disruptive and inherently problematic: 'Why design a system that people fall out of in the first place? Isn't that the point? That is unacceptable, just accepting the negative outcomes of development, justifying developmental activities ... ' (NGO leader). What was needed, the argument went, was to strengthen communities to allow people to become self-reliant, to enable them to look after their own, and so on. While all variants of this counter-narrative might reasonably be characterized as in some sense 'left', not all acknowledged leftists espoused it. None of the student political leaders we interviewed took an especially radical attitude to poverty, and one Communist Party youth leader even explained that economic growth would entail 'a trickle-down effect that will take care of poverty to some extent'. This is significant because in the past radical economic and political programmes have originated mainly from within student and youth political organizations.[11] No such radicalism is evident among contemporary student political groups; their views fit snugly within the dominant elite discourse about poverty.

How do Bangladeshi elites imagine their relationship to the poor?

Because they imagine Bangladeshi society to be cohesive and harmonious, it is easier for elites to imagine poverty as a shared national problem than as an issue of the clear deprivation of a distinct group. This image of cohesion and harmony is grounded in reality. Members of the elite have good reason to believe that their relationships with the poor are generally harmonious, or at least free of overt tension and conflict. We can explain that by exploring four dimensions to the notion that elite–poor relations are harmonious:

- beliefs about the moral integrity of village life, and by extension the integrity of the (rural) poor;
- an understanding that Bangladeshi society lacks sharp social, ethnic or cultural divisions;
- the absence of a perception of threat to the elite from poverty and the poor;
- elite beliefs about their role as important charitable benefactors to the poor.

The moral integrity of village life and the rural poor As was noted above, 'the village' is where the poor are believed to be made: the poor are the losers in resource struggles within an overcrowded, under-productive and outmoded agricultural economy, and also victims of their own superstition and ignorance. Yet at the same time, and in Bangladesh as in many other cultures, 'rural' also appears as a site of natural harmony and beauty, the repository of cultural tradition and morality, particularly when pitted against the modern, dangerous, dirty city, where antagonism and greed are bred (see Williams 1973, especially ch. 5). There is believed to be something innately simple and pure about rural society that makes 'the good life' possible:

> I lived in the village for nearly fifteen years. I think I was quite satisfied about it. It's hot, you go under the tree, you stay there for a while. Food, water you drink from the well, the pumps. Then you cook twice a day, so you don't need a refrigerator. Whatever little you have you cook, these are fresh things ... that sort of life, can be better. In Dhaka you drive, you have got all the tensions, you have got a *lakh* [100,000] of taka in your hand but you have accumulated a lot of funds. So you go for another *lakh*, and another – it's like a craze is going on. But that fellow, the meal for the next one or two days – he doesn't bother about the rest of it. I'm not naive, I'm just saying that is the sort of life they lead. And I think they are quite satisfied. (Former senior civil servant and diplomat)

Rural life should be easy, without greed, competition and stress. Some respondents referred to the lushness of the land. An MP said: 'You can just "scatter the seed and the crops come out".' It is safe in the village: people look after each other when they are sick; women are better protected than in the city; there are traditional systems for helping those in crisis (if only the rich would stick to their obligations!). But urbanization of both elites and the poor has altered relationships between them, and not for the better. As a newspaper editor explained, Bangladesh has to date lacked major social divisions between rich and poor, because all Bangladeshis are essentially from peasant stock. The 'kind of empathy' or 'natural bond with the rural poor' which this common origin once fostered, however, is being destroyed, mainly by the growing distance between the (urban) rich and their poor kin and others who remain in the village, but also because of the migration of the rural poor to towns. Our respondents, especially members of the national elite, frequently alluded to the decline of traditionally close, personalized relations between rich and the rural poor in the 'home' village.[12] They were not blind to the fact that something forces out or entices the poor into the morally impure environment of the city:

> That kind of pristine livelihood is no longer there in Bangladesh. Yes, there was a time when people were poor but even if they had a mere homestead or a small plot of land, they could still get by. And remain satisfied in that. Now I don't think it's possible. They see people growing richer, more

successful. He is being infected by various influences ... various influences, development, roads coming up, connecting the whole country ... (Newspaper editor)

Thus 'he', the archetypal peasant, once content with his tiny field and simple life, loses his refreshing innocence once 'infected' by urban and other unsettling influences.

By extension, the poor, who in the national elite imagination are all rural at heart even when forced to live in the city, are innately good and moral. It was made clear in the responses to our enquiries that questioning the moral character of the poor was indelicate and even transgressive. Rather, it is the elite itself – or at least some of its members – which is framed as immoral in public discourse. For members of the corrupt and decadent classes to question the morals of the poor is not only hypocritical and an insult to the dignity of the less fortunate, it is also missing the point. There is a problem of national morality, but it is located at the top of the pile. Most respondents suggested that it was a gross generalization to say that deprivation leads to immorality, even though the more common folk wisdom on the subject, quoted by one businesswoman, is that '*obhabhe shobhab noshto hoi*' ('deprivation spoils the character').

Although some respondents apparently felt constrained by the need to take a particular view in the interview situation, this faith in the morality of the poor did not seem feigned. It is the reverse of the assertion by some members of the Haitian elite of their civilizing mission in relation to the poor (Chapter 5). In Bangladesh, our various attempts to elicit relative moral judgements about different categories of poor people generally failed. Asked to identify groups of poor people as most deserving of assistance, most interviewees appear to have responded more in terms of relative productivity or economic worth than moral deserving.[13] There do not, in any case, appear to be powerful precedents in Bengali Muslim culture for categorizing poor people into 'deserving' and 'undeserving'.[14] Our respondents were unable or unwilling to make systematic moral judgements or assign blame when asked to compare the fate of poor people who had died from drinking illegal alcohol with those who had died during a severe cold spell. The ethics articulated by our respondents tend to put the poor above reproach: they are to be blamed neither for their misfortunes nor for their mistakes. There is a sense in which the affirmation of the higher morality of the poor denies their agency: they are more often victims than perpetrators, and if they transgress it is because they are almost childlike in their helplessness, and should not be held responsible for their actions. Nevertheless, the 'infection' of urban influences could change all that, as our respondents perceived that the innocence of the rural poor could easily be contaminated on contact with the city.

Social homogeneity The inability or unwillingness of members of the national elite to make or to admit to distinctions among the poor seems to be linked to the nationalist emphasis on the homogeneity of Bangladeshi society generally. Those of our respondents able to compare Bangladesh with other countries tended to insist upon and value this homogeneity. In contrast with other, more divided South Asian countries, it was seen as a basis for national progress. Perhaps partly because they lacked the basis for making such international comparisons, members of local elites were slightly more willing both to categorize poor people into more or less deserving groups, and to detect shades of difference within the national community.[15]

The denial of social distinctions affirms the basis for social cohesion between rich and poor in two ways. First, it highlights the putatively egalitarian aspects of Bangladeshi society, in implicit contrast to the dominant comparator case: India and Hindu caste. A few respondents noted that, in contrast to Hindu caste society, Islamic principles of social organization do not impose rigid obstacles to upward mobility. A realistic prospect of upward mobility may be a significant source of support for the existing social order in a country where much of the population is poor (see also Van Schendel 1982: 295). Second, the emphasis on social homogeneity also implies the absence of a basis for class conflict. 'Class' conflict has had a strong communal or ethnic character in recent Bengali history,[16] and is closely associated with other forms of social stratification. The protracted, two-part struggle for national independence meant liberation from 'foreign' oppressors – first from the British and Hindu landlords and moneylenders, and then from non-Bengali Muslims in the Pakistan era. Now that 'we are all Bangladeshis',[17] there are few of the sociocultural divisions that once helped generate class conflict.

The lack of a threat from the poor The image of a generally harmonious social order is not contradicted by any perception that the poor might be seriously criminal or rebellious. Indeed, elites are sufficiently confident of the absence of such threats that they talked of the inherent order and resilience of Bangladeshi society:

> [T]hat is still a question for me, that of how the people of Bangladesh are still so patient. How these needy poor people still tolerate the rich so much. How, in front of them, these brand-new cars are plying the streets of Dhaka,

and they are simply watching it. I find it difficult to understand. The senti-
ment of the people. Something says to me that given their level of poverty,
given their level of demand, given their level of wants, well, they should have
eaten up everything surrounding them! But that is not happening. And this
probably shows that this society is not rotten, that this society is there to
survive. (Political adviser)

Poverty is perceived as posing few overt or direct threats to the current
well-being of the elite; such concerns as exist are vague or focused on the
future. This is understandable: in recent history, the Bangladeshi poor have
rarely acted in ways that could cause elites much fear, or even anxiety; and
other social problems and groups have consistently proven themselves to
be greater menaces to elite welfare.

Crime, for example, is a major and apparently increasing source of
anxiety for elites, as with most sections of Bangladeshi society. Anecdotes
about theft at gunpoint are common in elite circles, and many affluent
people have modified their behaviour in response to the threat of violent
attack. Poverty in itself, however, is not viewed as a cause of crime. Although
extremely apprehensive about the effects of rural–urban migration, most
interviewees rejected the view that the rise in urban crime could be linked
to the presence of increasing numbers of poor rural migrants[18] (see Table
4.3). The causal link between poverty and crime that is routinely drawn in
other societies is largely absent from Bangladeshi elite thinking and public
discourse. This became clear when some local elites who claimed that
'there was no link between poverty and crime' then stated that the causes
of crime in their area included poverty and unemployment. In practice,
it is agreed, there are specific instances in which the poor may commit
some crimes; but 'poverty' is not instinctively or automatically connected
to 'crime' in any general sense. This understanding may be well founded:
police corruption can provide rich and powerful criminals with immunity
from the law, while poorer, small-time criminals tend to be caught (see
Ahmad et al. n.d.; and surveys by Transparency International, Bangladesh
chapter). An analysis of homicide statistics in neighbouring India supports
this perception: murder appears to occur least frequently in poorer areas
(Drèze and Khera 2000).[19]

The absence of an expectation that poverty leads to crime appears also to
reflect beliefs that the poor are more likely to be victims than perpetrators;
that it is not the petty crimes of the poor committed to feed hungry families
which affect elites, but organized attempts at extortion or violence; and
that, in any case, the poor do not have the means or opportunity to target
members of the elite. A businessman made this latter point, arguing that

TABLE 4.3 Understanding of the relationship between urban crime and the migration of poor people to urban areas (per cent)

Proportion of respondents according to response	National elites	Local elites
No link between crime and poverty	43	30
The poor are not the main perpetrators; or most criminals are not poor people	9	49
There is a link between urban crime and migration of the poor	26	15
Other	3	5
No clear answer	18	1
Total	100	100
Total number of respondents	65	100

crime was more likely to affect the lower middle classes than the rich. To the average poor person, he argued, he and his driver would both appear to be rich, but his driver would make a far easier target. Even if the poor do commit crime, it is not of the magnitude or type that are likely to worry elites to any great extent.

Those of our national elite respondents who agreed that the poor occasionally resorted to crime always added some qualification. There was a widespread concern that the poor, and in particular the poor of the urban *bustees* (shanty towns), were likely to be 'used by the rich'[20] either for material gain or political purposes. There was also a sense that urban life could taint the morality of poor migrants from the villages, and thereby encourage them to get involved in criminal activity. To the extent that elites do feel threatened by poverty, it is the urban poor on whom their concerns are focused. But it is the presence of other, more threatening social groups which offers the best explanation for the weakness of the perceived link between crime and poverty. Educated or semi-educated unemployed youth constitute the most problematic and threatening social problem to the elite. Politics and violence on university campuses, and organized crime linked to political activity, are attributed, in the words of one interviewee, to 'the drug addicts of the middle classes, or rich men's sons'. The rural poor are a relatively unthreatening social category, particularly compared to the unemployed, disaffected urban middle-class youth.[21] There is also an established discourse about the criminality of sections of the elite – notoriously corrupt politicians and businessmen who defaulted on multi-million-dollar industrial loans in the 1980s – which highlights the immorality of the elite compared to the rural poor.

So near and yet so far

The lack of concern about the potential for poverty to generate social unrest can be explained by similar factors. Major episodes of clearly class-based conflict, particularly involving the rural poor, have been uncommon in post-liberation Bangladesh. Memories may linger of the East Bengali peasant struggles between the depression of the 1930s and independence from the British in 1947, but these are unlikely to strike fear in the minds of contemporary Bangladeshi elites, as the class character of such struggles was frequently obscured by or politicized around religious and ethnic conflicts (Bose 1986; Hashmi 1994). As we noted above, the relative ethnic and religious homogeneity of independent Bangladesh may encourage the belief that the basis for such conflicts has now been successfully removed.[22] In any case, the political upheavals and struggles of the non-poor are more evident to elites and more likely to touch them directly. Party political competition is mainly in the form of confrontational extra-parliamentary activities such as *hartals*, i.e. attempts physically to bring economic activity to a close, within individual enterprises or the entire urban economy. These are costly for business and disruptive and dangerous for urban populations (World Bank 1999). Again, the sight of the educated middle-class youth engaged in increasingly militant student and party politics is a more prominent source of fear than the remote prospect of mass mobilization of the poor.

Nevertheless, elites may be increasingly sensitive to increasing inequality between rich and poor. An MP and member of the social elite reflected ironically on her position in society: 'You have to see the suffering of the people yourselves, and ask are they only here to suffer? Have you seen that nowadays the beggars bang on your windows when you're driving in your car? They used to tap gently and now they just bang. You know, I'm not going to still be sitting in my nice car with my diamonds on. Something will have to happen.' What that 'something' might be is rarely spelled out, and perhaps has yet to be imagined. But the contradiction between 'me in my nice car with my diamonds on' and the idea that the people are 'only here to suffer' is sharply felt, even if the greatest danger, to date, has been to the car windows. Although sensitive to the implications of increasing inequality between themselves and the rest of Bangladeshi society, surprisingly few members of the elite feel directly threatened by poverty. On the few occasions that such fears were articulated, they were nebulous and located somewhere in the future.

Concerns that poverty might adversely impact on the health of the elite were similarly absent. No member of the national elite independently raised the issue of health threats from the poor. Although, when we raised the issue of urban overcrowding and the lack of sanitation facilities, some respondents expressed concern about urban migration, they rarely raised these issues independently. Sanitation conditions were seen as highly distasteful, but not as a threat. The poverty–health link that does concern elites is high fertility rates. Even here, concerns seem to be abating. There is awareness that the population growth rate has slowed down in recent years; and more is heard of the potential advantages of a large population. Contemporary medical technology may provide elites with good reason not to worry much about the threat of infection and contagion from the poverty-related diseases that afflict the poor, such as cholera or tuberculosis. Curative treatment of many kinds is available for those who can afford it. Within elite circles, the main health fears relate to the degenerative diseases associated with wealth.

It is possible that members of the elite underestimate their vulnerability to diseases that are more common among the poor. They certainly appeared relatively ill informed about, and uninterested in, health issues. National elites knew less about the health of the poor than about their education. National achievements in increasing primary school enrolment were frequently mentioned, but very few interviewees referred to progress made in immunization coverage and reduced infant mortality rates. Local elites were asked more direct questions about health threats from poverty. When questioned whether they feared tuberculosis transmission from the poor, they generally responded that the disease was not communicable, as it was caused by smoking and was therefore unrelated to poverty. Relating health to sanitation, the living conditions of the poor provoked distaste rather than fear. It is possible that national elites hold similar misconceptions about poverty-related disease, and that this helps explain why they do not believe that poverty poses a threat to the health of their own families.

Just as members of the national elite have few fears that poverty will impact on them through crime, social unrest or disease, they have no concerns that national economic or military prowess will be undermined because so many people are malnourished, ill or uneducated. There is perceived to be a surplus of labour, and no scarcity of adequate military or industrial person-power. When owners of garment factories talked about improving working conditions for their labourers, they may have been motivated in part by productivity concerns; but they presented this to us purely as a matter of altruism.

Charity for the poor Belief in the essential harmony of inter-class relations had some basis in the understanding that the rich in general fulfilled their charitable obligations towards the poor. A former senior politician and bureaucrat suggested that the compassion of the rich helped to maintain concord: 'Maybe we are largely shielded because our poor are not so violent.

If they were violent it would affect us very, very much, because they are the majority ... I don't worry about it. Because I believe that we are not terribly insensitive. We do care. There are of course the super-rich and the defaulters who do not care. But by and large I think we do care.'

Displaying 'sensitivity' and showing that 'we care' are ideally achieved through acts of private charity:

> The tradition of charitable work in which I am involved has always been with moneyed people here – not all moneyed people all of the time, but some ...
> *Why do some wealthy people help the poor and not others?*
> It is a social problem – those who feel for the country do help. Some people spend thousands of dollars going to haj [pilgrimage to Mecca] and all that, but never think of opening a school. Look at my father-in-law, who helps his entire village. My husband's company is full of people from the village – they always get priority with jobs. We're always looking after the village – after all, charity begins at home. (Leading socialite)

This exchange touches on a number of recurrent themes about appropriate forms of private charity, and reveals continuing adherence to a 'traditional' Bengali rural model of patronage. One theme is an elite tradition of charity, which draws on an idea of the *zamindar* (landlord) as paternalistic, providing schools and direct assistance to tenants and the local poor in times of crisis. In the present day, the claim to be continuing a 'tradition' of philanthropy alludes to a (tenuous) distinction between an 'old' elite, who are assumed to be charitable, and a 'nouveau riche', who are not. A second theme is that the lack of compassion for the poor is the reason why current private provision is insufficient. It is partly for this reason that there was much agreement about the need for 'a social movement' to motivate elites to be compassionate towards the poor. A third theme is the personalized character of charitable responsibilities: obligations are not towards the poor in general, but to known, proximate individuals and categories of people. It is notable that (more rural, overtly religious, vernacular-speaking) local elites were less enthusiastic about private charity than their (urban, Westernized) national counterparts. Local elites appeared to feel that these responsibilities were a burden. Some complained of the persistent demands made on them by poor people.

National elites believe that class relations are relatively harmonious, that they are relatively close to the poor in a sociological sense, and that the rural poor are of good moral character. They have few actual interactions with poor people, however. As was noted in the introduction, they may not be physically distanced from the poor, but apart from domestic servants, they have little first-hand knowledge of them. Direct contact with rural 'home' districts is limited (Siddiqui et al. 1990). The national elite can idealize rural life from a distance. Local elites, by contrast, have far more contact and interaction with poor people, which may explain why they displayed less romantic views about their behaviour and attitudes. It is true that some national elites cited 'lack of awareness' as a motivational problem of the poor, but local elites were perceptibly more comfortable talking about laziness and 'the need for hard work'. Perhaps national elites are able to feel sympathetic towards the poor because, compared to local elites, they are largely insulated from the need for direct social interaction with them.

The success of indigenous NGOs also gave many national elites reasons for feeling satisfied about current efforts to tackle poverty, and therefore about the essential harmony of social relations between rich and poor. Bangladesh is unrivalled in the scale and importance of its development NGOs. Some of the larger and more established organizations trace their origins to the post-independence effort to rehabilitate the war-torn and famine-stricken rural population in the early 1970s. These organizations initially engaged in organizing and conscientization activities. Since the 1980s, most have turned their attention to the provision of services, in particular education, health and credit, with the support of aid donors. Some of the larger organizations now rival government departments in their scale and coverage of the rural population, and have become internationally renowned and imitated. The best known are the Grameen Bank[23] for its micro-finance programme, and the Bangladesh Rural Advancement Committee (BRAC) for micro-finance and non-formal primary education programmes. Most Bangladeshi development NGOs originated in and are led by members of the urban national elite. BRAC, for example, began in 1972 as a relief committee composed of young members of the elite. Many of the current leaders of large NGOs returned from a Western education to make their contribution to the nation-building effort. More recently, many top-ranking civil servants and other members of the elite are known to have established NGOs on retirement. NGOs are subject to intense public and media scrutiny, and some cynicism. But many members of the national elite enjoy some sense of pride in, and affinity to, the achievements of these NGOs. The record of the NGOs provides some confirmation that elites are performing, and being seen to perform, their duty towards the poor.

What can be done about poverty?

The dominant view among elites was that, given the scale of the poverty problem, the goal of anti-poverty activities should be limited to promoting the productivity of the poor. There was more dissensus about appropriate organizational means than about general strategies. Members of the national elite tended to display less faith in the role of the state and more in private and NGO efforts against poverty, while local elites took the reverse position, supporting state interventions while displaying considerable ambivalence about NGOs and some concern about the burden of 'charitable' demands. There was general agreement that the appropriate strategy for tackling poverty was through increasing the productivity of the poor, and thus simultaneously promoting national economic growth and development. Western notions of a welfare state enjoyed no support, and were seen to provide only warning examples. Members of the elite were more likely to make positive reference to their interpretation of the East Asian development experience, with the emphasis on promoting fast growth through market mechanisms and large investments in education. Again, elite views on anti-poverty strategy are largely in line with recent international development orthodoxies, especially the concern with productivity growth and scepticism about governments.

Increasing the productivity of the poor When asked how poverty could be reduced, members of the elite talked mainly about ideas of increasing productivity; medium- and long-term investments in the poor which should ultimately enable them to achieve self-sufficiency; avoiding dependency on state welfare; and the need for anti-poverty strategies to contribute to, rather than act as a drain on, national economic growth. To a substantial degree, this way of thinking appears realistic. Bangladesh has few resources of any kind in relation to the size of its (poor) population. Except for offshore gas fields only now being exploited, the country lacks significant mineral resources or industrial capacity. It still receives significant amounts of foreign aid. In comparative international perspective, income is relatively equally distributed. There are few resources or concentrations of wealth to redistribute.[24] The solution is thus seen to lie first and foremost in national economic growth. Issues of distribution are secondary. Although the poor must certainly be helped, any assistance they receive should encourage rather than constrain growth – credit to start small businesses rather than food or cash handouts, and education to enable them to take advantage of such opportunities.

Recognizing these constraints, some members of the national elite took the East Asian 'tiger' economies as realistic models, pointing out the similarities between the 'initial' conditions of these densely populated agrarian societies and the present condition of Bangladesh. Similar comparisons are made by organizations such as the World Bank (see World Bank 1999). The salient points of the East Asian model, as understood by national

TABLE 4.4 Percentage distribution of answers to the question: 'Will economic growth solve the poverty problem in time?'

Response	National elites	Local elites
Yes	33	52
Economic growth is necessary but not sufficient; 'potentially'	35	12
No	19	8
Don't know; other	13	28
Total	100	100
Total number of responses	70	100

elites, appear to be that (a) rapid growth can under some circumstances be sufficient to reduce poverty significantly; (b) the welfare state model has little relevance for Bangladesh; and (c) the emphasis should be on building human capital. The elite seem to have ignored potential lessons about the apparent benefits of asset redistribution from the experiences of land reform in Taiwan, South Korea and Japan. Instead, the emphasis is firmly on transforming a large population from a burden into an asset: '[The national priority is] to turn a burden into wealth. Population just by itself is a burden, but a trained population is wealth. And given the needs of the information age, the twenty-first-century technology revolution and all that, education, human resource development, skills training is really the only answer' (newspaper editor).

Faith in the poverty-reducing powers of economic growth was not universal: business elites were usually optimistic, and intellectuals and other groups usually sceptical. Although a third of our national elite interviewees were ambivalent about whether poverty could be tackled by economic growth, scepticism and uncertainty were not in themselves enough to produce alternative solutions. One might argue that it is the scale and severity of the poverty problem which limit the range of viable alternatives, so that, by default, a somewhat vague notion of *pro-poor growth* dominates elite thinking about solutions (see Table 4.4). The recent history of Bangladesh, however, also provides credibility to the 'growth-first' strategy. Although there are disagreements about how fast poverty has declined since independence, it is now generally agreed that there have been modest successes in tackling income poverty since the early 1990s. Human development and human poverty indicators have improved even faster (Government of Bangladesh 2000: 56), and the proportions of the population living in 'absolute' or extreme poverty have declined appreciably. Much of this improvement can be attributed to steady GDP growth averaging about 5 per cent over the last decade, and particularly to the acceleration of agricultural growth in the second half of the 1990s. Nevertheless, it is clear that at the current pace, a serious erosion of poverty is going to take a long time, given that economic growth has been both modest and unequalizing (Centre for Policy Dialogue 1997; World Bank 1999). One senior government minister felt that relying solely on economic growth in the short term could be a risky strategy:

> It's not just the growth, in a statistical sense, which will take care of poverty. It can to a certain extent – it is the long-term solution, no question about it – but in order to make sure that the condition is ameliorated in the short term or the medium term, you have to make sure that the prevalence of poverty does not destabilize the society. If it destabilizes the society, the very basis for long-term growth is gone.

The minister went on to make a case for state safety nets and human capital investments as a basis for growth. Similarly, local elites, which have more direct experience of and responsibility for tackling poverty than most national elites, saw the short-term or immediate problems of the poor as more pressing, and supported state safety nets despite clear preferences for more 'productive' investments. For most members of the national elite, however, even where the language of safety nets was used, it was not social security for the poor which was intended, but boosts to their productivity:

> Economic growth has never taken care of poverty anyway. Particularly with a massive poor population like in Bangladesh. We'll have to have a safety net, definitely.
>
> *In what sense a safety net?*
>
> Well, for example, government will always need to invest a lot of money in skills training and human resource development ... So economic growth will pull the country upwards, but for the bottom, for the 45 per cent of the population to jump on to that wagon of growth, there will have to be a push up from the bottom. Which means human resource development, training, a *massive* investment in education. And micro-credit. Micro-credit is that push from the bottom – you can picture this as a huge rocket going up towards the sky and people are not being able to reach it, and you give it a push from the bottom, and then they will reach it. (Newspaper editor)

The unattractiveness of safety nets (in the normal sense of the term) seriously limits the possibilities for thinking about action on behalf of the dependent poor – for example, the elderly and disabled. As we found when we tried to elicit moral distinctions between different categories of the poor, elites rank the poor not on the basis of need or deserving, but on 'productive potential'. Potentially 'productive' groups (marginal farmers, landless labourers, etc.) were more often selected over 'unproductive' groups (widows, the disabled, elderly, beggars, children), even when these might be seen as 'deserving' or morally appealing. One respondent explained that, although this seemed callous, it was a pragmatic response to the poverty situation in the country.

The most important direct state intervention the elite will countenance is investment in education. The need for more and better education dominated most discussions, and was rarely rejected as a solution to poverty. This faith in education draws in part, as we have seen, on understandings of the experience of the East Asian 'miracle' economies. It also relates, however, to the perception that one of the obstacles facing the development of the poor is their lack of 'awareness' or 'consciousness' – implicitly, a dearth of modern economic rationality. This is understood as a major cause of overpopulation, poor health practices, fatalism, and the 'inability to think beyond tomorrow' that is ascribed to poor people. Education is seen as the first step to achieving awareness, because without it the poor cannot make use of the opportunities available to them. It is also possible that one reason why the elite displays faith in education is that this is one sector in which the state has actually performed well. Real education spending increased fivefold between 1989/90 and 1995/96 (World Bank 1999). That the elite are extremely supportive of investments in primary education has undoubtedly eased this process: education is seen as a positive-sum intervention, one that is unlikely to arouse opposition, and also one that even the state is capable of implementing.

The emphases on a limited economic role for the state and on enhancing productivity also fit within national elites' perceptions of the success of Bangladeshi NGOs. Suspicion of the motivations and sources of funding of NGOs means they are closely scrutinized. Perhaps as a result of this scrutiny, many elites were aware of the international acclaim Bangladeshi NGOs have received, and perceive this as having played an important part in improving the international image of the country. Despite some ambivalence about NGOs, the dominant position among national elites was that NGO activities should be supported and promoted.[25] Local elites were comparatively unsupportive of NGO programmes, recognizing them as threats to their dominance as distributors of government resources to the poor, and to their local social authority. Members of local elites, however, also seemed to have accepted that NGOs were there to stay, and many admitted that they were effective at reaching the poor. Among NGO and Grameen Bank activities, micro-credit was singled out as particularly effective. The appeal of micro-credit for national (less so for local) elites seems to include the facts that it (a) helps the poor, and in particular poor women, to become entrepreneurial; (b) it does so without diverting resources away from other productive activities, partly because repayment rates are so high; (c) there is no danger of fostering dependency; and (d) it is a home-grown solution to the national problem of poverty.

Lack of faith in the state Moderately troubled by the persistence of widespread poverty, but not overly anxious about its impacts on their own welfare, Bangladeshi elites were ambivalent and somewhat divided about which institutions were most appropriate for tackling the problem. National elites tended to believe that appropriate non-state action was already being taken against poverty, and that the state was ineffective and should limit its activities to those of a facilitator. Local elites also lacked faith in state interventions on behalf of the poor, but were nevertheless more supportive of them, and correspondingly less supportive of the activities of non-state institutions than their national counterparts.

The success of NGOs and the desirability of private charity provide the basis for claims that responsibility for the poor should be broadly 'societal', rather than exclusively in the lap of the state. In discussions about responsibility for poverty, more than two-thirds of the national elite argued for a combination of societal and state responsibility. Even when government alone was allocated responsibility, it was usually expected to provide an 'enabling environment' rather than take direct action:

> Ultimately [responsibility] is government's. I am not advocating a welfare state, though, that didn't work. What has to be done is to create an environment which allows people to develop themselves. One [issue for government to tackle] is overcrowding – there have to be incentives to provide cheaper housing – and a second is sound economic guidelines. Then the individuals will take over. We have to give tax rebates. Individuals will then have more incentive.

The idea of the government as limited to the role of facilitator in poverty interventions was attractive to most members of the national elite. The role and responsibilities of government and the related issue of the role and effectiveness of NGOs were the only subjects on which the views of national elites diverged significantly from those of their local counterparts. Local elites firmly and almost unanimously supported the view that action against poverty was ultimately the responsibility of government. Few of them had faith in NGOs. These differences are consistent with the fact that sources of power and influence – the basis of 'eliteness' – lie more in positions in

TABLE 4.5 Answers to the question: 'Which agency is ultimately responsible for anti-poverty action?' (multiple answers possible; per cent)

Agency	National elites	Local elites
Government	50	89
NGOs	16	6
Everybody; society as a whole; private individuals	28	4
Other	6	0
Total	100	100
Total number of responses	105	105

the state apparatus at the local level than at the national level. With more direct links to and stakes in the state, local elites could be expected to favour state interventions. Ample evidence of local-level corruption in state programmes such as the Public Food Distribution System suggests that local political elites derive substantial direct benefits through 'leakages' (Adams 1998; reports prepared by the Bangladesh chapter of Transparency International; Abdullah and Murshid 1986). Another important reason why local elites may support state programmes for the poor is that these help safeguard their legitimacy and authority with respect to the local community, in particular the poor. As one long-term observer of rural Bangladeshi society has pointed out: '[i]n the rural areas of Bangladesh the perception of a good government depends on: whether a government is able/unable to feed its people in times of crisis' (Jahangir 1995: 93).[26] Local elites also have more direct contact with poor people than do national elites, however. The vulnerability and deprivation of the rural poor are starkly evident to them.

TABLE 4.6 Answers to the question: 'Would you support raising taxes to finance more and better state anti-poverty activities?' (per cent)

Agency	National elites	Local elites
No	25	38
Need better collection (combined with 'yes', 'no' or other response)	47	39
Yes	20	20
Other	8	2
Total	100	100
Total number of responses	60	94

National elites might be more willing to endorse state action if they had more faith in the capacity of the state. As it is, they are not confident that their state can adequately perform even its most basic functions of tax collection and the maintenance of law and order (see Table 4.6). The failure of recent governments to ensure the rule of law and judicial process has also become a major issue for concern. The national elite believes that state interventions against poverty have predominantly failed. This is not entirely warranted, given that moderate progress has been achieved on poverty reduction in recent years and that even direct state interventions against poverty are fairly well targeted and effective (see World Bank 1999). Members of the elite with more direct knowledge of anti-poverty activities (some civil servants, politicians and NGO leaders) displayed more optimism about state capacity, and also took more pragmatic, less ideological positions on what the state should be doing. Nevertheless, almost half of our national elite interviewees stated clearly that the government was ineffective at reducing poverty, and less than one-fifth felt that its activities were effective. This lack of faith in the state inevitably encourages the view that the state should limit its involvement to the provision of an enabling environment. It also promotes suspicion about direct public action in most forms, and especially in the form of safety nets.

The lack of faith in government action on poverty also contributes to profound suspicion about connections between politics and poverty. The dominant view is that to treat poverty as an issue for political competition amounts to 'doing politics with the plight of the people' – an accusation the major political parties frequently level against each other. Underlying this suspicion is the belief that political elites are not sufficiently committed to the concerns of the poor, and only use these when it suits their own political interests. The actual ideological and programmatic contents of the policies of the different political parties suggest, however, that, if anything, poverty is not an issue on which they compete. By the 1990s, the first decade of multi-party democracy in Bangladesh, there was an emerging political consensus on the need for continued economic reform; no substantive disagreement about the direction of economic development (Economist Intelligence Unit 1996; Baxter 1998); and equally little disagreement about poverty policy. Both the previous government of the ruling Bangladesh National Party (BNP) and the recent Awami League government (1996–2001) placed meeting the 'basic needs of the people' at the top of their agendas. In making their pledges, the parties used very similar language.[27] All recent governments have supplemented their basic emphasis on economic growth with a stronger focus on the social sectors, particularly education.[28] Their priorities are the same: a comparison of the last budget of the previous

BNP government with the first budget of the Awami League revealed a high degree of consistency in the way they ranked their spending priorities, indicating that 'the two major parties are not only committed to the same economic philosophy – but also share similar development priorities even at a more detailed level' (Centre for Policy Dialogue 1997: 100). Apart from some minor innovations in social security under the Awami League, such as the tiny old-age and widows' allowances, there are no major ideological or programmatic differences between the parties' approaches to poverty. In fact, it is not clear that there is much net political advantage to be gained from emphasizing political differences over anti-poverty policy. The charge of 'doing politics with the plight of the people' is potentially damaging. Combating poverty is viewed as a high-level moral imperative, above the realm of politics, and the responsibility of the entire Bangladeshi nation. Even NGO anti-poverty activities come under suspicion once they appear factional. NGO attempts to organize the poor receive far less elite support than what are seen as their 'charitable' activities. When NGOs are perceived to be 'getting involved in politics' they are roundly condemned.

Concluding comment: social consciousness?

Bangladeshi elites have a relatively homogeneous set of perspectives on poverty. They mostly talk about it using assumptions, ideas and even terms that one would expect to find in World Bank documents. The elites view poverty as a major problem, and an obligation. They have a relatively benign image of the poor, a strong sense that the poor are much like them in sociocultural terms (if not always in attitude and behaviour), and a relaxed perspective on social relations between rich and poor. The poor do not pose any great threat. The poor are deserving en masse. But there is nothing much to redistribute to them except the opportunity to become less poor through work and enterprise. Public institutions, especially state institutions, are not very capable. Since Bangladesh is a poor country, public action against poverty is most of the time equated with attempts to increase per capita GNP.

That summary is very focused on our specific case material. Let us try to generalize. Do Bangladeshi elites have social consciousness in the sense that Abram de Swaan originally defined the term? Yes and no. Each of his three components of social consciousness generates ambiguous answers.

Let us start at the end: do Bangladeshi elites believe that there are effective public means to help the poor, or that they might be created? When asked directly, they asserted little faith in the state – perhaps even less than would be justified by a close look at actual experience. But that did not prevent them calling for more and better education for the poor. And some were indeed aware that the Bangladesh state in recent years has made considerable advances in delivering basic education. So too have some of the country's well-known large development NGOs. Our respondents displayed considerable pride in these NGOs. It is difficult to avoid the conclusion that they are not quite so pessimistic about the scope for public action against poverty as is implied by their direct answers to direct but general questions on these issues. Scepticism about the state was internationally fashionable at the time the interviews were conducted.

Second, do the members of the Bangladeshi elite believe that they bear some responsibility for alleviating the suffering of the poor? Here again there is ambiguity. Two contrary narratives exist side by side. One is that the elites accept responsibility, and try to discharge it, whether through the 'traditional' charitable obligations that in the main they continue to fulfil, or through supporting state and NGO programmes directed against poverty. The other narrative is that many members of the elite – frequently characterized as in some sense nouveau (by an elite that is in comparative terms almost entirely nouveau) – not only fail to fulfil those obligations but, through their greedy, assertive and self-interested behaviour, share responsibility for many of the nation's ills.

The most significant ambiguity, however, is encountered in asking whether Bangladeshi elites are aware of their interdependence with the poor. The elites strongly believe (a) that they are the same kind of people as the poor – Bangla-speaking Sunni Muslim Bangladeshis with recent village roots; (b) that relations between them and the poor are generally good; and (c) that they have obligations to the poor. They do not, however, feel materially dependent on the poor: they neither need their labour or services in any very specific sense, nor do they feel any major threat from them. A strict interpretation of de Swaan's schema would force us to conclude that there is no strong sense of interdependence, and therefore no social consciousness. But to take that view is to dismiss the significance of the elites' own perception of their affinity with the poor, and may lead us to underestimate the latent potential for elites to be persuaded to put their money where their mouths are, and to give more active support to poverty eradication.

Notes

1 The reasons for the prevalence of this language of obligation to the poor are complex. They stem above all from the character of Indian nationalism, the nature of the 'social contract' forged in India at independence under the sway of the Congress Party and Mahatma Gandhi, and the influence in other South Asian countries of contemporary Indian ideas about politics and public

authority. That influence – and the extent of visible commitment to poverty reduction – is less in Pakistan.

2 See Deininger and Squire's (1996) data-set on income inequality.

3 In Bangladesh as elsewhere, the homogeneity and interconnectedness of the elite are no bar to deadly intra-elite political competition. Indeed, to the extent that competition is based on family rivalries, homogeneity may exacerbate it.

4 Some observers, however, are noting the apparent emergence of a distinct capitalist interest in politics (Kochanek 2000).

5 Chittagong is the only other significant metropolis in Bangladesh. It ranks far below Dhaka. We have no figures on the location of elites. The general population statistics do, however, illustrate the dominance of Dhaka in the urban hierarchy. We calculated an 'index of metropolitan concentration': the proportion of the combined populations of the four largest cities in a country which resided in the largest single city. This figure was 64 per cent for Bangladesh (Dhaka), with its population of 120 million, compared to 36 per cent for South Africa (Cape Town), with a total population of only 41 million, 49 per cent for Brazil (São Paulo) and 34 per cent for India (Mumbai). Among large poor countries, only Mexico has an 'index of metropolitan concentration' higher than that of Bangladesh (Mexico City, 75 per cent) (*The Times Atlas of the World* 1997: 64; Bangladesh Bureau of Statistics 1997).

6 According to the 1991 census, 88.3 per cent of the population was Muslim, and only 10.5 per cent Hindu, 0.6 per cent Buddhist, 0.3 per cent Christian and 0.3 per cent others (Bangladesh Bureau of Statistics 1999). The Minority Rights Group (1997), however, claims that 16 per cent of the population are Hindus and that there are between 250,000 and 300,000 Biharis, or Urdu-speaking Muslims, many of whom claim Pakistani nationality. They also claim that about 1,280,000 (1 per cent of the population) are Adivasis or members of indigenous tribal communities, and that 'it is widely believed that the Bangladesh government has deliberately undercounted the Adivasi population to emphasize its marginality' (p. 544).

7 This apparent unity can be illusory: even the use of the liberation struggle as an emblem of unified national identity is heatedly contested, with religion at times successfully competing to define nationhood. This competition over national identity is itself rooted in much deeper historical tensions relating to the culturally hybrid character of Bengali Islam (Ahmed 1981; Murshid 1995).

8 Social distance based on wealth and education has inevitably widened as elites have managed to establish and enrich themselves since independence.

9 Note that this national sample includes Members of Parliament representing non-Dhaka electorates. Interviewees were identified through reputation, and contacted largely through personal contacts. The interviews were semi-structured and conducted in Dhaka between November 1997 and April 1998, mainly by Naomi Hossain and Abul Hossain.

10 Almost all respondents willing to be committed to a figure estimated that more than half the population were poor, and many reckoned more than three-quarters were poor (Table 4.1). Two recent estimates put the proportion

of the population below differently defined poverty lines at 53 per cent and 45 per cent.

11 In the late 1960s, in particular, student groups formally associated with the Awami League were able to use their popular radical agendas and experience of mobilizing popular support to force leftward shifts by the mainstream or parent parties (see Maniruzzaman 1975; Lifschultz 1979).

12 That the harmony of rural social life is on the decline from an idyllic pastoral past seems to be a favourite moral precept of urban elites, famously documented for English culture by Raymond Williams (1973). Williams likens this perception to a backward-moving escalator: rural life is always seen to be on the decline, as far back in history as you go. Themes of rural decline may have been most resonant within English culture because of its early industrialization. Many such notions were translated into colonial policy discourse, finding their way eventually into nationalist political discourses on the ill effects of colonial rule (e.g. Spencer 1990: ch. 5).

13 The able-bodied, independent and young were favoured over the groups we had assumed would be found less deserving (drug addicts, prostitutes and beggars), but also over those we had expected would be deemed more deserving (the elderly, the sick and the disabled).

14 For a review of the treatment of the poor peasant in Bengali classical literature, see Beck and Bose (1995).

15 These tended to be familiar regional stereotypes ('Nohakhalis are stingy and cunning', 'Rangpuris are a bit simple', etc.) rather than more meaningful social distinctions, but the point is that they did not perceive the need to stress homogeneity or unity at the national level.

16 This is particularly true of the peak period of peasant revolts in East Bengal between the depression of the 1930s and partition in 1947, when the mainly Muslim peasantry mobilized against oppressive landlords and moneylenders as Hindus, although even then Hindu peasants took part, and Muslim landlords were also targeted at times (Bose 1986). Although it may not be appropriate to see class politics in that period as entirely communal, in most instances peasant rebellions had a strong communal character.

17 'Bangladeshi' (as opposed to 'Bangalee', 'Bengali' or 'Bengali Muslim') society is itself a politically interested construction, a neologism introduced by the Zia military government as part of a project to deny the 'Bangalee' character of the country and nationalist struggle. The term implies a clear distinction between the inhabitants of Bangladesh and those of (mainly Hindu) neighbouring West Bengal, and a rejection of a common – and implicitly largely 'Hindu' – Bengali culture. 'Bangladeshi' is preferred here (when talking about post-1971 East Bengal) merely to denote citizens of Bangladesh, regardless of ethnic/cultural background.

18 This view may be changing. Elite anxieties about rapid urban population growth mean that they are increasingly receptive to the view that slums may be breeding grounds for criminals (see conclusions).

19 Crime statistics are notoriously unreliable. Data on murder are assumed to be more accurate than data on other forms of law-breaking. These findings by Drèze and Khera challenge the assumptions of the standard

economic models of crime, poverty and inequality, which predict that the poor will be more likely than the rich to commit crimes as a result of their lower opportunity costs to jail time and greater incentives to commit crime (see review of Becker's and other theories of crime, poverty and inequality in Kelly 2000). Drèze and Khera (2000: 341) suggest that the Indian poor are more risk averse than the rich and run a higher risk of being caught if they do commit crimes. The same is likely to be true in Bangladesh.

20 The idea that it is outsiders who 'stir up trouble' or encourage the otherwise placid working poor has had considerable appeal for elites in other contexts (see Rudé 1981).

21 The term for 'unemployment' (*bekaroto*) is usually used to denote formal-sector unemployment – in effect, the unemployment of the educated middle classes. *Bekaroto* is not generally applied to the underemployment of the unschooled poor, for whom lack of 'work opportunities' (*kajer shujog*) is more usually used. Notably, the unemployment rates of the educated classes rose faster than those of less and uneducated people during the 1990s, despite the moderately good performance of the economy (Bangladesh Bureau of Statistics 1999). While this may be a reflection of these issues of definition, it may also be due to the expansion of secondary schooling and higher education.

22 Continuing insurgency of tribal groups in the Chittagong Hill Tracts may give support to the assumption that conflict coincides with communal identity.

23 The Grameen Bank is not actually an NGO, but a bank, originally funded by the government of Bangladesh (which retains some influence over its activities). There is a tendency to discuss it with NGOs because its programmes are similar to those of many large NGOs.

24 Mass redistributive land reform may in any case have little impact on poverty on a national scale because of the size and rapid increase of the landless rural population, and the small size of even 'large' farms (Taslim 1993; Wennergren 1986). Even an influential early study, widely cited as promoting the need for land reform, actually admits that the net effects of redistributive reform on poverty would be limited, although it might raise agricultural productivity (Jannuzi and Peach 1980).

25 The former prime minister, Sheikh Hasina, has publicly acclaimed Bangladeshi NGOs, linking micro-credit programmes directly to the 'mission' of her father, Sheikh Mujib, the leader of the struggle for national independence, speaking of 'the war against poverty' launched after independence, and of the pride that 'We in Bangladesh' feel about 'the outstanding work done by Professor Mohammed Yunus and the Grameen Bank he founded' (speech delivered to the 1997 Micro-credit Summit in Washington, DC).

26 See also Greenough (1982: 19–20) on the mundane traditional basis of political authority in Bengal, and Huque for a contemporary example of the basis for political and social leadership (1986: 971).

27 These are 'food, clothing, education, medicare and shelter', according to the BNP (1991 election manifesto, cited in World Bank 1994: 43), and 'food, clothing, shelter, education, medical facilities and a clean and safe

environment', according to the Awami League (budget speech 1996, in Centre for Policy Dialogue 1997: 108).

28 Recurrent expenditure on education increased by 58 per cent between 1990/01 and 1998/99; the share of total recurrent spending on education also increased from 16.4 per cent to 18.6 per cent over the same period (Government of Bangladesh 2000: 62).

References

Abdullah, A. and K. A. S. Murshid (1986) 'The Distribution of Benefits from the Public Food Distribution System', Bangladesh Institute of Development Studies Research Reports, no. 60, Dhaka: Bangladesh Institute of Development Studies

Adams, R. H. (1998) 'The Political Economy of the Food Subsidy System in Bangladesh', *Journal of Development Studies* 35 (1): 66–88

Ahmad, M. with A. M. R. Khan and S. Nazneen (n.d.) *Corruption as People See It,* Dhaka: Transparency International Bangladesh Chapter

Ahmed, R. (1981) *The Bengal Muslims, 1871–1906: A Quest for Identity*, Delhi: Oxford University Press

Bangladesh Bureau of Statistics (1997) *Statistical Yearbook*, Dhaka: BBS

— (1999) *Statistical Yearbook*, Dhaka: BBS

Barua, T. (1978) *Political Elite in Bangladesh*, Berne: Peter Lang

Baxter, C. (1998) *Bangladesh*, Boulder, CO: Westview Press

Beck, T. and T. Bose (1995) 'Dispossession, Degradation and Empowerment of Peasantry and the Poor in Bengali Fiction', *Economic and Political Weekly*, xxx (9): 441–8

Bertocci, P. J. (1970) *Elusive Villages: Social Structure and Community Organization in Rural East Pakistan*, PhD thesis, Michigan State University

— (1982) 'Bangladesh in the Early 1980s – Praetorian Politics in an Intermediate Regime', *Asian Survey*, 22(10): 988–1,008

Bose, S. (1986) *Agrarian Bengal: Economy, Social Structure and Politics, 1919–1947*, Cambridge: Cambridge University Press

Broomfield, J. H. (1968) *Elite Conflict in a Plural Society: Twentieth-century Bengal*, University of California Press

Centre for Policy Dialogue (1997) *Growth or Stagnation? A Review of Bangladesh's Development 1996*, Dhaka: University Press

Deininger, K. and L. Squire (1996) 'A New Data Set Measuring Income Inequality', *World Bank Economic Review*, 10: 565–91

Drèze, J. and R. Khera (2000) 'Crime, Gender, and Society in India: Insights from Homicide Data', *Population and Development Review*, 26 (2): 335–52

Economist Intelligence Unit (1996) *Bangladesh Country Report*, London: Economist Intelligence Unit

— (2000) *Bangladesh Country Report*, London: Economist Intelligence Unit

Ghosh, S. (1990) *The Awami League: 1949–1971*, Dhaka: Academic Publishers

Government of Bangladesh (2000) *Memorandum for Bangladesh Development*

Forum 2000–2001, Government of the People's Republic of Bangladesh, Ministry of Finance (Economic Relations Division) and Ministry of Planning (Planning Commission)

Greenough, P. R. (1982) *Prosperity and Misery in Modern Bengal: The Famine of 1943–1944,* New York and Oxford: Oxford University Press

Hashmi, T. I. (1994) *Peasant Utopia: The Communalization of Class Politics in East Bengal,* Dhaka: University Press

Huque, A. S. (1986) 'Politics and Administration in a Periurban Community in Bangladesh', *Asian Survey* XXVI (9): 959–72

Jahangir, B. K. (1995) 'Famine and Politics', *Journal of Social Studies,* 68: 91–101

Jannuzi, F. T. and J. T. Peach (1980) *The Agrarian Structure of Bangladesh: An Impediment to Development,* Boulder, CO: Westview Press

Kelly, M. (2000), 'Inequality and Crime', *Review of Economics and Statistics,* 82 (4): 530–39

Kochanek, S. (1993) *Patron–Client Politics and Business in Bangladesh,* Dhaka/New Delhi: University Press

— (2000) 'The Growing Commercialization of Power', in R. Jahan (ed.), *Bangladesh: Promise and Performance,* London/Dhaka: Zed Books/University Press

Lewis, D., B. Sobhan and G. Jonsson (1994) 'Routes of Funding, Roots of Trust? An Evaluation of Swedish Assistance to Non-government Organizations in Bangladesh', SIDA Evaluation Report

Lifschultz, L. (1979) *Bangladesh: The Unfinished Revolution,* London: Zed Books

Maniruzzaman, T. (1975) *Radical Politics and the Emergence of Bangladesh,* Dhaka: Bangladesh Books International/World University Press

— (1980) *The Bangladesh Revolution and Its Aftermath,* Dhaka: University Press

Minority Rights Group (eds) (1997) *World Directory of Minorities,* London: Minority Rights Group

Murshid, T. M. (1995) *The Sacred and the Secular: Bengal Muslim Discourses, 1871–1977,* Calcutta: Oxford University Press

Rahman, M. S. (1991) *Administrative Elite in Bangladesh,* New Delhi: Manak

Rudé, G. (1981) *The Crowd in History: A Study of Popular Disturbances in France and England, 1730–1848* (revised edn), London: Lawrence and Wishart

Sen, R. (1986) *Political Elites in Bangladesh,* Dhaka: University Press

Siddiqui, K., S. R. Qadir, S. Alamgir and S. Huq (1990) *Social Formation in Dhaka City: A Study in Third World Urban Sociology,* Dhaka: University Press

Sobhan, R. and A. Ahmad (1988) 'The Structure of DFI Sponsored Investment in Bangladesh', BIDS Research Report no. 76, Dhaka: Bangladesh Institute of Development Studies

Sobhan, R. and B. Sen (1988) 'The Social Background of Entrepreneurship in Bangladesh: An Occupational Profile of Borrowers from the DFIs', BIDS Research Report no. 71, Dhaka: Bangladesh Institute of Development Studies

Spencer, J. (1990) *A Sinhala Village in a Time of Trouble: Politics and Change in Rural Sri Lanka*, Delhi: Oxford University Press

Taslim, M. A. (1993) 'Redistributive Land and Tenancy Reform in Bangladesh Agriculture', *Journal of Developing Areas*, 27: 341–76

The Times Atlas of the World (1997) London: Times Newspapers

Toye, J. (1999) 'Nationalising the Anti-poverty agenda', *IDS Bulletin*, 30 (2): 6–12

Van Schendel, W. (1982) *Peasant Mobility: The Odds of Life in Rural Bangladesh*, Delhi: Manohar Publications

Wennergren, E. B. (1986) 'Land Redistribution as a Developmental Strategy in Bangladesh', *Land Economics*, 62 (1): 74–82

Williams, R. (1973) *The Country and the City*, New York: Oxford University Press

World Bank (1994) *Bangladesh: From Stabilization to Growth*, Washington, DC: World Bank

— (1999) *Bangladesh: From Counting the Poor to Making the Poor Count*, Washington, DC: World Bank

5 | Haitian elites and their perceptions of poverty and of inequality[1]

OMAR RIBEIRO THOMAZ[2]

Extreme poverty prevails in Haiti. In terms of gross domestic product (GDP) per capita, it ranks 167th out of 174 countries; neighbouring Jamaica ranks 109th (World Bank 1999). Life expectancy is far lower for Haitians than for their neighbours: 52 years for men and 57 for women, compared to 69 and 72 in the Dominican Republic and 72 and 83 years in Jamaica. Sixty per cent of the adult population of Haiti is illiterate (Chapter 1, Table 1.1).[3] Approximately 65 per cent of Haitians live in absolute poverty, immersed in a subsistence economy and/or dependent upon international cooperation and assistance from the Haitian diaspora. Compared even to Bangladeshis, who have similar per capita income levels and much less international aid, few Haitians go to school or have access to protected drinking water supplies (Chapter 1, Table 1.1).

Little is known of the Haitian elites, and of their perceptions of the country and its devastating poverty and related problems.[4] The subject is especially interesting because, while Haiti is the poorest country in the western hemisphere, there have been, since the country was created through successful anti-colonial revolt in 1804, persistent visions of establishing a national elite that could dialogue on an equal footing with the European metropolitan centres. In this chapter I will suggest that, in their discourse on poverty and social inequality, the Haitian elites create a *native theory* concerning otherness and, ultimately, a native theory on the 'nation' itself.

Before discussing the perceptions of the elite in Section 5, I will briefly explain the conditions under which this research was undertaken (Section 2), look at the history of the country (Section 3) and present a schematic macro-social picture of Haitian society (Section 4). My intention in summarizing this history is not simply to provide the context for this study: the historical data also provided clues to the appropriate questions to ask about elites in the Haitian context. Haitians frequently find an explanation for the country's current situation in its history, through a process that highlights certain events and conceals others, erases or exalts certain personalities and, ultimately, rewrites history itself.

Research

In April and May 2000, I conducted sixty-four interviews in Port au Prince (the nation's capital, which has 2,500,000 inhabitants) and Cap Haitien (the second-largest city, which has approximately half a million inhabitants). In Cap Haitien, the entry routes were local traditional families. In some cases, contact went well beyond the first interview, sometimes extending to daily conversations at the end of the afternoon – conversations about the old days, the war of independence, American occupation (1915–34), the era of 'Papa Doc' Duvalier, the harrowing years marked by the coup d'état (1991–93) and, finally, the period of the occupation by the 'blue helmets', the United Nations peacekeeping forces (1993–99). It was these traditional families from Cap Haitien who suggested I should interview the nouveaux riches (often people who had accumulated fortunes in the United States), and introduced me to a complex local ethnic code: blacks, light blacks, dark blacks, mulattos (*wouj*), light mulattos, dark mulattos, Lebanese, Dominicans, and so many other categories as to merit a study in its own right. This complex code revealed the way a system based on colour gradations was used to explain existing inequality. The correct use of French was obligatory among these families: all were proud to express themselves adequately in Creole, but many stressed that they had been obliged to use French at home during their childhood, for Creole was the language of the servants. While the small size of Cap Haitien and the lifestyle of its inhabitants facilitated my investigations there, conduct-ing research in Port au Prince was very different. With the help of local contacts, I was able to make appointments with well-known intellectuals, ex-presidents of the republic, ex-ministers, bankers and businessmen. These interviews were scheduled for an appointed time and could not extend beyond an hour or so.

Keeping up with the news in two important local newspapers, *Le Nouvel-liste* (Port au Prince) and *Tribune d'Haiti* (Cap Haitien), was very helpful. The newspaper section of the National Library allowed me a closer view of the last few years of *Le Nouvelliste*, though not in a systematic way. Reading the weekly newspaper, *Petit Samedi Soir*,[5] helped me to comprehend the twilight years of the Duvalier regimes (1957–86) and the hectic first years of democratization. Both papers confirmed that, within the limited confines of public debate in Haiti, 'poverty' was a concern.[6]

From colony to nation: the constitution of contemporary Haiti

Michel-Rolph Trouillot calls attention to the silences that surround the historiography of Haiti. According to him, until recently, and with the exception of the classical work by C. L. R. James (2000 [1938]), the deep meanings of the Haitian revolution were systematically disregarded by Western historiography. Yet Haitians of diverse social origins refer continually to their history. The exceptional character of national independence in 1804 – the sole liberation from direct European colonialism that was achieved, at that point in history, through the forcible expulsion of the colonizers – seems to justify the almost daily recollection of the nation's symbolic figures: Toussaint L'Ouverture, Dessalines and Henri Christophe. Some interviewees claimed that all Haitians should, at least once in their lives, visit the ruins of the Cidadela and the Palace of Sans Souci, national symbols of resistance to French invasion and surprising avatars of a projected civilization in the midst of the rainforest. At the same time, these edifices are manifestations of delusions of grandeur, personified in the figure of Henri Christophe, the self-proclaimed Emperor of Haiti. According to one interviewee, this obsession with history causes poverty in Haiti: the great deeds of the past are part of daily life, whereas poverty and chaos have become secondary.

When asked about their past, Haitians first recall the fabulous wealth and opulence of the French colony of Santo Domingo (Saint-Domingue) – the island now divided between Haiti and the Dominican Republic.[7] During the seventeenth and eighteenth centuries, slave labour and the European demand for tobacco and sugar seemed to guarantee immense profits and a prosperous lifestyle for the French and their descendants in the west of Santo Domingo, i.e. contemporary Haiti. Hierarchy within colonial society was based upon colour, liberty and property. Accounts of this period note the coexistence of two notably different societies on the island, each with internal tensions. On the one hand, a white minority tried to reproduce a European way of life in the colony, but ended up 'inventing' another society quite different from Europe. Associated with this white minority were the black *afranchis*, and mulattos.[8] On the other hand, there was a black slave majority, amorphous and uncouth from the perspective of the European colonizers who depended on their labour in the plantations. In addition, another society was being constituted on the island, distant from the European social order and different from the one of African origin. This society, increasingly distinguished by the power of those who controlled the knowledge associated with voodoo, had found in the Maroons (communities of escaped slaves) a form of rebellion and insurgency against slave labour. It was a complex social order, in which slaves were divided into two categories: the *esclaves noirs bossales*, or those who had come directly from Africa, and the *esclaves noirs créoles*, who had been born in Santo Domingo (Barthelemy 1996: 28).

This society emerged in a surprising manner following the 1791 uprising against the French. Voodoo, the cosmology of the slaves, had dominated and accompanied the confrontations of the incendiary, insurgent masses, placing itself at the service of the blacks in their struggles against the whites. And what of the mulattos and the *afranchis*? The characteristic tension resulting from their position in colonial society would express itself throughout the decade following the French Revolution and the crisis of the *ancien régime*, which lasted until Haiti's independence, in 1804. The unfolding of events, as described by James (2000 [1938]), reveals the ambiguities of mulattos and *afranchis* in their relation to the revolution: seen as friends of the whites by the black masses, they feared their fate in an independent Haiti. Conversely, confronted with the colonizers' desire to reconstruct pre-revolutionary colonial society on the island, they were ambivalent about reconquest by the French. Confronted with the existence of black Haitian heroes, and massacres of the white population, the mulattos and the *afranchis* attempted to find their place in independent and 'creolized' Haiti.

Independence brought the unprecedented challenge of constructing a state in a country in which former slaves of African descent constituted the great majority. During this process, the social dynamics of colonial society were reordered (Pluchon 1991; Barthelemy 1996; Hurbon 1987). The mulattos and *afranchis* took over the state apparatus. Between them and the 'uncouth masses' were the Creoles, an intermediary group that had been born into slavery in Haiti. The civilizing project in post-colonial Haiti emerges from two contradictory movements: on the one hand, the assertion of the *perfectibility* of black Africans and their descendants; on the other, the claim by mulattos and *afranchis* that they were the legitimate heirs of Enlightenment civilization. The latter ended up transforming themselves into the new French, assuming the hierarchical superiority that the French had enjoyed during the colonial period. Two aspects of Trouillot's (1995, 1997) insightful analysis of the Haitian revolution deserve attention here. First, this was the only slave rebellion that resulted in the expulsion or death of the entire population of colonizers, an event that spread fear throughout the Americas where slave labour still existed. Second, the movement failed to fulfil a truly emancipatory project. From the beginning of the nineteenth century, Haitian society was characterized by the reproduction of inequalities similar to those of the slave period. This process reached absurd proportions during the Duvalier period (1957–86), and led scholars such as Hurbon (1987) to affirm that the relationship established between those who came to dominate the state apparatus (and were aligned with sectors of the bourgeoisie) and the masses of the people was similar to the relationship between masters and slaves.

If the state and the sectors of society with which it was associated seemed to have inherited forms of behaviour typical of the old colonial masters, the evidence suggests that the popular reaction was also similar to that of the slaves in the old days: 'marooning' (escaping). Once again, there emerged a divided society, with the state perceived as the site of pure, unrestrained, illegitimate violence, because it treated citizens not as legal persons, but as 'slaves' in a strict sense (ibid.). Throughout the Duvalier period – and, quite possibly, since – the Tontons Macoutes came to represent the materialization of this state of affairs, incarnating a local power structure and at the same time a kind of repressive all-embracing praetorian guard to the presidency. Although persecuted and prohibited in public, voodoo was associated directly with the power of the Macoutes and the Duvalier family itself. The Creole language was banned from state institutions. Language became the great symbol of differentiation and inequality between the elites, with their good knowledge of French, and the Creole-speaking masses. Paradoxically, it was 'Papa Doc' Duvalier who, with the intention of gaining mass political support, devised *noirisme*, a political discourse that depicted the black majority as in constant struggle with the white world. Distinct from the universalistic ideals of 'black is beautiful', *noirisme* postulated an eternal conflict between whites and blacks, oppressors and oppressed. The implication of this was that the blacks should ensure that a black man – Papa Doc – should hold the monopoly of power within Haiti. At the same time, the black and mulatto elites built their power on their mastery of European culture and the only language taught in school – French. And the Catholic Church claimed to be the only legitimate and universal public religion in Haiti.

Starting in the nineteenth century, emigration became the alternative to either life in misery or marooning. The number of Haitians in the Dominican Republic rose from 19,000 in 1950 to 300,000 by 1970. By the 1970s there were also 30,000 Haitians in the Bahamas and approximately 200,000 Haitians in the United States, a figure that has risen since, as indicated by the phenomenon of the Haitian boat people (Lundhal 1979: 624–35). There were only 9,000 Haitian immigrants in Paris in the 1970s, but an additional 30,000 were in French-speaking Guadeloupe and French Guyana. The rural–urban exodus has also been significant since the 1970s. Misery in the countryside was followed by misery in the cities: the capital city faces acute shortages of drinking water, sanitation and health facilities, housing, land for building, and educational institutions.

It would be untrue to say that certain sectors of Haitian society have never expressed their dissatisfaction with this state of affairs. Besides the explosions of violence, there was the period of immense artistic and

131

intellectual creativity following the timid liberalization under the Jean-Claude Duvalier 'Baby Doc' regime. Tourism also grew in this period, and brought some improvements in economic welfare. After the Duvalier family was expelled in 1986, following popular riots, a wider range of cultural and political activities surfaced, and non-governmental organizations (NGOs) began to appear and work with the poor. In addition, the diaspora brought increased interaction with and knowledge of the world beyond national and Caribbean frontiers.

The end of the Duvalier era in 1986 brought a short, troubled period during which attempts were made to institutionalize democracy and attract foreign investment. The endeavour to establish a democratic government – with the 1990 election and Jean Pierre Aristide's ascension to power – was interrupted by the coup d'état of September 1991. The ensuing violence was indescribable: personalities from the Duvalier period reappeared; the Tontons Macoutes returned; many people who had supported the democratic transition or were suspected of acting against the old regime were killed. There were reports of torture and of thousands of murders. The international community responded with an embargo: between 1991 and 1993 Haiti was isolated from the rest of the world, and dependent on smuggling from the Dominican Republic. The embargo had devastating consequences for the weakly structured society. In addition to the violence of the army and the Tontons Macoutes, the few existing institutions were dismantled. Governmental institutions were closed, the university suffered 'intervention', and tourism, which had become an important source of income, stopped. This was the situation Aristide encountered when he returned to Haiti in 1994, with the support of the United Nations. Ironically, while throughout the embargo the threat of an American invasion had mobilized groups and individuals around a historical anti-American nationalism, it was the American army and the United Nations peacekeeping forces which combined to re-establish peace and to erect democratic institutions.

A contemporary social map

Establishing democracy has been costly and difficult. Although formally abolished by decree after the coup d'état in 1993, old institutions such as the army continue to make themselves felt through indiscriminate violence. Confrontations between the legislative and executive branches of government and the fragility of the judiciary create obstacles to truly democratic elections. There are also allegations of open corruption: the ruling party led by Aristide, the Lavalas family, has been accused of using terror during the years of Macoutisme and of misappropriating aid funds. Haiti has opened its markets to international trade, but life has not become easier for Haitians. Local production remains highly traditional and uncompetitive, while the majority of the population lacks access to basic goods.

To give an idea of the current situation in Haiti, I provide some basic economic and social indicators. Comparisons with other countries in the region, such as the Dominican Republic and Guatemala, show that the current situation in Haiti cannot be seen solely as a consequence of its colonial past, troubled political history or geographic and environmental conditions – although these factors play a role. Haiti's structural characteristics reproduce misery. Comparison is important, as Haitians speak about 'their poverty' on the basis of information about the quality of life in neighbouring countries spread by travellers, images in the media and via the relatively porous border with Haiti's much wealthier neighbour, the Dominican Republic.

The first contrast that strikes the eye when entering Haiti by land from the Dominican Republic is the landscape. The environment as a socially constructed space is a theme of central importance to understanding the country's recent history and future prospects. The contrast between the eastern and western parts of the island is startling: crossing the border from Haiti into the Dominican Republic means encountering nature of such abundance that the country seems like the tropical paradise of Western tourist imagery. Haiti, by contrast, looks more like a desert. The country is on the brink of ecological disaster, as the use of charcoal, the only local source of energy, is promoting deforestation. This process dates from the colonial period (Ans 1987: Part 1), but recent history has aggravated the situation. Deforestation and the construction industry have led to soil erosion and landslides, and the sea is also eroding part of the coast. The current environmental situation is connected with the flagrant disregard for law and order during the last few decades. Throughout the Duvalier period, the public patrimony, including the natural environment, was appropriated by powerful individuals and families. The international embargo affected the import of energy sources: oil products were smuggled across the Dominican border at exorbitant prices, and charcoal became the main domestic source of energy. The startling growth of Port au Prince must be understood in the context of a human and environmental disaster (Girault and Godard 1983). Daily life in the capital involves uncollected garbage, inadequate drainage of the water that flows down from the mountains, untreated sewage, lack of adequate drinking water for most people, and the frequent collapse of the precarious townships (*bidonvilles*) affected by soil erosion.

Haiti's ecological problems are especially serious considering that the population is largely dependent upon traditional economic activities. The economic activities of the inhabitants of the urban *bidonvilles* are agrarian and largely self-provisioning. Industry employs no more than 7 per cent of the economically active population, mainly in food processing and the manufacture of cement and other products for the building sector. The service sector employs less than 25 per cent of the economically active population. Agriculture, herding and traditional fishing absorb – or should absorb – the large majority of the population. Recurrent economic crisis, however, means that the vast majority of the population are unemployed or underemployed as, for example, vendors of charcoal or craft products, domestic servants, collectors of old newspapers, glassware and other garbage. Fast urban population growth does not reflect any labour demand from industry or the service sector; it is mainly due to the severe crisis in the countryside. In addition, the numerous international organizations established in the cities may act as pull factors, to the extent that prospective migrants look to them to supply social services.

A major concern of the Haitian elites is the 'demographic explosion'. Population growth rates have remained high in Haiti, while, as in other Latin American countries, the neighbouring Dominican Republic has seen growth rates decline since the 1960s. Many people interviewed considered high birth rates to be one of the major causes of poverty in the country.[9] The Haitian population is locally estimated at 8.5 million, and is distributed unevenly throughout the 22,000 square kilometres of the country. In the view of Haitians, the population exceeds the productive capacity of the country, a perception that is widespread across different sectors of the elite: the country is small and has a limited productive capacity, so that the demographic explosion must be curbed by any means. This perception seems realistic enough when one is confronted with the crowds in Port au Prince, or with news concerning the boat people or illegal migration to the Dominican Republic. Indeed, the statistics show high birth rates, high infant mortality rates and low life expectancy – a demographic pattern characteristic of underdeveloped countries that have not gone through the demographic transition. As Table 5.1 shows, there has been a slight improvement in these indicators during the last three decades, but crude mortality and infant mortality rates remain very high, while life expectancy at birth remains exceptionally low.

The indicators used by the international agencies reveal a devastating education situation. The literacy rate of adults over fifteen years of age is 48 per cent – lower than the average for countries with low rates of human development, and well below the Latin American and Caribbean average of 88 per cent (UNDP 2000: 196–7). The evidence suggests that the situation

TABLE 5.1 Haiti's population

	1970–75	1975–80	1980–85	1985–90	1990–95	1995–2000
Estimated total growth rate (per thousand)	17	21	24	25	19	18
Rate of growth of the population at an active age (between 15 and 64 years of age) (per 100 people in active age)*	...	...	2	2	2	3
Rate of estimated global fecundity	6	6	6	6	5	4
Crude estimated rate of birth	39	41	43	42	34	32
Estimated life expectancy at birth	48	51	52	54	55	57
Estimated rate of infant mortality (per thousand)	152	139	122	100	74	66
Estimated crude rate of mortality (per thousand)	18	16	16	14	12	11
Estimated rate of migration (per thousand)	–4	–4	–4	–3	–3	–3

* CEPAL (2000b)
Source: CEPAL (2000a)

is unlikely to improve in the next few years, given the low enrolments in elementary and secondary schools during recent years. We should also keep in mind Hurbon's estimate that the number of functional illiterates – individuals who have passed through a formal educational institution but who have only minimal reading and writing skills – may be as high as 90 per cent of the population.

When we speak of 'formal educational institutions', or about learning to read, we refer to the French language. Unfortunately, there are no data available on the percentage of individuals who are fluent in French, which is supposedly taught in schools.[10] Apart from being a status symbol, knowledge of French is a basic requisite for access to bureaucratic offices, and therefore a key mechanism of social mobility.[11] Lack of knowledge of French is thus a mechanism of social exclusion that affects the majority of the population, who speak only Creole.

Clearly, public schools are not capable of meeting the needs of Haitian youth. Their material fragility is frequently accompanied by a lack of adequately trained teachers. The situation gets worse the farther the distance to urban centres. Alongside the public school system, there are private schools in the capital which enrol the children of the nation's elites and of foreigners. Children in these schools not only learn French, they also have daily access to English, which creates an even greater gap between them and the majority of the population.[12]

The elites and their perceptions of poverty and inequality

Who are the elites in Haiti? Elite groups are those who control a wide range of material, symbolic and political resources (de Swaan et al. 2000: 46). This control differentiates them from the rest of the population and transforms them into groups that may be aware of their particular role as 'elites'. Who are these groups and what are these symbolic and material goods? This theme is briefly addressed here, to better define the group under study.

Possession of material goods that allow consumption patterns well above the average is an obvious trait of the elite. A member of the elite has other attributes, however, beyond material advantages: control of social and political resources and a prominent position within society. This prominent position is reinforced through bureaucratic position, a strategic situation or the greater ease with which the individual understands the functioning of society itself, as well as the state and the formal and informal institutions with which he is associated. Subscribing to Pierre Bourdieu's perspective, I would say 'the different positions within social space correspond to life styles, systems of differential deviations which are the symbolic re-translation of differences that are objectively inscribed in the conditions of existence' (Bourdieu 1983: 82).

In Haiti one of the most important of these symbolic goods is knowledge of French. Distinct from the rest of the population, who speak almost exclusively in Creole, the elites prefer to use French, which they learned at school in Port au Prince or abroad. Knowledge of French is necessary for access to public office and for social mobility in general. The inability to speak and write in French is one of the main mechanisms of social exclusion: the poor, whether they are of rural or urban origin, are immersed in a universe that expresses itself in Creole, and perceive that all doors to social mobility are closed.

The process of adoption of French by the elites, along with their control over key positions in the economic and political structures, suggests a 'colonial situation', in Balandier's sense (1963). In the Haitian case, however, French is not only the language of the capital, in contrast to the countryside, as is common in many African colonial contexts. In addition, the relationship between French and Creole also lies at the basis of a hierarchical social structure. Although Creole had previously been repressed and banned in schools, it has recently been gaining respectability. The democratic constitution established it as one of the country's official languages. The new celebration of Creole has led to its use by poets, schoolteachers and popular actors. It should be noted that the elites have always known how to speak this language, for it is necessary in order to be able to take a walk down the street, go to the market, speak to employees, or walk into a voodoo temple through the back door.[13] While it is evident that this is a society divided between the 'country' and the 'city', between state and society, it is important to keep in mind that the different social groups constitute themselves in their interrelations. While the use of French is a means of exclusion, it is in Creole that the relationship is established. It is not Creole's resilience, however, which seems to characterize its peculiar permanence, but the exclusive nature of the relationship that a specific group establishes with the French language.

Following the clues given by anthropologist and historian Gerard Barthelemy, we can affirm that the constitution of Haiti as a modern state occurred in the midst of growing ill feeling provoked by an 'original debt' of the *afranchis* and mulatto elites in relation to the 'uncouth masses', who were remembered only from time to time in moments of crisis. Uncertainty and insecurity have marked the history of the mulatto elites and the resources that they draw upon to maintain their economic and social situation. This insecurity has led them to adopt a series of survival strategies. They favour commercial activities over investments in the plantations, so that they can easily transfer capital to banks abroad and guarantee their security in the face of a possible forced exile. Consequently, and like the Lebanese – the only group of immigrants who came into Haiti from the end of the nineteenth century to the present – they are constantly accused of being leeches, because they charge high prices. They are believed to have acquired other nationalities, and to possess North American or French passports.[14] Their vulnerability has also led many of them to establish matrimonial alliances with black families that have close ties to those in power.[15]

During the period of authoritarian rule it was the intellectual elites which suffered most. Universities and schools were subjected to 'intervention' and professors, physicians, journalists and writers were systematically persecuted. Many abandoned the country for the United States, Quebec, France and, eventually, the newly independent francophone countries of Africa. The universal ideals of *négritude* appealed to the intellectual elites much more than the pettiness they saw in *noirisme*. Furthermore, members of the Haitian intellectual elite felt that, by helping solve the lack of skilled cadres in African countries, they could play their historic role in the modern world.

The end of the Duvalier regime in 1986 and the crisis of Macoutisme transformed Haiti into an attractive place for many of these exiled intellectuals, who came back to their partly destroyed native land. All intellectuals interviewed were unanimous with respect to one of the causes of poverty: the long period in which the Duvalier family was in power deprived the country of intellectual and cultural life. They believe that the 'transition to democracy' can only occur piecemeal. There is a serious shortage of qualified personnel with knowledge of the country. The enthusiasm for the new constitution, however, and the return of Leslie Manigat – an internationally acclaimed historian, particularly well known in France, where he is a full professor of the history of Latin America at the Sorbonne – as president of the republic in 1987 was soon destroyed by the turbulence to which the country succumbed.

The period following the promulgation of the constitution in 1987 seems, however, to have revived an old tradition among the Haitian elites: their sense of mission.[16] Writings of an almost confessional nature by intellectuals such as Leslie Manigat (1995), the experienced politician Marc Bazin (1995), Robert Malval (1994), a businessman from a traditional family, and the internationally renowned film director Raoul Peck (1997) attempt to re-establish connections with this tradition as set out in the classic text by Jean Price-Mars, *La Vocation de l'Élite*.[17] We could define the elites in Haiti as that group which attributes to itself a mission and a vocation: to prove to the world the perfectibility and civilizing capacity of the 'black race', at the same time as it proposes to erect a new *black France* (*France noire*) in a small island in the Caribbean. This process is fraught with paradoxes and contradictions, not least because the construction of a black France would have as its most immediate consequence the extinction of the elite itself as a group.

Haitian elites: a lifestyle Two attributes are therefore central to the definition of the elites in Haiti: the adequate use of French and the sense of mission. Other traits are also relevant: the social setting in which these groups are situated, and the economic basis of their reproduction and of their lifestyle. The analysis of the social setting in which these groups are situated and their economic activities is based on the interviews conducted for this study. As already pointed out, the definition of 'elites' used here points to a group that is heterogeneous in terms of social composition and economic base. I interviewed many well-known politicians from different political parties, including two former presidents of the republic, public servants, businessmen, merchants, store owners, intellectuals, professionals, artists and students. While diverse in terms of their lifestyles and livelihoods, they all had in common an awareness of a 'Western' cultural patrimony to be preserved and a sense of mission with respect to the country and its population.

Perhaps the most obvious differentiation line within the elite is the one that separates Port au Prince from Cap Haitien. Big businessmen, top public officials and professionals within the financial sector are based in the capital, occupying the elegant suburbs of Pétion-Ville and nearby towns. Adjoining Port au Prince, high in the mountains, Pétion-Ville serves as a refuge not only from the heat, but also from the decayed, crowded streets of Port au Prince. Many elite families live in large mansions surrounded by high walls, and under the surveillance of one or more heavily armed private guards.

All the evidence suggests that individuals who occupy positions of prominence, whether in the political or business spheres, also have close ties with the so-called 'traditional families', both black and mulatto. The significance of this relationship is multiple. The traditional families derive their wealth and prestige from rural estates or the import-export trade. Many own big coffee, sugar or fruit estates. Others are associated with the enterprises that import manufactured goods and export primary products. The crisis that affected these economic sectors forced them to channel part of their resources into the financial market, as well as to ensure that some of their members were recruited for professional positions in large international organizations, including NGOs and large banks.

This sector of the elite maintains close relationships with the outside world. Some have spent part of their lives abroad, either as political refugees or as students in French or North American universities. This cosmopolitan orientation is maintained not only through travel to the United States – a way of ensuring a certain level of consumption – but also in the relational universe established in Port au Prince. They are part of a sophisticated circuit that includes diplomats, professionals and foreign aid workers. Their children study in French or North American schools, before attending foreign universities.

During the 1930s, 1940s and 1950s, the civil service tended to be dominated by educated blacks, admitted when the state bureaucracy expanded after the American occupation of 1915–34. This coincided with a sort of 'resistance movement', in which groups of blacks criticized what they saw as the ethnic exclusiveness of the mulattos, and demanded channels of social mobility. Some of the people interviewed in Port au Prince derived their livelihood from public offices maintained to a large extent through funds provided by international cooperation. While salaries are low, securing these seems to be crucial to maintaining the dynamics of a middle sector that still supplies the cadre of liberal professionals.

Among the intellectuals, we encounter a world that is marked by a greater degree of diversity, including individuals from the traditional wealthy families, members of the middle classes and others who occupy positions within the state apparatus. This group resists classification by 'colour' or 'race': in it we find blacks, mulattos and mestizos of Lebanese origin. In general they are associated with some international organization, teach in the universities or work in bookstores, radio stations or the press. Although they cultivate an exceptional fluency in the French language, they also spawn very articulate narratives about the fundamental importance of the 'African heritage' within the country.

In Cap Haitien, the range of elites is more restricted. Among the businessmen, special emphasis should be given to those who dedicate themselves to tourism: the owners and managers of the few remaining hotels and restaurants in the city. Proximity to beautiful beaches, such as Abadie, and the magnificent historical patrimony (the ancient Spanish ruins, the Cidadela complex, and the Palace of Sans Souci), guarantee its inclusion on the Caribbean tourist circuit. Unlike in the capital, businessmen here may be encountered in the city streets or in front of the cathedral: they have a much less busy lifestyle, and appear less interested in consumer goods. As in Port au Prince, however, they come from traditional families whose first source of wealth was the ownership and exploitation of land. The limited possibilities of investment within Cap Haitien help to explain why many of these families have become impoverished without ever questioning or being questioned about their social status.

Cap Haitien's physicians, journalists and professors are also from the traditional families. Their lifestyle seems to be centred on their love of sitting and conversing in front of their houses – something that would be unthinkable in Port au Prince. In contrast, members of non-traditional families have achieved upward mobility through the state, politics, the Catholic Church and, more recently, the rapidly proliferating Protestant sects. Amid such diversity, something seems to unify all members of the elite and define part of their lifestyle: they all possess a more or less extensive number of servants.

'Right to the state' There is consensus across the various elite sectors interviewed that poverty is Haiti's biggest problem. When I enquired about the number of poor people in the country, the answers varied, but estimates were always higher than 60 per cent of the population. Approximately 70 per cent of the people interviewed stated that eight out of ten Haitians find themselves on the threshold between 'poverty' and 'misery'. In other words, from the perspective of the elites, Haiti is a 'poor' country with a large portion of 'miserable' citizens.

The majority of people interviewed appeared to consider the difference between 'poverty' and 'misery' to be 'dignity': 'poverty' can be 'dignified', but 'misery' cannot. The traditional peasant way of life is associated with poverty, while misery is associated with the urban poor who lack work, decent shelter and adequate food. The poor are seen as individuals who have broken away from their families, and therefore from the traditional systems of self-regulation defined by age and gender.[18] In the view of Port au Prince elites, the miserable urban population is not subject to any kind of traditional social control, and it is this which makes them vulnerable to the ailments of modern Haiti: criminality, violence, prostitution and the transmission of diseases. In this respect there is a marked difference between the interviewees from Cap Haitien and those from the capital. Whereas the latter associate misery with violence and the rupture of traditional society, the Capoises seem less concerned about violence, crime and prostitution. This is easily explained: in the second-most important city in the country rural ties are still very strong, and with them elements of the self-regulation characteristic of traditional Haitian society: strong age and gender hierarchies. Thus, while 80 per cent of the Port au Prince elites interviewed viewed violence, criminality and corruption as the causes and consequences of poverty, the elites in Cap Haitien gave greater emphasis to the crisis of traditional values, even though they do not point to violence

Haitian elites

141

or criminality as the country's 'greatest problems'. Only 15 per cent of Cap Haitien elites mentioned violence in the interviews.

When asked about the possibility of a 'social explosion' as a consequence of poverty and misery, the differences between interviewees from Port au Prince and Cap Haitien are significant: the former displayed no doubt that there would be an explosion in the near future, and many even asserted that they were already living through such an 'explosion'. The Cap Haitien elites, by contrast, are more sceptical, claiming that 'conformity' is part of the Haitian 'state of mind'. In both cities, however, the contemporary lack of a 'firm hand' emerges as a perceived major cause of contemporary chaos and poverty. The entire elite was extremely nostalgic for strong government. They felt that institutions such as the executive, legislative or judicial branch of government have nothing to do with Haitian reality – 'people just don't understand'; 'everyone wants to be the president of the republic'; 'going to the parliament is a way of getting rich'. The 'people', in short, are not prepared for democracy, and are an easy target for populist discourses such as *noirisme* and *lavalasianisme*, which have characterized Haiti during the past few decades.[19] Also noticeable is the nostalgia among members of the old traditional families for an earlier Haiti that was 'poor but dignified', whose government was in the charge of 'capable men',[20] independently of their colour. Artists, professionals, people working in NGOs and members of the Catholic Church tended to emphasize democratic values. Their criticisms with respect to methods of governance of the Lavalas Family party do not imply so much a critique of democracy as a denunciation of the abuses committed by those who, once in power, reproduce the repressive and coercive methods of their predecessors. A large portion of this elite sector expressed profound disillusionment with the Lavalas Family government. It should be recalled that popular groups, intellectuals and leaders of public opinion enthusiastically welcomed both Aristide's initial election and his later return to power. Discouragement, disillusion, lack of hope: these are the sentiments of those who once saw a means of overcoming Haiti's secular misery in the power of the Lavalas Family party and the figure of Aristide.

The only thing that unites critics and supporters of the democratic system is a desperate demand for some sort of 'right to the state'. The perception that the state has collapsed, does not exist or is in the hands of corrupt people is all the more serious when we realize that, for the majority of those interviewed, the only possible solution to poverty in Haiti is the state itself. It is the state which should guarantee a decent education and a reasonable health system, even if, to meet this end, it must antagonize large sectors of Haitian society. How can drinking water and sewage systems be provided for all citizens in an overpopulated city such as Port au Prince without the abrasive presence of state power?

From the perspective of the elites, the state should have a civilizing role over a society that is still backward and largely rural. It is the state which should carry out mass campaigns to combat illiteracy, and teach both adults and children how to read and write. It is the state which should promote vaccination and teach people measures for preventing diseases and epidemics. It is also the state which should prevent the rural exodus by creating better living conditions in rural areas and controlling migration. What is lacking in Haiti, according to about 70 per cent of the people interviewed, is a strong, authoritative state.[21]

How should this lack of adherence to democratic values be interpreted? I have no definitive answer to this question. In any case, it is important to take into account the fact that Haiti lacks a successful recent experience with democracy. Moreover, the state has made itself present in fits and starts, rather than through a long process of power consolidation. Even the long period of *duvalierisme* was not an era of a strong state. While it is true that in some sense it resembled Latin American state authoritarianism, its characteristic traits were the privatization of the state, the formation of a violent praetorian guard (the Tontons Macoutes) to guarantee the defence of the president-for-life, and the destruction or systematic co-optation of any social group that expressed misgivings about the regime.[22] The fall from power of 'Baby Doc' Jean-Claude Duvalier in 1986 did not give rise to democratization, but rather, according to the elites, to the anarchy and chaos that culminated in the last era of Presidents Preval and Aristide, who combined a populist discourse, appealing to the masses for support, with the systematic dismantling of democratic institutions.

Another recurring element in the discourse of different sectors of the elite is the expression of shame about the situation: more than half of the interviewees stated that nothing works because the elites do not exert any pressure on the state. Why should they? When faced with an illness, the best hospital is American Airlines, which ensures arrival in Miami in an hour and a half, or the regular flights to Cuba – a country held in great esteem by Haitians of all ideologies for its public health system.[23] As for the educational institutions, the elites rely on the French and American schools in Port au Prince, and some of those who continue on to higher education do so in the United States, Canada or France, with a small minority going to the Dominican Republic or Cuba. In short, the collapse of whatever is public is perceived as the result of several factors, including the explicit neglect of the country's public institutions by its elites.

Who is poor in Haiti? While defining the elites was a problem for the researcher, defining the poor was difficult for those who were interviewed. Who is poor in Haiti? The most common definition among interviewees was that the person who does not have access to the minimum necessary to live a dignified life is poor. The urban elites interviewed, however, did not feel comfortable with this definition. When asked 'Who is poor in Haiti?', there seemed to be a certain consensus that this term referred to those who lacked material goods, but not only this: to individuals who do not speak French; or, as former President Manigat told me without hesitation, 'poor is that person who does not have access to Western culture'. The lack of knowledge of the French language would be a signal of the lack of access to that which, he felt, all should be entitled: Western culture, the only culture capable of providing people with universal values and, above all, the only culture capable of 'liberating' people from 'slavery'. I would like to stress the importance that Haitian elites accord not only to knowledge of the French language, but to everything that this presupposes: the notion of *rights*, of *free will*, the possibility of perceiving the world as other than controlled by vengeance, fear or magic spells. Whether or not a certain clearly Western code, expressed exclusively in French, was shared seemed, for most of the people interviewed, to constitute the frontier between the elites on the one side and the poor and the miserable on the other.

There is no consensus as to what to do with the 'African heritage', which some of the interviewees held as the 'true Haitian national identity'. A certain discomfort became evident when the term 'race' emerged. I enquired whether we could define a poor person according to his/her race. The answers indicate that for many people being a mulatto would indicate that one belongs to the urban elite, which is fluent in French. Rarely, however, did a member of the elite explicitly use the theme of 'race': only 20 per cent of those interviewed asserted that race was an indicator of poverty or wealth, and all of those were black. These black interviewees felt that all mulattos were members of the elite, whereas, among the blacks, the reality was different. While the term race was avoided as an apparent indicator of wealth or poverty, it was introduced into the dialogue through other channels and was present in nearly all interviews.

When asked about solutions to poverty, the idea of unity emerged as crucial. To what degree were the Haitians (historically) disunited? The answer is a puzzle, leading to different native views of the country. The first concerns the division between mulattos and blacks: while the majority of people interviewed did not consider being mulatto or being black an indicator of social status, the dissension between these two sectors was pointed out as the major cause of poverty in the country. Some people, particularly in Cap Haitien – where mulattos are more of a minority than in Port au Prince – were quite emphatic when they pointed out that racism among the mulattos, and the desire to become whiter among the blacks, were reasons for dissent and, consequently, for poverty in Haiti. Others – mulattos – signalled continual concerns that one of the reasons for their insecurity in the country was the capacity of populists to manipulate the 'black masses'. Emphasis must be laid on the perceived role of the discord between 'blacks' and 'mulattos' in moments of crisis, and the consequent disunity, which was mentioned by almost all interviewees when asked about the causes of poverty in the country.[24]

There is more to the issue of disunity or dissension, however: voodoo, according to the elites, is in part responsible. On this the young intellectual elites differ from the rest of the elite. A significant number of young intellectuals presented this religion as a belief that should be respected, as it is in fact presented in the most recent constitution, and even as one of the symbols of nationality. The older intellectuals and other elite members perceive voodoo as a problem. In their view, it not only imprisons the individual in fear and superstition, but is also responsible for the cycles of magic spells and vengeance that contribute to the disunity that has characterized Haiti since the foundation of the nation-state. Furthermore, it generates distrust, since suspicion becomes widespread because of voodoo: anyone can be the subject or the object of magic spells.[25]

Cultural diversity, social inequality While the definition of the 'poor' among the Haitian elites leads us to their images of social inequality, the constant references to language and religion lead us into the centre of a debate that torments these elites: a dispute about the cultural diversity of their country, and a rupture between those who dominate Western codes and those immersed in rural life, marked by *hierarchies* (and not by equality) and, above all, by *fear* (and not by freedom).

All were unanimous concerning one point: the need to guarantee formal education to all Haitians. When asked about the causes of poverty, the most common answer was the 'lack of education' and the lack of schooling of a considerable part of the population. The large number of illiterates and the high rates of school repetition and drop-outs are singled out as important causes of poverty. The only way of overcoming these problems would be state investment in this sector: around 90 per cent of the people interviewed expressed the opinion that basic education should be universally guaranteed by the government.

When I enquired about the potential role of the Catholic Church or of other churches in basic education, 60 per cent were sceptical. Historically, the Catholic Church played a central role in education. An agreement between the government and the Vatican, made in the middle of the nineteenth century and renewed at the beginning of the twentieth century, conceded the Catholic Church much of the responsibility for providing basic education. From the perspective of the elites, however, this has not guaranteed the emancipation of Haitians. Today the good image of the Church and of its cadres is due to the fact that it was one of the few institutions to openly oppose the Duvalier regime, especially from the 1970s onwards. It was during this period that a series of popular organizations, originating in the Grass Roots Ecclesiastic Communities, emerged throughout the country. The fact that bishops, priests, nuns and lay people fought together against the 'old regime' did not, however, improve the institutional image of the Catholic Church. The elite believes that the Church should act in the field of education, but that it should not be the major actor in an arena that should be 'run by the state', 'public' and 'free'.

The elites are ambivalent about the heavy presence of national and foreign NGOs. While some express their sympathy for any kind of effort to diminish the suffering of the population and to attend to their needs, above all in health and education, at least 60 per cent of those interviewed revealed a profound distrust of and even indignation about the NGOs' presence. On the one hand, there is the idea that the state has no control over their activities: no one has any idea how many NGOs there are or what they do, nor is there any attempt to coordinate their activities, even among themselves, nor any guarantee of continuity. On the other hand, there is the perception that foreigners working in the country in NGOs or international organizations seek to assure themselves the *'belle vie'*. They live in palaces with swimming pools, satellite dishes, fancy modern cars; their children are educated in the French Lycée or the American School; and they frequent the same restaurants, hotels and exclusive milieus as diplomats resident in the capital. In cities such as Cap Haitien, there are neighbourhoods almost exclusively for professionals from the World Food Programme (WFP), the United Nations Development Programme (UNDP) and the Organization of American States (OAS).[26]

What seems to annoy the elites – from the richest businessmen to those closest to what would be a well-to-do middle class such as professionals working in NGOs, traditional families and professionals – is the difference in the salaries paid to foreigners as compared to Haitians. The former earn in foreign currency and deposit most of their earnings in banks outside the country; the latter earn much less, and in *gourdes*, the local currency. The former have advantages such as housing, first-class cars, schools for their children, constant trips to the United States or to Canada; while the latter must live exclusively on their wages. The recurrent observation was that these differences should not exist, since both Haitians and foreigners do the same work. Why should a North American physician earn more than a Haitian?

When I enquired about the 'goodwill' of foreigners, around 70 per cent of the people interviewed expressed deep scepticism. A Catholic priest from Cap Haitien claimed, 'they are in search of the exotic and the *belle vie*'. A member of one of the traditional families from Cap Haitien claimed that international cooperation actively participates in this 'death dance of poverty' in Haiti: it ends up destroying the structure of production and Haitian society, without guaranteeing true local development, and it deepens the dependency of Haitians on international generosity.[27]

None of the people interviewed altogether denied the useful role played by NGOs: it is the intentions of their staff which are in doubt. Are foreigners here to help or to earn some money so they can maintain a high standard of living in their countries of origin? It is clear that those Haitians interviewed who were associated with NGOs had a more mixed perception of the problem: their work depends on the presence of these organizations and their resources. Resentment provoked by the differences in wages is none the less evident.

The vision that the NGOs and their professionals have of the country was frequently criticized. According to about 40 per cent of interviewees, the foreigners working in Haiti view the country as 'exotic' or 'authentic'. Once again, language appears as an object of dispute. Some of the people interviewed, as I have already mentioned, perceive Creole as almost a 'cause' of poverty in Haiti, whereas it seems that a good number of the NGOs and North American and Canadian institutions propose a complete creolization of the country. This prospect terrifies the majority of the members of the elite I interviewed.

The issue of Creole divides the elite. Some consider it to be the only language that expresses the Haitian 'soul', and consequently believe it should be fully incorporated in all spheres of social life. Creole should dominate in all public institutions, businesses, communication media, churches and schools. French is perceived by exponents of this view as a language of domination which, strictly speaking, should be used only in international relations, and gradually substituted by English. Haitian children should complete their education in Creole, overcoming the long-term view of this language as 'minor', as belonging to the 'masses', repressed by the schools and by the 'good families'. This opinion was mainly held by politicians, religious leaders and businessmen. A larger proportion of the elites, however (around 60 per cent of those interviewed), expressed

147

the opposite view: Haiti would be able to overcome the present situation only if reading and writing in French were to become universal. For them, French language and culture represent a historical heritage, which should not be discarded in favour of English or Creole. Most Haitian works of literature, as well as the country's laws and its historiography, are written in French. Abandoning the stigmatization of Creole should not imply banning the French language, which would not even be a realistic policy. Where would one find teaching material of good quality in Creole? How should one translate the classical works of literature into this language? How could important concepts be conveyed in a language which, it was claimed, is based on a highly material and narrow universe of concerns and depends heavily on proverbs to expound broader ideas?

Discussing formal education means talking about whether or not to incorporate the only language spoken by all Haitians. This is a true Pandora's box, taking into account the secular elite's control over decisions, the prejudices of class and origin, and the myths that surround notions such as 'culture' or 'spirit', so cherished in discourses on the nation. The discussion about Creole and formal education also involves a debate about the gap between the world of writing and literacy and that of oral expression. The inclusion of all Haitians by teaching all French would in the long run entail the loss of a mythical universe associated with the authentic and the rural – and with poverty. The opposite strategy – which is to an extent under way in contemporary Haiti – involves the incorporation of Creole into the formal education system. But this would lead to a more inward orientation to Haitian culture, the distortion of Creole away from the focus on oral expression that currently defines it, and a break with a tradition of cultural universalism that is dear to the elite of this small country, and which they believe makes it the daughter and direct heiress of the Enlightenment.

Solutions What kind of solution can be imagined in order to minimize poverty and inequality in Haiti? From the perspective of the elites, there seems to be a single source of consensus, and this concerns the need to (re)construct the modern bureaucratic apparatus that embodies the 'state'. This state would be required to: attend to the health and educational needs of the entire population; promote public health and vaccination campaigns; build water supply and sewage systems, at least in cities such as Port au Prince and Cap Haitien; give expression to the century-long vocation of the elites;[28] and promote the unity of all Haitians.

What kind of state did the majority of my interviewees actually refer to? It was evidently not a contemporary Western democratic state. With more or less emphasis, the great majority have in mind a 'strong state', staffed with competent cadres able to take unpopular measures for the good of the people. Many, especially intellectuals and artists, referred to Cuba as a contrasting experience that should be taken into consideration. Others – political leaders attuned to the United States, or top businesspeople – look at Cuba with distrust and link the current chaos of the Lavalas Family regime to the influence of the Cuban model. They argue for a strong state, but one that will gain the confidence of the population, by promoting bureaucratic rationalization, fighting corruption, ending tax evasion, restoring business confidence, and attracting foreign investments. Nearly half the interviewees believed that the state should play a civilizing role, by expanding the use of the French language and discrediting voodoo, a cause of disgrace among Haitians. The other half proposes a solution based on the promotion of Haitians' self-esteem, the valorization of Creole and even the promotion of voodoo and of the secret societies. The latter tend to believe that the emphasis on national symbols does not exclude the need to learn good French: Haitians should unite and learn to live with both their African and French heritages.

When I asked about concrete solutions for reviving the national economy, more than 90 per cent of respondents were emphatic that tourism was the solution. Apparently the successful experience of the Dominican Republic and of other islands in the Caribbean, including Cuba, is well known in Haiti. For this to be successful, however, a strong state is once again considered necessary. In their view, only a strong public authority could create the infrastructure adequate to attract foreign tourists.

Final remarks

Do the Haitian elites have a 'social consciousness'? Do individuals, aware of their condition as members of the elite, feel any responsibility for improving the living conditions of the socially excluded? The prevalence of the idea of a 'vocation' suggests a degree of consciousness with respect to elite responsibilities. The notion is very abstract, however, and does not help to establish a real debate about the possibilities of reducing poverty or of identifying groups within the elite responsible for aspects of the current situation. More broadly, the interviews indicate limits to the social consciousness of the elite which are implicit in the attribution of poverty to causes well beyond their control – either to history, or to 'the international community'. Within this framework, there is little scope for realistic discussion about the possibilities of intervention on the part of the Haitian elites themselves.

The perception of Haiti as a fundamentally poor country is the dominant theme in all the interviews. Poverty is one of the central elements in the definition of the nation. The Haitian elite's experience of contrasts is built on the observation of the poverty of the majority of the population, contrasted with the situation of the old colonial metropolis, the neighbouring Dominican Republic, the United States or Cuba. Why there is poverty and how to solve these problems constitute challenges to the nation and frame the basis of a major debate: 'Why are we poor?' My research subjects direct their gaze to history, to culture and to their political institutions. Often, poverty is explained in the light of the failure of the rest of the world to comprehend a revolution and an independence movement that arose two hundred years ago: it has not been possible to realize the project of Haitians ('blacks') to fight against slave labour ('a white man's invention'). Throughout two centuries we have seen the constant reproduction of a struggle of 'blacks' against 'whites', or of 'blacks' against those who wished to replace the 'whites'. From this perspective, poverty is not only the consequence of a century-long embargo, but also of the lack of unity inside Haitian society.

Disunity is interpreted as a consequence of a set of misfortunes that occurred at the onset of the history of the nation, notably the distance separating *afranchis* from the masses. But there are also other causes. Culture reproduces this 'disunity', by promoting cycles of vengeance expressed by means of magic spells, or through the existence of a 'national' language that encloses the mass of Haitians inside a world of beliefs and proverbs, far removed from the conceptual universe of the French language. Voodoo and Creole, frequently viewed as the translation of the 'soul' of the people and the nation, come to be seen as the causes of its material poverty.

Finally, the explanation for poverty is seen as lying in the absence of a modern state in Haiti. For the vast majority of Haitians, the existence of the nation is unquestionable and the proof is the revolution that occurred two centuries ago. The revolution did not, however, guarantee the construction of a state that could translate the desires of the Haitians to improve their conditions. The state emerged as a sphere of power coveted by all in the sense of guaranteeing their private interests, and not public welfare. For many, it is this state which became aligned to the ('white') international community so as to halt the development of a nation that is, in its essence, revolutionary.

How can poverty be overcome? By constructing a strong state, authoritarian if necessary, and capable of translating the desires of the nation instead of destroying the nation itself. A state fashioned by 'capable people' (from the elite), able to confront the world (of whites), to unite all Haitians (blacks and mulattos), and to reveal to all the site of the revolution, the island through which history passed.

Notes

This chapter was translated by Peter Fry

1 The research upon which this essay is based would not have been possible without the support of Elisa Reis, Abram de Swaan and the entire *Perceptions* team, who generously welcomed a late arrival among the researchers. In the field, I received assistance from Hérard Jadotte, Gart and Mureen, whose contacts made it possible to conduct the interviews in Port au Prince. In Cap Haitien, the Lubin family made me feel at home. I would like to thank Gabriel Barbosa, Sebastião Nascimento and Silvana Nascimento for their assistance in the organization of the data. Jean-Phillipe Beleau introduced me to Haiti and opened the way for this research.

2 Professor of the Department of Anthropology of UNICAMP (the University of Campinas) and researcher at the Brazilian Centre of Analysis and Planning (Centro Brasileiro de Análise e Planejamento, CEBRAP).

3 According to Laënnec Hurbon, in 1987, among the so-called 'literate', those that had writing skills would not represent more than 10 per cent of the total population (Hurbon 1987: 71).

4 Although there are few quantitative and qualitative studies concerning the elites in Haiti, the subject constitutes a kind of obsession in the intellectual history of the country. A number of sources – the intellectuals of the nineteenth century (Hurbon 1987: 53–76; 1989: 240–56), the classic text by Price-Mars (1919) and the recently published essay by Michel Soukar (2000) – both emphasize the historical mission of Haitian elites to demonstrate to the world the capability of the black race to govern itself well, and reproach these same elites for ignoring the real Haiti, marginalizing the allegedly uncouth blacks, and reproducing French colonial lifestyles.

5 Dr Lubin's private collection, Cap Haitien.

6 A review of press material reveals that besides 'poverty' and 'misery', the following themes dominate the pages of these newspapers: 'nation', 'diaspora', 'corruption', 'AIDS', 'international community', 'international aid', 'crisis' (economic, political, institutional and national). This is not exhaustive, for many other themes, such as *duvalierisme* and Macoutisme, were also prominent in the daily newspapers.

7 As C. L. R. James recalls in the first edition of *The Black Jacobins*, in 1789 the French West Indies colony of Saint-Domingue represented two-thirds of all the external commerce of France, and was one of the great markets for the European slave trade (2000 [1938]: 15).

8 *Afranchis* and mulattos are native categories. *Afranchis* included Africans who had been in Haiti for two or three generations or more, spoke French, and adopted French behaviour patterns. Many were free men, although none had the same rights as whites. Mulattos were of mixed African and French descent. They were often free, sometimes presented themselves as more French than African, but enjoyed fewer rights than whites.

9 This finding was confirmed by the Haitian sociologist Pierre Joseph Florival, who conducted research on 'the population issue' in 1999. He interviewed fifty individuals in Port au Prince from civil society, political parties,

financial institutions, the media, etc. Roughly 95 per cent of interviewees gave Haiti's 'overpopulation' as one of the major explanations for the country's poverty (Florival 1999).

10 Many of those interviewed asserted that the official recognition of Creole in the 1987 constitution formalized reality: that Creole was anyway consistently used in rural schools in place of French, in which many rural teachers are not fluent.

11 While for the large majority of the population learning French is only possible in educational institutions, many elite families use French when speaking to their children, who end up learning Creole with the servants or on the streets.

12 I did not have access to much data concerning higher education. I visited the universities of Haiti (the oldest in the country), of Port au Prince, the Catholic universities (at Port au Prince and Cap Haitien) and the Henri Christophe University (in Cap Haitien). I spoke to students, professors and academic officers. Although I did not gather enough material for a systematic analysis of higher education, some conclusions were evident. Students in private universities, particularly those at the Catholic universities, come from the elite. By contrast, the Henri Christophe University is less prestigious. The National University of Haiti faces funding problems, a lack of professors and limited facilities, but still preserves a certain prestige.

13 Throughout the research it became evident to me that the status of voodoo among the elites is a source of great controversy. I did not come upon a situation like that in Brazil, where the religions of African origin were transformed during the twentieth century into national symbols and points of contact between groups of different social origins (Fry 2001). Some of the Haitian elite consider voodoo to be the essence of the 'Haitian soul', whereas for many others it constitutes one of the main causes of backwardness in the country.

14 This is illegal according to the Haitian constitution. It is frowned upon by a large part of the population, and seen as proof of disloyalty to the nation. The idea that mulattos carry more than one passport is a suspicion rather than a proven fact: there are no data on the subject.

15 The most notorious alliance was the wedding of Jean-Claude Duvalier (Baby Doc) and Michèle Bennet, the daughter of a mulatto tradesman, in May 1980 (Malval 1994).

16 On this sense of mission during the nineteenth century, see Hurbon (1987).

17 Leslie Manigat was the first legitimate president to take office after the fall from power of 'Baby Doc' Jean-Claude Duvalier; his international reputation makes him an unassailable public figure. Marc Bazin is a more controversial figure: besides the fact that he has occupied important offices in institutions such as the World Bank – which confers on him respect among businessmen – he was minister of the economy in one of Jean-Claude Duvalier's last cabinets and accepted the office of (illegitimate) prime minister during a short period of time when Aristide was in exile. Robert Malval was the first (legitimate) prime minister to prepare for Aristide's return to power.

Owner of a publishing company and other businesses in the country, member of a traditional mulatto family, he offers testimony that is honest to a degree that is, at times, disconcerting. Finally, Raoul Peck, the great film director who made his career in Africa and the United States, was minister of culture during Aristide's government. He later became disappointed and broke off relations with the Lavalas Family party. A good contemporary essay on the elites in Haiti is by Michel Soukar (2000).

18 The idea of self-regulation within the rural Haitian universe was discussed by anthropologist Gerard Barthelemy (1989). While his description of traditional Haitian structure is convincing, I believe his application of Pierre Clastres' (1974) concept of the society against the state is not appropriate to the Haitian context. The notion of the 'state' as an ideal is strong in Haiti.

19 Clearly, those who were aligned with or sympathetic to the Lavalas Family party, the winner of the last three elections – which some alleged were won fraudulently – would not agree with these remarks.

20 The idea that the power of the state should be handed over to 'the most qualified' people was reiterated by all members of the old Capoises traditional families, and is echoed in the contemporary constitution: ' ... sur l'initiative des intellectuels "mulâtres", soutient la nécessité de remettre le pouvoir aux patriotes éclairés et instruits appelés "les plus capables" ... ' (Republic of Haiti 1987: 62).

21 A young businessman who went to school in New York – the son of a traditional Capoise family, married to a French woman – was more emphatic: when confronted with the systematic failure of his business endeavours, he suggested that the only possible solution for Haiti was recolonization, for it was not prepared for self-government. He asserted more than once that nothing works in the country. After the period of the coup d'état, he had returned with his wife and daughter to the city where he was born and took risks in different business ventures: bars, restaurants, importing firms. In his view nothing worked because the Haitian businessman cannot rely on the state. If he pays his taxes properly – and these are exorbitant – he is aware that he is financing a corrupt machine. The solution is to take on the tasks that should be responsibility of the state, such as paving the streets in front of his business, installing private electricity generators because of constant power cuts, and planning to send his daughter to study abroad, either in France or in the United States. Finally he reminded me that in Cap Haitien not even ice could be produced locally: the trucks arrive at different times of day from the neighbouring Dominican Republic, with large ice cubes that are then sold in smaller pieces.

22 The opposition created between 'state' and 'nation' throughout the authoritarian period was Michel-Rolph Trouillot's (1989) object of analysis. In keeping with his analysis, the testimony gathered throughout the fieldwork presented here does not corroborate Barthelemy's (1996) observations concerning the existence of a society that is resistant to the logic of a state. What I did find were men and women who expressed fear, misgivings or exasperation with respect to the instituted powers, and demanded the constitution of a true state in Haiti.

23 The majority of intellectuals and liberal professionals interviewed asserted their sympathy for a strong government, stressing the accomplishments of Fidel Castro's government in the fields of health and education. Among politicians empathetic to the Lavalas Family party, praise for Cuba was also frequently voiced, although not among businessmen and politicians more closely aligned to the United States. Among all of the above, however, a 'strong state' was a recurrent image.

24 In many moments of Haitian contemporary history, political and economic crises were followed by threats to mulattos and even by massacres.

25 In many interviews, I found a representation of 'tradition' very similar to that detected by Peter Fry in Mozambique (2000): it was the 'African traditions' which were truly responsible for the country's backwardness.

26 Another source of criticism of foreign professionals who have established themselves in the country is their geographic concentration in the capital city. Many of those interviewed observed that all foreigners want to stay in Port au Prince, where there is a sophisticated lifestyle connected to the world of business and diplomacy.

27 In a well-structured narrative, this individual told me about his misfortunes when he was a small farmer. How could he compete with imported corn or chicken that was subsidized through international aid? The competition led him to give up growing corn and rice, and breeding local chickens, which were more costly than frozen chicken. In addition, this farmer had never fully recovered from the slaughter of his pigs during an outbreak of swine fever in the 1980s. These conditions led many peasants to abandon their land and head towards the cities, where they would never find regular employment.

28 Price-Mars (1919).

References

Ans, A.-M. d' (1987) *Haïti. Paysage et société*, Paris: Karthala

Balandier, G. (1963) *Sociologie Actuelle de l'Afrique Noire*, Paris: PUF

Barthelemy, G. (1989) *Le Pays en dehors: essai sur l'univers rural Haitien*, Port au Prince: Henri Deschamps

— (1996) *Dans la splendeur d'un après-midi d'histoire*, Port au Prince: Henri Deschamps

Bazin, M. L. (1995) *Haïti 92: Démocratie sous Pression*, Port au Prince: Henri Deschamps

Bourdieu, P. (1983) 'Gostos de classe e estilos de vida', in R. Ortiz (ed.), *Pierre Bourdieu*, São Paulo: Ática

Clastres, P. (1974) *La Societé contre l'état: recherches d'anthropologie politique*, Paris: Minuit

CEPAL (2000a) 'Boletín Demográfico: América Latina: población por años calendario y edades simples – 1995–2005', Santiago de Chile

— (2000b) 'Anuario estadístico de América Latina y Caribe 1999', Santiago de Chile

de Swaan, A., J. Manor, E. Oyen and E. Reis (2000) 'Elite Perceptions of the

Poor: Reflections for a Comparative Research Project', *Current Sociology*, 48 (1)

Florival, P. J. (1999) 'Rapport d'enquête sur les perceptions et les attitudes des décideurs des différents groupes et secteurs de la société sur la question de population en Haiti', Mimeo, Port au Prince

Fry, P. (2000) 'O espírito santo contra o feitiço e os espíritos revoltados: "civilização" e "tradição" em Moçambique', *Mana*, 6 (2)

— (2001) 'Feijoada e *soul food* 25 anos depois', in N. Esterci, P. Fry and M. Goldenberg (eds), *Fazendo antropologia no Brasil*, Rio de Janeiro: CAPES/DP&A Editora

Girault, C. and H. Godard (1983) 'Port au Prince: dix ans de croissance (1970–1980): la métropole comme reflet de la crise haïtienne', in M. Birckel, B. Lavallé, Y. Aguila, B. Chenot, W. Casanova, A. M. De La Mota, C. Girault and H. Godard, *Villes et nations en Amérique Latine*, Paris: CNRS

Hurbon, L. (1987) *Comprendre Haïti: essai sur l'état, la nation, la culture*, Paris: Karthala

— (1989) 'Sobre una antropología haïtiana en el siglo XIX', in B. Rupp-Eisenreich, *Historias de la antropología (siglos XVI–XIX)*, Barcelona: Júcar

James, C. L. R. (2000) [1938] *Os jacobinos negros: Toussaint L'Ouverture e a revolução de São Domingos*, São Paulo: Boitempo

Lundhal, M. (1979) *Peasants and Poverty: A Study of Haïti*, London: Croom Helm

Malval, R. (1994) *L'Année de toutes les duperies*, Port au Prince: Regain

Manigat, L. (1995) *La Crise haïtienne contemporaine (une lecture d'historien-politologue) ou Haïti des années 1990s: une grille d'intelligibilité pour la crise présence*, Port au Prince: Editions des Antilles

Peck, R. (1997) 'Monsieur le Ministre ... Jusqu'au bout de la patience', Port au Prince: Velvet

Pluchon, P. (1991) *Histoire de la Colonisation française*, Paris: Fayard

Price-Mars, J. (1919) *La Vocation de l'élite*, Port au Prince: Presses Nationales d'Haïti

Republic of Haiti (1987) *Constitution de la République d'Haïti*, Port au Prince

Soukar, M. (2000) *Entretiens avec l'histoire: radiographie de la 'bourgeoisie haïtienne'*, Port au Prince: Le Natal

Trouillot, M. R. (1989) *Haiti: State against Nation. The Origins and Legacies of Duvalierism*, New York and London: Monthly Review

— (1995) *Silencing the Past. Power and the Production of History*, Boston, MA: Beacon Press

— (1997) 'Silencing of the Past: Layers of Meaning in the Haitian Revolution', in G. Sider and G. Smith (eds), *Between History and Histories: The Making of Silences and Commemorations*, Toronto: University of Toronto Press

UNDP (2000) *Human Development Report 2000*, United Nations Development Programme, New York and Oxford: Oxford University Press

World Bank (1999) *World Development Report 1999/2000: Entering the 21st Century*, Washington, DC: World Bank

6 | Elite perceptions of poverty and poor people in South Africa

NOUSHIN KALATI AND JAMES MANOR[1]

One contrast between South Africa and most of the other cases examined in this book is especially striking. In many (perhaps most) less developed countries – and in most of our other cases – the governing political elite does not possess in any full sense what Abram de Swaan has called a 'social consciousness', while certain other elites do. In South Africa, that pattern is reversed.

The ruling ANC elite and its close allies tend to believe strongly in the interdependence of all social groups, and in the responsibility of all elites for the condition of poor people. They also believe in the third element of a social consciousness – the existence of efficacious means for tackling poverty (although, as we shall see, their views on this third point are both diverse and disputed). Other South African elites, however, tend not to share these beliefs so fully or, in most cases, at all. To make matters worse, most members of the non-ANC elites also feel that they have little influence on public affairs and even that they are unfairly discriminated against in a new democratic system based on mass suffrage. They feel alienated and inclined to stand on the sidelines as the government seeks to pursue national integration and greater social justice. And yet the non-ANC elites continue to exercise immense power in many sectors. Their perceptions of poverty and poor people – which include some colossal *mis*perceptions – thus pose serious dilemmas and dangers for the new South Africa.

Methodology

Our research in South Africa closely paralleled the approaches used by colleagues in the other countries addressed in this book. During the first half of 1998, we conducted semi-structured interviews with 108 members of a range of South African elites in four cities – Durban, Johannesburg, Pretoria and Cape Town. Follow-up interviews with a further twelve respondents followed in 1999 and included prosperous farmers in rural areas. We raised questions from a pre-determined list similar to those used in the other countries. But we gave respondents a good deal of latitude to take the discussion where they wished.

We interviewed members of eleven elites. These were: politicians in power, politicians in opposition, people working in the media, educators and professionals, union leaders (in both blue- and white-collar unions), business executives, leaders of voluntary associations (including those which exist to serve the needs of women, minorities and the poor), civil servants, military and police officers, prosperous farmers, and religious leaders. In each category, we sought out fairly senior people who were capable of having an impact on events.

We conducted fewer interviews than in some other countries with certain elites that had less importance in South Africa than elsewhere. For example, we met fewer members of the military elite than did our counterparts in countries that had experienced military rule. Our purpose was to obtain a reasonably accurate picture of the perceptions of a roughly representative sample of South Africa's elites.

We deliberately interviewed a slightly larger number of non-whites, especially 'Africans' (see below), than was strictly justified by their repres-entation in most elites. We did so because a sample reflecting the current composition of many elites would have excluded non-whites entirely, and because the numbers of non-whites – especially Africans – within most elites are on the rise.

If South African society is broken down (as it often is in public dis-course) along such lines, the main groups and their percentages of the total population[2] are roughly as follows.

- Africans – 73 per cent
- whites – 15 per cent
- coloureds – 9 per cent
- Asians – 3 per cent

Profiling poverty and inequality in South Africa

Both poverty and inequality are severe problems in South Africa. An admirably objective government report on the subject opens with a sober-ing sentence: 'In per capita terms South Africa is an upper-middle-income country, but despite this relative wealth, the experience of most South African households is of outright poverty or of continuing vulnerability to being poor' (May 1998). The core problem is not that the nation, taken overall, is poor, but inequality within it. For many years, South Africa had the highest (that is, the worst) Gini coefficient – a measure of inequality – in the world. The latest figures on this place it just behind Brazil, the other sizeable country in which inequality is most extreme – but only just.[3]

Figures from 1994 placed South Africa 90th in a ranking of nations on the United Nations' Human Development Index. It stood below many other countries with lower gross domestic products (GDP) per capita, including Lebanon (whose GDP per capita is just 15 per cent that of South Africa), Suriname, Ecuador, Turkey, Tunisia – and Brazil, its rival as the most inequitable major country (UNDP 1997: 158–60).

The extent of inequality in South Africa is startling. Consider, for example, that 'the top income decile [10 per cent of households which include just 7 per cent of the population] earns approximately half of the total income, or 100 times the share of the bottom income decile' (Nattrass and Seekings forthcoming). The poorest four deciles, which contain around 19 million people or just under half of the population, receive only 11 per cent of total income. This leaves 60 per cent of children in poor households (May 1998: 4). Roughly 40 per cent of the population are in households that consume, per capita, fewer than 2,000 calories each day (Nattrass and Seekings forthcoming). Just under half of the population lacks access to electricity (May 1998: 19).

Inequality is predictably very marked among racial groups. Sixty-one per cent of Africans live below the official poverty line, as against 38 per cent of coloureds, 5 per cent of Asians and 1 per cent of whites. Ninety-three per cent of the unemployed poor are Africans. Among whites, wealth is more equitably distributed than among the other three groups. This subjects the non-white poor to two kinds of disparities (Wilson and Ramphele 1989: 21).

When we break society down in other ways, other important dimensions of inequality become apparent. Gender is important. 'The poverty rate for female-headed households is 60 per cent, compared with 31 per cent for male-headed households.' Fifty-six per cent of the unemployed poor are women (ibid.: 4, 11). The rural/urban divide also counts significantly. Just under half of the country's population is rural, but fully 72 per cent of its poor are rural dwellers. The median incomes of Africans and coloureds living in rural areas are roughly half of those earned by their counterparts in urban centres. 'Average wages in agriculture are well below the minimum living level', and many rural folk cannot find employment – 58 per cent of the unemployed live in the rural sector. Households that are not just poor but severely poor are concentrated on white-owned farms and small villages (ibid.: 25). In many rural areas, people have little or no access to welfare services or basic amenities. Over 80 per cent of rural households have no access to piped water or sanitation, and 74 per cent need to fetch water every day (ibid.: 4, 10, 11, 16, 18).[4] And yet, despite these startling rural/urban disparities, South African elites (as we shall see) almost unanimously regard poverty as an urban problem – rural poverty is, in effect, invisible.

Elite perceptions

Let us contrast in a little more detail the differences between the perceptions of poverty and poor people among elites outside the ruling ANC, and the perceptions of the ANC elite. The term 'ANC elite' refers to senior leaders in the ruling African National Congress, and to prominent figures in the Congress of South African Trade Unions (COSATU), which is part of the ANC (that is, most of the union leaders we interviewed, although we also consulted some who stand outside COSATU). It also refers to a relatively small number of influential people who are closely allied to the ANC and exercise some influence over public policy and political strategy. Some of these allies are senior bureaucrats – almost always political appointees selected by ANC leaders – and others are intellectuals in universities, the media, etc. The term 'non-ANC elites' refers to nearly all members of elites other than those included under two categories: 'politicians in power' and 'union leaders'.

Non-ANC elites' incomplete social consciousness Poverty, as an issue, has only recently become a matter of some concern to most members of South African elites. Only since the early 1990s has it figured much in their vocabulary.[5] There are two ways to look at this, both of which have a certain validity. On the one hand, it is fair to say that elites have never been more aware of poverty, as it is experienced by *all* South Africans,[6] than now. On the other, they have reached this awareness from an exceedingly, even dismally low base.

A comment from an African woman who heads a non-governmental organization proved an accurate summation of the understanding of most white members of elites. 'It's only now that most whites are getting to know what was happening in other parts of South Africa [under apartheid] ... the pain and hunger of the poor ... and they still have much to learn.'[7] A distinguished African editor of an indigenous-language newspaper explained part of the problem. He said that the English-language press, on which much of the white elite relies, ' ... used to ignore the problems of ordinary Africans. In recent years, there has been some improvement. That press now *does* report serious issues, but poverty is still a somewhat secondary issue.'[8]

Most of our respondents had a reasonably accurate estimate of the *numbers* of South Africans who lived in poverty – they usually gave figures in the 60–70 per cent range. But these fairly accurate estimates were accompanied by a number of other curious perceptions. They tended *not* to see poverty as an urgent issue or even as an especially severe problem for the poor. Most believed that even those people who face extreme poverty manage to survive at a very basic level thanks to a combination of things: resourcefulness and reliance on others, a sense of community and collective responsibility which is regarded as very strong among the African population.

Coupled with this view are a startling *mis*perception and a remarkable *non*-perception. The misperception concerns levels of inequality in South Africa. *Nearly all* respondents firmly rejected the idea that theirs is a particularly unequal society. Many regarded Brazil and India as worse – despite evidence which clearly shows that Brazil (an extremely unequal society) is roughly similar to South Africa, and that India is far less unequal.[9] They therefore felt that they need not be any more embarrassed about inequality than elites in many other countries. They (especially but not only white respondents) tended to believe that as long as basic needs are met, the fact that a thin layer of very wealthy people remains should not be considered objectionable.

Many pointed to other countries in Africa where some equalization has taken place, the top layer has been pulled down, and standards have dropped for everyone. In their view, this has not helped to reduce poverty and is an approach that they wish to avoid. Indeed, they view South Africa's poor as well off, at least relative to other parts of Africa – partly because the top layer has not been pulled down. For a large majority of our respondents, the existence of what they refer to as a 'First World community' alongside a Third World majority in South Africa is a source of optimism and pride, not of concern. They believe that their First World economy, infrastructure, education and skills give the country hope for the uplift of the poor.

Their colossal misperception of inequality is accompanied by a remarkable non-perception – their failure to recognize the extent and the gravity of *rural* poverty. Respondents seldom referred to this issue – and those who did so were overwhelmingly Africans, who had relatives and friends in rural areas. When we raised the problem of rural poverty, it was usually greeted with incredulity. Non-ANC elites tended strongly to see poverty in purely urban terms. As one African woman who works among convicts put it, 'they have not been there'. They have not visited the places where poor rural dwellers struggle to survive, so they cannot and do not see rural poverty as a problem. Rural dwellers were usually seen by elites as having easier access to the means of survival – especially food – than their urban counterparts. The invisibility of rural poverty is a deeply serious concern, given the widespread and grievous nature of that problem.

All of this informs a discussion of a social consciousness that exists when elites develop

1 an awareness of the interdependence of all social groups;
2 a realization that elites bear some of the responsibility for the suffer-
   ings of the poor; and
3 a belief that efficacious means of assisting the poor exist or might be
   created.

Let us consider the first two of these items. The efforts of the ANC elite
and others who seek to promote national reconciliation and integration
have begun to persuade some members of other elites of the interdependence of all social groups in South Africa, including the poor. But most
elites outside the ANC circle still stop well short of a full acceptance of
that idea. We found them much more inclined to focus on and to accept the interdependence of the country's diverse *elites* – across ethnic
lines (despite some inevitable tensions).[10] This is hardly surprising, since
events since 1990 have thrown diverse elites together. Inter-elite links are
perhaps a step towards a fully fledged social consciousness, but they have
also served as a potent distraction from a more thoroughgoing sense of
interdependence.

Some in the ANC – not least President Thabo Mbeki – are inclined to
press elites (especially whites) to accept an all-embracing social consciousness. But white elites tend to recoil from this as anti-white posturing. Many
whites feel threatened by affirmative action and other recent changes.
Even though they have retained many of their former privileges, and even
though the old socio-economic order has been largely preserved, many
of them have reacted in a way that Africans regard as unreasonable. On
several occasions, white respondents told us that because they continue
to possess great economic power but now lack concomitant political influence, they feel unfairly discriminated against. In response, many felt
inclined to stand on the sidelines, to make no contribution to society, and
to leave problems such as poverty to the government.

In the West, a belief among elites in the interconnectedness of all social
groups was encouraged by elite perceptions of *threats* to their well-being
from the poor. Three such worries were particularly important – a belief
that epidemics might develop among the poor which could spread to elite
areas, fears of insurrection by the poor, and crimes against elites committed by desperate poor people. Let us consider each of these in turn in the
case of South Africa.

EPIDEMIC/DISEASE Most respondents were surprised by questions about
this threat. The issue had not occurred to them before. They did not regard
it as a possibility. Poor health for much of the population was both a cause

and a consequence of poverty, but this was not seen to pose a threat to the rest of society. This indicates an elite ignorance of the seriousness of health issues in South Africa. Tuberculosis is a widespread and increasing problem among Africans. There have also been outbreaks of cholera in cities such as Cape Town, and malaria is reportedly making a comeback. The migration of poor people to cities has intensified these problems. Squatter camps on the periphery of metropolitan centres pose a health hazard. But elites regard these as diseases of the poor, which pose no threat as health and sanitation services improve. Despite the growing exposure of elites to other groups since the end of apartheid, there is still little close contact between these groups. And if elites fall ill, they can purchase first-rate treatment. Their only real concern is the spread of AIDS, which many believe has reached epidemic proportions. AIDS, however, is not viewed as a threat to the non-poor by the poor but as a problem extending right across different groups in society.

For many of our respondents, the real threat of disease is not the possibility of contagion, but that the costs to government of dealing with such problems will erode its financial resources and perhaps result in higher taxes. Some respondents, however, held the cynical view that an epidemic that wiped out large numbers of the poor might serve the government's interests by easing the demand for services.

It must be stressed, however, that African members of elites – many of whom live closer to the urban poor and understand the wretched conditions they face – are less sanguine. One of them told us, for example, that epidemics are a 'real possibility' and that it is 'just luck' that nothing significant has yet happened.[11] But Africans still fail to figure sufficiently in the elites more generally to drive this message home among others of elite status.

REBELLION/POLITICAL INSTABILITY Few respondents thought that the poor were likely to rebel in the medium term. There was a widespread perception among non-ANC elites that they are in what one senior bureaucrat described as 'a post-revolutionary phase'.[12] It is more accurate to say that they have come through a transfer of political power, a negotiated settlement that was intended to head off a revolution.[13] Most elites believe that their democracy is stable enough, their institutions are resilient enough and their country is too well developed for the African majority to rebel against a government that they elected. For these reasons, most members of elites tend not to accept the warning by Archbishop Desmond Tutu that unless the needs of the poor are effectively addressed, elite privileges will eventually be swept away.

CRIME The only threat that *might* be linked to poverty which produces acute anxiety among elites of all ethnic backgrounds is crime. Indeed, it is difficult to over-state the alarm on this issue, especially among white and Asian elites. For many respondents, crime has come close to replacing apartheid as *the* national problem. It is perceived as damaging the economy, by deterring tourism and discouraging foreign investment, thus hindering growth.

Elites' perceptions of crime vary somewhat across racial lines. White elites showed a much greater fear of crime and worried more about the crime rates constantly going up. They firmly believe that crime has worsened since 1994, despite statistics showing either a stabilization or a decrease in serious crime. While many whites acknowledged that not all poor people are criminals, some took the view that Africans and the poor think that crime is an acceptable form of redistribution or vengeance. In reality, the poor are the victims of crime far more often than the middle class or elites, but this has not entirely registered with the latter.

Anxiety over crime tends not to persuade South African elites of the interdependence of all social groups – for several reasons. In so far as the poor are perceived to be perpetrators of crimes, this tends to produce alienation from the poor more often than a sense that something must be done about poverty. Most respondents tended to see the *non*-poor as the source of a great deal of crime, particularly those types of crime which they regard as most threatening. They tend to distinguish between *crimes of need* and *crimes of greed*. The first category, which may be linked to poverty and blamed on the poor, includes petty crimes. Most of our respondents did not feel gravely threatened by this, because they think that they can buy the necessary protection from it. Fortified houses and businesses, sophisticated alarm systems and private security guards are a visible feature of life in affluent neighbourhoods in South Africa. Crimes of greed include white-collar crimes such as corruption and tax evasion and, much more importantly, serious violent crimes such as hijacking, heists, drug smuggling and murder. This type of crime is mainly attributed to the dramatic rise in well-organized criminal syndicates. As a result, where crime is the issue, poverty alleviation is not seen as a solution.

Crime is also seen to have been caused, in part, by things that have little to do with poverty – the perceived failure of the government to take forceful action, difficulties in a judicial system adjusting to a new culture of rights, popular distrust (for historical reasons) of the police. So elites' threat perceptions tend not to incline them towards either a belief in the interdependence of all social groups, or a conviction that action must be taken against poverty in order to reduce threats.

Let us now turn to the third element of a 'social consciousness', the belief that *efficacious means* either exist or might be created to reduce poverty. Most respondents were sceptical about the efficacy of redistributive anti-poverty programmes as antidotes to poverty – for four main reasons (apart from their fear that redistribution would mean an increase in what they see as an excessively high tax burden).

The least important is a belief among a minority of respondents that South Africa lacks the financial resources to make a substantial impact on poverty – a dubious notion in an upper-middle-income country. Since most saw huge numbers of people living in poverty, they felt daunted by the scale of the problem. Second, some (again a minority) regarded the bureaucracy as too rigid and inefficient. But most crucially, many more respondents worried that corruption in (and beyond) government would cripple its capacity to achieve much of anything, including poverty reduction. The empirical evidence indicates that elites tend substantially to over-state corruption's importance. The problem receives more attention now partly because the present government is far more transparent.[14] But even though this is something of a misperception, it still fosters doubts in elite minds that efficacious means can be created to tackle poverty – unless economic growth takes off.

We discuss growth further below, but elites' belief in it as the main answer to poverty has one attraction for them which – together with another idea – has impeded the development of a full social consciousness. It requires little action and no fresh sacrifices from elites, and thus allows them to distance themselves from a sense of responsibility for tackling poverty. That distancing is reinforced by their explanation for the origin of poverty in South Africa. It can be summarized in one word – apartheid, which was something from which nearly all respondents also distanced themselves. Their thinking on this subject proceeds as follows.

Apartheid was an immense experiment in social engineering which deliberately fostered structural inequalities in society and, in the process, caused massive poverty. It had the unintended effect of impoverishing South Africa more generally, by denying opportunities to many talented people to contribute to the nation's economic well-being, and by cutting South Africa off from many markets. Hardly any respondents felt personally responsible for apartheid. It was something that a rather small Afrikaner elite had developed. They therefore did not see themselves as contributors to the problem of poverty in South Africa. And most reasoned that since apartheid was the main cause of poverty, the dismantling of it should – on its own – open the way to a reduction in poverty. This optimistic view stands incongruously alongside their pessimism about efficacious means of addressing poverty. But we none the less encountered this incongruity quite often. This logic – like their belief in growth – enables elites to remain comfortably at one remove from the immense problem of poverty.

The ANC elite: redistribution versus growth Despite all this, many members of South Africa's *ruling* elite – the ANC elite and its allies and network of advisers – possess something close to a fully developed 'social consciousness'. A large majority of them accept the first two of its core elements. Their difficulties in tackling poverty arise partly from the need to operate in a democratic system amid other elites with an incomplete 'social consciousness'. But their main problem is their own uncertainty about the most 'efficacious means' of addressing poverty, about which anti-poverty strategy to employ.

The ANC elite consists of three main groups: (i) senior figures who went into exile to sustain the struggle from havens elsewhere, (ii) those who were imprisoned on Robben Island, and (iii) leaders of the mass campaigns within South Africa during the 1980s, who emerged from the United Democratic Front and the Congress of South African Trade Unions (COSATU). Since the late 1980s, the first two of these groups have largely taken control, and those from the third have been relegated mainly to secondary roles.

The ANC, after its arduous struggle against apartheid, is a highly centralized organization. Since taking power, ANC leaders have consolidated their control over the wider organization. All major policy decisions have been made at or near the top, and members are required to stick closely to them. Internal dissent is highly unusual, and when dissenters emerge, they tend to be marginalized rather than expelled. Urban professionals dominate the party, and most stand at a considerable distance from the poor, especially the rural poor.

This is ironic, since the ANC's greatest electoral support comes from the poor, especially the rural poor. It has attracted that support by projecting itself as a body representing the nation – and the greater part of the nation consists of impoverished people. Despite the loyalty of the rural poor (or paradoxically, because it is so dependable), the ANC elite pays greater heed to two other groups: urban dwellers in general, including the poor, and (more importantly in their eyes) the much smaller, upwardly mobile and overwhelmingly urban socio-economic elites – most of whom do not share its fairly well-developed social consciousness. The ANC elite has sought to foster a fuller social consciousness among these others, but this will take time. For the present, they seek to carry these groups with them in the tasks of national reconstruction and reconciliation – and this means that they cannot confront their social attitudes aggressively. They must therefore restrain themselves from pursuing the redistribution of wealth as forcefully as many of them might wish. They are further restrained from such redistributive efforts by (i) international pressure to maintain fiscal discipline, an open economy and a drive for economic growth, (ii) the limited financial resources available to them, and (iii) the perceived inadequacy of the administrative instruments available to them.

Most members of the ANC elite would like to redistribute resources in this exceedingly unequal society – both because it would promote social justice, and because it may become politically necessary if it is to retain mass support. Commitments to redistribution are evident even in South Africa's 1996 constitution,[15] but our main concern here is the government's development strategy.

The government initially set out to stress redistribution over growth, through its Reconstruction and Development Programme (RDP).[16] But this was soon superseded by a more growth-oriented strategy that has imposed tight fiscal constraints in order to attract foreign investment – the 'Growth Employment and Restructuring' (GEAR) programme. This has curtailed redistributive efforts under the RDP, which in theory lives on. In the 1999 budget, for example, all but one redistributive department under the RDP suffered cuts in real terms. Water and sanitation programmes were cut by 19.9 per cent, rural development by 14.3 per cent, housing by 14.4 per cent, health by 2.2 per cent, education (national and provincial) by 0.7 per cent, and pensions by 3.6 per cent. By contrast, taxes on corporations were reduced, and the overall exercise was described by a Deloitte and Touche manager as 'a very good budget for the wealthier'.[17]

Pro-growth forces in the ANC argued that, despite the shortfall in redistribution, enough would have been achieved in reversing the racist practices of the old regime and in providing some basic goods, services and benefits to needy people to persuade poor voters to back the ANC again in the election of 1999. The results of that election proved them right.[18] They were mightily helped by the grotesque character of the apartheid regime. As long as it remains the main point of comparison in the popular mind, even minimal achievements offer a glittering contrast. But growing restiveness since 1999 suggests that in the future the ANC's performance will be increasingly judged against its own promises of greater social justice, and not against the apartheid era. That increases the pressure for redistribution, but thus far the ANC government has stubbornly stressed the drive for growth.

The international context has had a significant impact on the decision of the ANC elite to rely mainly on growth to combat poverty. International aid has been relatively unimportant. South Africa depends less (sometimes far less) on aid than the other countries assessed in this book, and all elites recognize this. But pressure from the international economic order to pursue policies that are market friendly, in order to attract foreign investment, has had a huge influence. The government since the mid-1990s has gone to great lengths to comply, and has persisted with these measures – even though investment flows and the growth that might follow from them have been sorely disappointing.

As a senior banker told us, the government 'has done everything right except on privatization (which has been tardy) and introducing greater flexibility into the labour market'.[19] GDP growth was 3.1 per cent in 1996, but dropped to 1.7 per cent in 1997, a dismal figure. It was 0.5 per cent in 1998. The latter two figures are below the population growth rate, and have next to no impact on unemployment. Since then, growth has picked up but only a little. The key issue, however, is not the current rate, but whether growth will accelerate.

There are, crudely speaking, two broad views on this. *Optimists* argue that the economy is temporarily at a low point in an adjustment process and that, once South Africa has made the painful transition, it will play a dynamic role in the global environment. They expect a take-off of perhaps 7–10 per cent by 2005 – if the rains are plentiful, if the gold price does not decline, and if there is no major downturn in the world economy.[20] *Pessimists* doubt that growth will accelerate much, even if those conditions are met. Anxieties about the potential for growth (and about jobless growth) were expressed even by social scientists in Thabo Mbeki's office.[21]

They wonder whether South Africa can prosper as a low-cost producer with cheap labour when unions have such political influence and when concerns over human rights protect the interests of workers in the organized sector. They note that domestic savings rates are low, which limits resources for growth-oriented investment, because taxes are deemed to be high. The legacy of apartheid includes low levels of human resource development, which further curtail the country's capacity to be productive and competitive. The current growth-oriented strategy holds back investment in education that would promote growth over the longer term, and the management of education funds has been poor.

Even some optimists, including senior government officials whom we interviewed, fear that growth may not generate many jobs. This argues for two things, which receive little emphasis from the GEAR strategy. Both were occasionally mentioned by African members of elites. The first is funding and advice to poor peri-urban and rural folk, to enable them to develop small enterprises. The second is land reform, to enable some of the rural poor to become self-sufficient owner-cultivators. If either of these things is to be pursued vigorously, it will require a shift in emphasis from growth to redistribution, and greater attention to rural poverty.

One other element of the ANC elite's outlook is noteworthy. If other elites look mainly to the state to tackle poverty, the ANC elite is strongly determined to claim that role for the government it heads. This may sound incongruous coming from an elite that has sought to promote market-led growth. But the ANC has fostered corporatist arrangements that are intended to bind industry (and organized labour) closely to it. This is partly intended to ensure stability during a difficult transition. But it is mainly driven by the ANC elite's suspicion of pluralism, and of autonomous power centres. It has successfully built on its position as the dominant party to draw major industrial firms and banks – along with COSATU – into consultative structures that give the government the upper hand on grand policy questions. The ANC elite's discomfort with pluralism is also evident in its exclusion of most important non-governmental organizations from the policy process and from resource flows – including those from international donors which, under apartheid, often went to those organizations. It takes this line even with those organizations that served as its allies in the anti-apartheid struggle. Many now criticize its reliance on growth to reduce poverty, as does COSATU – although the latter has been substantially co-opted within corporatist structures.

This discussion of the alternatives available to the ANC is warranted by the strong belief among all elites that the government carries the main responsibility for anti-poverty initiatives. Even those who see its main role as creating conditions for market-led growth have serious doubts about whether growth can benefit the poor. This suggests a need for greater redistribution, with the state taking the lead. To understand why elites look to the government as the main anti-poverty force, we must consider another reality that shapes their thinking – social segmentation.

Social segmentation

South Africa is a *segmented* society. It is divided by lines running vertically down through society from elite to mass levels, fragmenting it into distinct social blocs (or segments). In South Africa, segments tend to be groups with similar primordial or 'ethnic' origins – Xhosas, Zulus, Afrikaners, other whites, people of mixed race, Asians, etc. Some readers might prefer the use of the term 'ethnic' groups to describe these collectivities, but this term tends to be rather unhelpful in several ways.[22] So the alternative term 'segmentation' is used here.

We saw above that South African elites' incomplete social consciousness undermines support for efforts to tackle poverty among *all* South Africans. But in such a segmented society, do elites possess a more immediate and compelling sense of obligation to the poor within their own social segment? It is important to stress that if they did, their perceptions would fail to conform to de Swaan's concept of a 'social consciousness' in two ways. First, their concerns would *not* be focused on the poor of their country *in general* – and thus they would lack the universalistic quality that de Swaan's concept requires. Second, their concern might be seen to be motivated more by a sense of identity with the poor of their particular segment, rather than by considerations of elite self-interest – which is another feature of de Swaan's concept.[23] So this analysis of elite attitudes to poor people within their own social segments focuses *not* on an alternative means of developing a social consciousness, but rather on a set of perceptions that would *undercut* a social consciousness. If such perceptions loomed large in the minds of South African elites, they would thus be a counterweight to a social consciousness worth noting.

So let us return to our question: do elites possess a more immediate and compelling sense of obligation to the poor within their own social segment? In most cases, the answer is 'not to any great degree'.

To explain why that is true, we must understand four distinctive features of social segmentation in South Africa:

1 it is not always clear what a given person's social segment is;
2 the *distance* (geographical, social, educational, economic, psychological) between elites and the poor within segments in South Africa is greater than in many other countries;
3 the social segments that are most real to South African elites tend to be larger than similar segments in many other countries – in, for example, South Asia;
4 Two imperatives – to develop (a) broad political alliances within South Africa's new democratic system, and (b) an inclusive new national identity that transcends segments – are seen to be more urgent in South Africa than they are in many other countries.

All four of these things undermine elites' sense of obligation to poor people within their segments. Let us consider each in turn.

Confusion about what one's social segment is What social segments do we encounter in South Africa? This is not an easy question to answer. If we consider the usual list of social categories – whites, 'coloureds', 'Africans' and Asians – we find that most are divided internally. To speak of 'Asians' is to ignore divisions between Hindus and Muslims. The term 'whites' ignores the division between Afrikaners and English speakers. To speak of 'Africans' is to ignore various 'ethnic', linguistic and other divisions among them. But to focus on those 'ethnic' groupings[24] is to ignore the sense of commonality, born of shared oppression, among different groups of Africans and among non-whites more generally.

In other words, all South Africans have available to them a diversity of identities which compete with one another for their attention. A person may, for example, be a Xhosa, but s/he will also be aware of pan-African, national, regional, local, clan or family, class, urban/rural, political party, religious and other identities. Some of these identities can be seen as 'segmental' while others cannot. But since many cut across one another, their larger 'segmental' loyalties to the Xhosas, Zulus, Afrikaners or whatever tend to be undermined at least somewhat. People sometimes shift their preoccupations from one to another of the various identities available to them, according to circumstance and recent events. So to ask people what social segments they belong to tends to elicit somewhat different answers at different times, and answers are sometimes multi-faceted. Elite perceptions in these matters are less clear than those of people of lesser status. If a member of an elite is unclear about the boundaries of his/her social segment, this tends to undermine his/her sense of obligation to poor people within that segment.

Distance between elites and the poor within segments Consider also the various types of distance that separate elites from poor people within social segments. This problem is more marked in South Africa than in South Asia. Members of elites often find themselves distanced from the poor geographically – (i) in terms of urban/rural or urban/peri-urban separations, and (ii) in terms of inter-regional separations.

The urban/rural divide is discussed in detail elsewhere here, so let us merely note that poverty is particularly serious in rural areas while elites are overwhelmingly concentrated in towns and cities. Thus elites within social segments that contain large numbers of poor rural folk are spatially cut off from the poor within their own segments.

Within the great conurbations of South Africa, geographical distance between areas inhabited by elites of all descriptions (usually leafy suburbs) and those inhabited by the poor (squatter colonies and townships in other suburbs or in city centres) also separates elites – spatially and psychologically – from the poor in their own segments. This is especially important among Africans and people of mixed race. Our encounters with members of African elites indicate that far more of them remain in townships, and are thus concerned about poor neighbours from their own social segment, than is often supposed. But the movement to the suburbs is still a significant reality that will continue. So the problem of African elites being cut off from poverty among others in their segments is quite genuine.

The distances between the regions of this large country also play a role here. In the apartheid era there was considerable spatial mobility among elites, mainly whites. In recent years, as non-whites have been freed from racist restrictions on their movements, such mobility has greatly accelerated. It is important to note that South Africa lacks a single, pre-eminent city in which elites are mainly concentrated. It is thus common to find members of South African elites – of all descriptions these days – living at great distances from most of the people in their social segments. Spatial distance – within conurbations and between regions – further erodes a sense among elites of personalized obligation to the poor within their segments.

Other types of distance compound the problem. Most members of elites stand at a considerable (and often a vast) economic distance from the poor within their social segments. Most members of elites have acquired high-quality education which puts another sort of distance between them and the poor within their segments. Economic and educational distancing fosters and is reinforced by an enormous psychological distance between elites and poor people within various segments. We found that, contrary to prevailing clichés, many members of the emerging African elites still live modestly by the standards of white South Africans (often in townships) and cannot imagine driving BMWs. But most of them still enjoy substantially greater incomes and far greater access to the abundance offered by South Africa's 'First World' milieu than their poor brethren. Most have internalized many 'First World' habits of mind. All this has (usually, though not always) had a deracinating impact on them and has created considerable psychological distance between them and even the urban and peri-urban poor within their segments.

This is true even within the segment that was most cosseted by the apartheid regime – the Afrikaners. From the 1920s onwards, the Afrikaner elite was concerned with the problems of the poor within their own segment. They had a well-developed but perverse 'social consciousness' towards the Afrikaner poor, and they sought to use state power to generate a 'sponsored bourgeoisie' that included as many Afrikaners as possible.[25] By the early 1990s, however – after many (but by no means all) Afrikaners had been enriched – the Afrikaner elite 'peacefully negotiated away their position of ethnic dominance' on the assumption that this would prevent the emergence of a radical new order. They reckoned that the 'rights culture of a liberal democracy' and 'the global predominance of a competitive market economy' would protect their material comforts. 'However, it meant that the poorer Afrikaners were left to fend for themselves in a vastly more hostile and competitive environment.' They 'sold out' the poor Afrikaners (Adam et al. 1997: 58, 61).

The size of segments Most social segments in South Africa are quite large – far larger, for example, than the endogamous caste groups that preoccupy elites in much of India, or the kinship networks that preoccupy Bangladeshi elites. These South Asian collectivities are usually small enough to make face-to-face relations between elites and many poor people within the segment possible. The sheer size of South African categories – Xhosas, Zulus, Afrikaners, etc. – makes it difficult for a member of an elite from one of these groups to feel personally obligated to the generality (or even to a sizeable proportion) of the poor within his or her segment.

Efforts to transcend segmentation Most of South Africa's political parties seek to develop broad-based social coalitions which require loyalties and alliances that cut across social segments. They do so because the imperatives of electoral politics demand it, and because it is in the interests of national integration and of the democratic process. Most members of elites are also preoccupied with the need to create a new, all-inclusive national identity that transcends segments. There is clear evidence that these efforts are meeting with a degree of success, and they are reinforced by other processes that are at work.

All these things are, in most respects, immensely valuable. But we also need to recognize that such transcendence undermines the already weak sense of obligation to poor people within their social segments which elites perceive. Elites have become preoccupied with the impersonal obligation of the government and the ruling party to provide for the needs of the poor – which implies a de-emphasis of their more personalized obligations to the poor within their social segments. It also shifts the burden from private philanthropic efforts within segments to impersonal, government programmes and policies to address the needs of the poor in all segments.

The four things discussed above do not erase social segmentation in South Africa. It retains enough importance to impede both the full development of a social consciousness among most elites and the emergence of a commitment among those elites to initiatives that address the needs of all the poor. At the same time, these four things possess enough potency to undermine elite efforts to address the needs of the poor within their social segments. Even where certain agencies seek to promote this – the African Zionist churches stand out as a rare example – the scattering and social dislocation that the poor within most segments have experienced make it very difficult to achieve. So we should not expect anti-poverty efforts within segments to do much to compensate for the incomplete social consciousness that prevails among most South African elites. This implies that initiatives to tackle poverty will have to come from the government.

The invisibility of rural poverty

Poverty in rural South Africa is widespread and deeply serious. Our respondents consistently estimated that 60 to 80 per cent of the population qualify as 'poor'. Since huge numbers of people live in rural areas, it follows logically that rural poverty should be a serious concern. But our respondents seldom drew that inference. The poverty that is visible to them is urban, and most of them scarcely recognize the existence of rural poverty. This was especially true among white elites. Elite Africans often have at least tenuous links to relatives on the land (or know other Africans who do), so that they are more conscious of the seriousness of the problem. But even they give it relatively little attention.

Most members of urban elites whom we interviewed told us that even the worst-off rural dwellers do not face extreme difficulties because they can subsist adequately on food that they grow themselves. This notion enjoys currency in most of the other countries examined in this book.

Political elites have developed programmes to assist the rural poor, but such efforts are not as widespread as they might be. Inter-party competition, at and between elections, tends to be much more closely contested in urban areas than in the rural sector. So the urban sector is seen as the main political battleground, and ruling parties at both national and provincial levels usually pay more attention to urban than to rural needs.[26] Additionally, the three key elites within the ANC (COSATU, the South African Communist Party and those who spent years in exile) are all preoccupied with urban issues.

Non-ANC urban elites – including African elites in townships – also tend to regard the rural poor, particularly women, with condescension and even distrust. When an official commission recommended an extension of child benefits (at, inevitably, a much reduced per capita rate) to mothers in rural areas, howls of outrage emerged from these elites. This reaction revealed elite doubts that such recipients could manage such money responsibly, and their lack of awareness of how severe the destitution of rural households actually is. Our elite respondents also strongly resisted the idea that a redistribution of rural lands should occur, because it would undermine agricultural productivity. Even efforts to restore lands that had been seized from Africans during the apartheid era were frowned upon.[27]

The need for national reconciliation was often invoked as a reason for this. Predominantly white elites saw this in terms of reconciling whites rather than poor people to the new order.

Non-ANC elites, resource issues and poverty

Let us now examine the views of non-ANC elites on three critically important resource issues: on poverty and South Africa's economy, on the current use by the ANC government of public funds, and on the thorny matter of taxation.

Poverty and the South African economy Non-ANC elites see widespread, severe poverty as a drain on the economy and on the government, which has to provide for the poor. It is thus regarded as something that holds back the rest of society. There was general agreement that in the long run everybody suffers from extensive poverty because it entails a serious waste of human potential. (We see here the beginnings of a belief in the interdependence of all social groups.) The economy as a whole suffers because poor people are capable only of low productivity, and because the presence of large numbers of indigents implies that internal markets will be small, limiting the opportunities for businesses to expand.

The use of financial resources Does this then imply that financial resources should be used to attack poverty – by way of programmes to provide housing, primary healthcare, vaccinations, clean water, sanitation and sewage, education, pensions, child support, etc.? Most non-ANC respondents were unenthusiastic about programmes such as direct cash transfers to the poor, but more sympathetic to longer-term programmes such as education, which was seen to have promise in equipping the poor to lift themselves out of poverty and in enhancing human resources required for accelerated economic growth.

While there was general agreement among most of these respondents that in principle the poor should have access to housing, water, electricity, education, welfare, etc., the limited resources available to the government mean that some programmes need to be prioritized over others. This led members of non-ANC elites to question, for example, the importance of healthcare or housing schemes – because in their view, if the poor lack the funds to maintain their houses or pay for such services, these programmes would merely add to their problems. Many thought that such schemes should not be given priority – because they were expensive, and because (however beneficial they may be in improving living conditions) they do little to help the poor escape from poverty.

Taxes When discussing policies that could help the poor, scarcely any members of non-ANC elites volunteered the idea of tax increases as a way to fund them. Instead, they put their trust in economic growth, which would (if it occurred) generate the necessary revenues. When the question of further taxation was put to them directly, it met with emphatic rejection by a large majority of respondents. Tax increases were viewed as 'controversial', 'problematic', 'counterproductive' and 'a dangerous idea'.

They were vehemently opposed to further increases in direct income tax, and they showed little support for most other forms of taxation. But many were prepared to entertain proposals for greater taxes on very high incomes and on luxury goods.

Most respondents acknowledged their obligations towards the state, and were aware both of the resource problems facing government and of the need for a degree of redistribution. They felt strongly, however, that they were very heavily taxed and that a very small section of society is being asked to fund everything and carry the burden for the whole country. The payment of taxes was viewed as a form of sacrifice which citizens are rightly expected to make, but respondents felt that this was a sacrifice they were already making in abundance. Many white respondents saw this sacrifice as a way of atoning for the errors of the past, for apartheid – but they also tended to argue that this cannot go on for ever and that there comes a point when taxes simply become too prohibitive. Most of those who expressed this view felt that they had already reached this point. Their solution to this problem was the expansion of the tax base by creating more middle-income earners and by targeting people currently operating outside the formal economy.

The perception that one of the weaknesses of the South African tax system is the high degree of tax evasion and avoidance was strongly held among most white respondents. A degree of racial bias came into play here. While it was acknowledged that many Africans were excluded from the tax base simply because they have little income, many white members of elites felt that a section of the African population was getting away with not paying any taxes and living off the white minority who do. Indeed, African families on middle incomes were sometimes viewed as having considerably more disposable income than their white counterparts because they were not locked into the same tax system – a dubious proposition. Many white respondents attributed this to the culture of non-payment fostered among Africans during the struggle to end apartheid, which continues to influence attitudes towards taxes. As a result, many Africans were seen as wanting to enjoy public services without paying for them. White respondents repeatedly insisted that Africans must learn to understand the link between giving and receiving.

A restructuring of the tax system and more effective collection of taxes were widely seen as alternatives to higher taxes. Devolving power from national to provincial government over taxation was suggested as one way of ensuring that people share in the perception that their taxes are being spent efficiently – although some respondents were concerned at reports that certain provincial governments were highly inefficient or worse. Introducing a specific tax for a direct programme of action such as housing, education or poverty relief might also find some support among elites. For example, plans for a one-off windfall tax on the future demutualization of two large insurance companies, which will be used to create a new fund aimed at job creation, were welcomed as an innovative way to raise revenue. There was also some support for the Skills and Development Bill, which entailed a levy of 1–1.5 per cent on business to fund industry-specific education and training and a national skills fund.

Implications

Let us now consider the implications of all this. It is important to stress that while much of our evidence will make depressing reading for those who want to see poverty and inequality tackled in South Africa through redistribution, it also offers them some encouragement.

To begin with, the bad news: South African elites believe that they are well informed both about their own country and about how it compares to other similar cases in the wider world, but some of their misperceptions or non-perceptions are still quite startling. They are so startling that it is arguable that the gap between what they think they understand and what they actually grasp is greater here than in the cases analysed in other chapters of this book.

They do not regard the existence of the First World milieu in which they live as a problem for poor people. They do not grasp that inequalities in South Africa are greater than almost anywhere else. They do not see that such yawning inequalities create a clear threat of political instability which could test both the strength of South Africa's liberal institutions (from which elites derive both pride and reassurance) and the capacity of the ruling ANC elite to maintain some sort of settled order.

It is encouraging that most members of the ANC elite possess something like a fully developed social consciousness. But the incomplete social consciousness of non-ANC elites remains troubling, for several reasons. The ANC elite mixes constantly with members of other elites, and the perceptions of the latter could – over time – undermine the ruling elite's social consciousness. This could become more likely if the ANC breaks its links to or distances itself from the South African Communist Party and/or COSATU, since those groups help to maintain the ANC elite's social consciousness. Indeed, since the turn of the millennium the ANC has indeed begun distancing itself from COSATU. ANC leaders are also acutely aware of the need to keep many in those other elites from becoming alienated. They have increasingly aligned themselves with an emergent group of wealthy Africans whose social consciousness scarcely exists. Some analysts fear that these trends may cause senior leaders in the ANC to dilute their efforts to tackle poverty and inequality.

But our evidence also indicates that things could go the other way – there is also good news here for those who favour redistribution. Despite their incomplete social consciousness, the comments of many non-ANC elite respondents strongly suggest that they might become more amenable to efforts to address poverty and inequality. A discussion of how this might occur will reveal another, intriguing side to elite perceptions of poverty in South Africa.

Our interviews clearly showed that non-ANC elites would respond powerfully to a realization that they live in one of the most inequitable societies on earth. There is plenty of evidence that could persuade them that the end of apartheid and the political transformation have not solved this problem. Indeed, these things have made the problem more urgent, since they have created expectations among many poor people that economic betterment will ensue.

It is also entirely possible to persuade elites that poverty is an exceedingly serious problem in terms not just of relative deprivation, but in absolute terms for vast numbers of their fellow citizens. Abundant evidence of this has also been collected. Our interviews plainly indicate that if this were publicized in a non-confrontational tone (more in sorrow than in anger, through appeals to the better nature of elites) the message would not alienate prosperous South Africans. They could also, and without great difficulty, be convinced by the substantial evidence on the extent and depth of poverty in *rural* areas.

Our interviews further demonstrate that elites would respond to evidence that poverty poses both a greater *threat* to their well-being than they usually suppose and that poor people constitute an important potential *resource* for the nation. Both ideas would help to persuade them of the interdependence of all social groups – one element of a social consciousness. Their threat perceptions could be made more acute and realistic if they were acquainted with evidence of the extent to which certain communicable diseases afflict poor people in South Africa – for example (there are others), tuberculosis. But the main emphasis here could be placed on the *potential* that poor people offer. A sizeable minority of our elite respondents already saw the poor as a source of considerable potential. They believe that their country is not productive enough and that its human resources are being under-used. They told us that, if it had not been for apartheid, which damaged the potential of the vast majority of the population, South Africa would have become a much more productive country. And even elites that have not voiced such views are open to the idea that it is in their interests to develop this potential by bringing the poor into the development process. Many of them believe that, in this information age, basic education is a priority for every country.

Elite doubts that efficacious means exist or might be created to tackle poverty are reinforced by the failure of economic growth – one possible means – to accelerate. But since many members of elites cling to a belief in growth because it absolves them of further responsibility, an erosion of that belief has positive implications for those who favour redistribution.

There is clearly a need to address elites' lack of faith in their government as a satisfactory instrument in the struggle against poverty – and again, our evidence suggests that many of them are open to this. Despite constraints on investment in anti-poverty programmes, the government has plainly made significant headway in certain key sectors. If elites became more aware of this, our interviews indicate that many would become more inclined to regard government as an effective force for poverty reduction, and even to tolerate somewhat higher taxes – especially on luxury items and very high incomes – to fund anti-poverty programmes. Many were also prepared to accept higher taxes with good grace, if headway is made on bringing prosperous people in the informal sector into the tax net. The government's efforts to achieve this are again worth publicizing.

It is also worth stressing that much of the popular perception of corruption in government is the result of the greater transparency that has existed since the end of apartheid. Our evidence indicates that this would also help to persuade many members of elites that they are getting a more satisfactory return on their tax payments.

Finally, our evidence demonstrates that most members of elites would respond to arguments that persisting inequalities discredit South Africa and its 'First World' achievements in the eyes of the wider world. More crucially, elites might be persuaded by evidence that these inequalities add up to an inherently unstable socio-economic order which threatens both national reconciliation (in which most elites feel that they have a stake) and South Africa's political settlement (about which most elites feel mightily relieved and, often, proud).

Notes

1 We are grateful to the British Department for International Development for funding this study under a grant for poverty research to the Institute of Development Studies, University of Sussex. Thanks are also due to the University of Natal, Durban, and the University of Pretoria for assistance during our field research. A great many people helped us in the field. We cannot thank them all, but we are especially grateful to Mike Morris, Francine Lund, Johan van Zyl, Christophe Heyns and Andre du Toit. We must also thank colleagues who assisted in the preparation for this study – Abram de Swaan, Else Øyen, Elisa Reis, Mick Moore, Naomi Hossain, Raphael Kaplinsky, J. E. Spence and Saul Dubow.

2 A comment is needed about two terms used here. After taking advice from many people, we have decided to use the word 'coloureds' when referring to people of mixed race. This and all other terms that might be used are problematic and subject to contestation. Some people understandably object to this word because it might be seen to imply a belief in racial purity (which we are not suggesting), because it was in use within the apartheid regime (with which we do not identify), etc. But despite its problems, we use it here as the best of a bad range of possible terms. Second, we use the word 'Africans' to refer to people who are sometimes called 'black' – but as it is used here, this term does not refer to people of Asian origin, to 'coloureds' or to white South Africans. This carries us into another minefield. Some whites regard themselves as genuine 'Africans', and the black consciousness movement in the apartheid period used the term 'black' to refer to all non-whites, etc. If any readers take offence at our choice of terms, we apologize. We understand the problems, but we need some means of identifying the groups under discussion.

3 This was acknowledged in May (1998: 4). For the best guide to different countries' Gini coefficients, see the Deininger and Squire dataset on 'Measuring Income Inequality' at <www.worldbank.org/html/prdmg/grthweb/ dddeisqu.htm> See also Wilson and Ramphele (1989: 17–18).

4 For more on rural poverty, see Nattrass et al. (1986).

5 We are grateful to the historian Saul Dubow for stressing this.

6 From the 1920s onwards, there was an intense awareness among white Afrikaners of poverty among disadvantaged groups within that narrow group. But that is not the same thing as an awareness of poverty more generally.

7 Interview, Durban, 25 February 1998.

8 Interview, Durban, 26 February 1998.

9 See the Deininger and Squire dataset at <www.worldbank.org/html/ prdmg/grthweb/dddeisqu.htm>.

10 We are grateful to Andre du Toit for stressing this.

11 Interview with an African woman who is an upper-middle-level official of the Inkatha Freedom Party, Durban, 24 February 1998.

12 Interview, Durban, 27 February 1998.

13 This has, for example, been argued by Shapiro (1998: 33).

14 Indeed, South Africa has (unusually) gone to the extent of including a requirement that procurement processes must be fair, cost-effective and transparent – Constitution of South Africa, Chapter 13, Section 217 (1). The problems arise in implementation.

15 Constitution of South Africa (1996, sections 9: 26–9, 38–9; and interview with Christophe Heyns, Pretoria, 3 March 1998.

16 'A Basic Guide to the Reconstruction and Development Programme' and 'The Reconstruction and Development Programmes: A Policy Framework', available at the South African government website <www.polity.org.za/gnuindex.html>.

17 *Mail and Guardian*, 19–25 February 1999; and *Business Day*, 22 February 1999.

18 Here are the totals of parliamentary seats won in a house of 400 at the last two elections:

	1994	1999
African National Congress	252	266
Inkatha Freedom Party	43	34
Democratic Party	7	38
New National Party	82	28
United Democratic Movement	0	14
Others	16	20

19 Interview, Johannesburg, 6 March 1998.

20 This last point was stressed by an economist in Thabo Mbeki's office, Pretoria, 4 March 1998.

21 Interviews, Pretoria, 4 March 1998.

22 See, for example, Brass (1989).

23 I am grateful to Mick Moore and Elisa Reis for raising these issues.

24 It should be noted that some of these 'ethnic' categories are seen by elites within them to have greater reality than others. This emerged from our interviews, but see also Welsh (1996: 477–92).

25 We are grateful to David Welsh for this point.

26 Interview with Johan van Zyl, Pretoria, 2 March 1998. This point was later corroborated in discussions with several political scientists and political journalists.

27 Interview with an official in the Ministry of Lands who was eager to see such restitution, Pretoria, 3 March 1998.

References

Adam, H., F. Van Zyl Slabbert and K. Moodley (1997) *Comrades in Business: Post-Liberation Politics in South Africa*, Cape Town: Tafelberg

Brass, P. R. (1989) *Ethnicity and Nationalism*, London, New Delhi and Newbury Park, CA: Sage

Constitution of South Africa (1996) Pretoria

May, J. (ed.) (1998) 'Poverty and Inequality in South Africa: Report Prepared for the Office of the Executive Deputy President and the Inter-Ministerial

Committee for Poverty and Inequality', Pretoria, available on the government's website at <www.polity.org.za/govdocs/reports/poverty.html>

Nattrass, J., J. May, A. Peters and D. Perkinset (1986) 'The Anatomy of Rural Black Poverty: The Challenge to a New Economic Order', Rural-Urban Studies Unit Paper no. 4, Durban: University of Natal

Nattrass, N. and J. Seekings (forthcoming) *From Race to Class: The Changing Nature of Inequality in South Africa*, New Haven, CT: Yale University Press

Shapiro, I. (1998) 'On the Normalization of South African Politics', *Dissent*, New York

UNDP (United Nations Development Programme) (1997) *Human Development Report 1997*, New York

Welsh, D. (1996) 'Ethnicity in Sub-Saharan Africa', *International Affairs*, July

Wilson, F. and M. Ramphele (1989) *Uprooting Poverty: The South African Challenge*, New York and Cape Town: W. W. Norton

7 | Elite perceptions of the poor: reflections on a comparative research project

ABRAM DE SWAAN

In the course of the last century, fully equipped welfare states emerged throughout western Europe and in North America, but with a few exceptions similar developments did not take place elsewhere, in Asia, Latin America or Africa. This is, of course, first of all a consequence of the lower levels of per capita income in those countries. But if the societies of the 'South' and of the 'East' were compared to those in the 'West' (or the North), not today but, say, fifty or a hundred years ago, many have now achieved levels of industrialization, of education or per capita income as high or even higher than those of their Atlantic counterparts in the past. And yet no movement towards encompassing welfare arrangements is in sight. The comparison is, clearly, unfair. The Industrial Revolution in Europe and America was without precedent, and even though there was stiff competition between industrializing countries, they did not have to confront rival powers that were way ahead of them. By contrast, those countries that started industrialization after the First World War, and, even more acutely, those that began only in the 1950s and 1960s, had to face the overwhelming advantages of the established industrial nations, which in the meantime had evolved towards post-industrial economies. The challengers had and have hardly a chance to compete through innovation; they are compelled to compete by keeping their production costs low. Since they depend on the Western powers for advanced technology and machinery, they can lower their costs only by holding wages down. Social security and other insurance schemes for the working population necessarily add premiums or taxes to the wage bill and are therefore generally avoided. If countries in the South and the East do have substantial social security arrangements, these are limited to government employees and workers in the 'spearhead' industries. In the past ten years or so, international trade and credit policy has strengthened this downward pressure on total labour costs, first by opening up national economies to international price competition and, second, by insisting on a reduction in the share of government expenditure in the national income, in the process also reducing what little social benefits were available. At this global level of analysis, there is another circumstance that needs to be taken into account: the presence after 1917 of the Soviet Union, and from

1948 of the Chinese Democratic People's Republic, and their numerous satellites. These communist regimes provided some material support but above all huge moral encouragement to the workers' movement in the industrializing nations, and inspired considerable anxiety among rulers and owners in these countries. The blessings of communism, if any, may not have materialized in the people's democracies, but they did accrue in some measure to the workers in all those other countries who were emboldened while the ruling and propertied elites were deterred by the example of 'actually existing socialism'. This non-military, Soviet threat certainly helped to keep social reform (and agrarian reform) on the political agenda in many parts of the world. Equally, the demise of the communist system has taken much of the impetus out of the workers' movement: it now appears as if there simply is no alternative to the neo-liberal recipe for economic growth. The result has been political paralysis in the workers' movement and among the partisans of social and Christian democracy from where the support for the welfare state used to come.

At present, not much is left of the body of ideas known as 'social thought', a tradition of social reform, fair wages, education of the workers and protection of the weak. This ideological current certainly did not remain restricted to Europe, and never was the monopoly of socialism. It was also manifest on other continents, nourished quite often by Christian as well as Islamic teachings. Today the mainstream, neo-liberal conception of social policy may be summarized as 'trickle-down': if government is minimized through deregulation, privatization and retrenchment, and markets are opened up to free and global competition, economic growth will necessarily ensue, especially in low-income countries. This in turn will gradually lead to higher wages for the workers, increasing opportunities for the unemployed and better circumstances for those who cannot work to earn their living. Indeed, free market policies have brought about economic growth across the globe, but less so or not at all for the poorest countries, and within each national economy less so or not at all for the poorest citizens. In other words, granted that neo-liberal economic theory provides a recipe for economic growth – albeit not for sustainable development, or for steady, 'non-volatile' expansion without periodic downturns, recession or stagflation – it does not come with a prescription for a feasible and fair social policy.

Summing up, several developments at the global level help to explain the relative absence of welfare arrangements in the Southern and Eastern world: competitive disadvantage due to the relatively late industrialization of so many non-Western countries, and the demise of the communist system with the attendant rise of neo-liberal doctrines and institutions. But, of course, developments within each national context were also decisive for the emergence, or rather non-emergence, of welfare arrangements in the societies of the South and East. The relatively low level of per capita income has already been mentioned. It is in great part the consequence of global relations of power and exchange, but it also depends on the natural resources and the geo-political location of a given country. The development of welfare arrangements is equally determined by the political culture in a particular society. In this respect, what count especially are the relations between the elites and the masses who possess neither economic means nor political resources, and who for the sake of brevity will be called 'the poor'. In this context, the core issue is how the elites perceive the poor in their society. If, because of tradition, habitus and mentality, the elites experience the presence of the poor as mostly irrelevant, neither much of a threat nor much of an opportunity, they will tend to be indifferent towards the fate of these masses and hardly inclined to initiate any kind of welfare measure, be it assistance for the needy and the elderly, security for the workers, healthcare for the sick or education for the young. There may be various reasons for this imperturbability on the part of the elites. Their religion may hold that material means do not count for much next to spiritual values, which may even be enhanced by poverty, or that deprivation in this world is more than compensated by rewards in the hereafter. Members of the elite may also believe that the poor are simply different from the rich, that they do not mind hardship, that they are content with less, or that their emotional make-up is wholly different. The rich may hold that the poor deserve no better because of their laziness, stupidity, prodigality, improvidence or the incapacity to manage their own affairs. A few members of the elite may even perversely subscribe to the old Marxist immiseration theory, that the poor should not be succoured at all so as to instil better in their minds the revolutionary spirit.

On the other side of this multi-dimensional continuum of elite attitudes is the perception of the poor as political and economic agents that do matter, for better or for worse. They may constitute a threat to the social order or represent a variety of opportunities. The threats are mainly of four kinds: rebellion, crime, contagion and migration. The opportunities are also fourfold: the poor may benefit the rich in their roles as workers, soldiers, consumers and voters. The elites will attempt to control the threats emanating from the presence of the poor in their midst and try to exploit the opportunities that the poor also represent. At this point, however, the elites face a particular predicament, very familiar in the theory of the collectivizing process.[1] Any entrepreneur or ruler who might wish to put in place some arrangement to diminish the menace that the poor evoke, or exploit the opportunities that they provide, might find that other members of the elite will also profit from these efforts without contributing to their cost. Thus, some benefactors might decide to establish a school, hospital or charitable foundation in order to improve the lot of the poor. But their wealthy peers, who did nothing to aid the effort, will nevertheless reap the benefits of a more agreeable and more efficient workforce. Clearly, for the rich the improvement of the condition of the able poor constitutes in many respects a collective good, with all the attendant dilemmas of collective action and the paralysis these may entail when there is no entity that can effectively coordinate the individual efforts. In the last analysis, for the rich the problem of poverty is a problem of collective action.

The history of poor relief, education and healthcare illustrates how these dilemmas of collective action were overcome, initially at the parish level, later in the urban context and finally within the framework of the nation-state. In essence, individual actors are confronted with the dilemmas of collective action in a transitional situation. They are already aware of their interdependence, of the consequences that the action or inaction of the other parties may have for them, but there is as yet no agency that may effectively coordinate their actions. Collective action may nevertheless get under way owing to the intervention of outside initiators, through manipulation of expectations about the behaviour of the other parties and because of illusions about the outcome and its costs. Once the collective effort begins the parties interact and in the process come to constitute a collectivity.

In other words, in the course of collective action a collectivity emerges which in turn supports the collective action: this twofold process is called the collectivizing process. Such a sequence of events is not difficult to imagine. Once collective action gets under way, participants will meet more frequently, will be in a position to inspect and judge more easily one another's contributions to the common cause, will compliment or criticize, praise or ostracize one another, and in the course of their interaction reinforce existing norms and develop new rules for the distribution of tasks. This collectivizing process may occur among individuals trying to organize poor relief at the parish level, or among villages attempting to counter vagrancy in their region, or between regional capitals striving to control epidemics on a nationwide scale. In essence, the very same process occurs between national governments in a worldwide effort to control the global ecology. In other words, the collective good and the collectivity that realizes it emerge more or less simultaneously in a 'collectivizing process'.

The very broad connotations of the concepts 'elite', 'perceptions' and 'poverty' allow us to adapt them to the wide array of circumstances that prevail over the very long time period in which Western welfare states took shape, or at a specific moment in time in the very diverse societies studied in this comparative project. For the sake of analytic coherence, a more precisely defined concept is introduced: 'social consciousness'. This term refers to a set of perceptions, which were used in de Swaan (1988) to characterize the mentality of the welfare state. Here the notion is adopted to analyse the ways in which poverty affects the elites and to interpret their efforts to control it. Members of the elites possess social consciousness to the degree that:

1 They are aware of the interdependence among social groups in society – and, most relevantly, of the external effects of poverty upon the elites, which they may perceive either as threats or as opportunities.
2 They realize that as members of the elite they bear some responsibility for the condition of the poor.
3 They believe that feasible and efficacious means to improving the lot of the poor exist or might be created.

When, as is often the case, individual members of the elite are unable on their own to ward off the threats or to exploit the opportunities that the presence of the poor holds for them, and when they are unable to alleviate poverty individually, the presence of the poor in their midst confronts the elites with a problem of collective action: to coordinate their efforts, either through voluntary agreement or by seeking a compulsory arrangement, i.e. public action. In the history of Western welfare states, elite initiatives and elite consent have been pivotal in bringing about (and equally in holding off) collective and public arrangements for remedying ignorance, disease and deprivation.

The three elements of a 'social consciousness' refer to three different types of thinking by elites. Point 1 entails a factual assessment of the condition of the society in which they live. It calls for a 'proto-sociological' insight on the part of elite members. Point 2 entails both factual assessments – the identification of a causal chain linking their (in)action to the living conditions of the poor – and moral evaluations of what they ought to do about them. Point 3 requires the elites to accept the interventions of some collective or public agency (governmental or non-governmental), in order to reform the prevailing situation

It should be said at the outset that altruistic dispositions and a general climate of social compassion greatly facilitate collective and public initiatives to alleviate poverty (Bendix 1964: 286–90). But the problem of coordination, i.e. the distribution of burdens within the elites, must somehow be resolved if remedial arrangements are to be put into effect. This requires that the mutual suspicion of inaction or desertion, in short the fear of 'free riders', with its paralysing impact, be overcome. If this is indeed achieved, it is most often in the course of tentative yet successful collective efforts that in the process strengthen mutual confidence. To the degree that elites possess a social consciousness in all three respects listed above, and this awareness resonates with personal and societal moral concerns, the outcome should be voluntary and public action to tackle poverty.

My argument implies that we will encounter among the elites three basic attitudes to poverty and poor people. First, they may be wholly indifferent to the issue. Second, they may be concerned with the problems of the poor because they believe that these pose threats to their own well-being, or because they think that the poor might provide them with opportunities, individually and collectively. Yet they may still remain inactive and resign themselves to the existing state of affairs, because they believe that no effective remedies are available. And, third, their concern and confidence in the efficacy of their actions may impel them to undertake remedial, collective action. Of course, elites are not monolithic, and will tend to be divided in their perceptions of the poor in all relevant aspects. In the course of time, the nature of the debate and thus of perceptions may change – for example, the idea that the poor are responsible for their own fate had long been abandoned for all practical purposes in Europe, but was reintroduced in public debate with a vengeance in the 1980s. Since then, a paradigmatic split in European elite perceptions has occurred, and similar divisions may be found in the studies of non-Western societies in this volume.

To sum up: what is presented here is an elite theory of welfare arrangements, developed originally to explain the emergence of welfare states in Europe and the United States in the period 1870–1970 (de Swaan 1988). The theory holds that the more elites are aware of the threats and opportunities represented by the poor in their midst, the more pronounced will be their social consciousness and the more they will be inclined to act to bring about collective arrangements to ward off the threats and realize the opportunities that the poor present them with. This, however, creates dilemmas of collective action. These dilemmas occur in a transitional situation and must therefore be analysed from a dynamic perspective. The paradoxes of collective action are resolved in the dynamic conception of the collectivizing process. In other words, the logical paradox is replaced by a sociological dilemma.

These theoretical ideas have been elaborated in de Swaan (ibid.), a book-length discussion of the emergence of welfare arrangements in Europe and the United States over the course of five centuries. Applying the same notions to non-Western countries does not at all imply that these societies will travel the same road and are simply a few stops behind. On the contrary, making a comparison means assessing both similarity and difference. In this case (as in others) it would be a great loss for social science if the extensive knowledge that has been assembled about Europe and the USA were not brought to bear upon the study of Southern and Eastern societies.

The first general observation is precisely one of difference: there are hardly any welfare states outside of North America and western Europe. If social security or other provisions have been established at all, they are usually limited to government personnel and a workers' elite. How far can the material in this volume explain this difference? In so far as I can find an explanation, it lies at two levels: first in terms of differences in the general, global and historical conditions of these countries in comparison with western Europe and North America; and, next, in terms more specific to the political culture of each country, namely the manner in which its elites perceive the poor in that society.

The history of welfare states in western Europe and North America was closely connected with the emergence of the nation-state. The evidence collected in this volume suggests two related but distinct hypotheses about the way these processes played out in the non-Western countries.

First, in the non-Western countries a sense of national identification nowhere swamps other loyalties, of class, caste, region or religion. Of all countries under study, Brazil most closely approaches the model of the nation-state. Countrywide mutual identifications seem relatively strong in Bangladesh, with its rather homogeneous population, which still vividly remembers the struggle for national independence. But its significant minorities, especially the Hindus, who might account for a sixth or more of the population, still struggle to be accepted as Bangladeshi. Although intense national feelings seem present in South Africa, even stronger cross-cutting cleavages, which date from the apartheid era and before, divide the different population categories. The Philippines is divided by linguistic barriers, and different ethnic origins distinguish different sections of the elites. National identifications seem lowest in Haiti, where, despite the fact that most of the population is rather homogeneous, there are intense divisions around language (Creole versus French) and skin colour (mainly black versus a very small mulatto minority). As a result, the sense of a generalized interdependence between all the groups that constitute society is also rather weak. Thus, in most countries the urban elites have only the haziest notion of the way the rural poor live. They tend to idealize village life in a rather sentimental way: the villagers are often perceived as simple, honest and frugal, caring for one another and not wanting much as nutritious plants spring up everywhere in the countryside. The rural elite is more knowledgeable about conditions in the countryside but at the same time can be quite hostile to the poor since its interests are so clearly opposed to those of the landless farmhands, as Clarke and Sison have shown for the Philippines. The urban elites have a more realistic perception of the urban poor and a more acute sense of the degree of deprivation in the cities. Yet this awareness need not lead to a pronounced social consciousness among the elites. The urban rich generally do not see their own existence as somehow interdependent with the living conditions of the city's poor. The potential dangers or the possible opportunities that the poor represent do not figure vividly in the perceptions of the elites.

The second hypothesis is suggested by Elisa Reis in Chapter 2: the elites of Europe and North America first created states and then converted them into welfare states. This was a process of their own making, under their control. They could identify quite strongly with their creations. By contrast, the elites of the non-Western world have largely inherited, from colonialism, states that they did not create and which, because of international dependency relations, they often felt that they did not control. In those circumstances, their willingness to extend to the state a general welfare role – a role that would inevitably require giving the state wider authority, including the authority to tax the elite themselves – was definitely muted.

Both these hypotheses about the comparative histories of welfarism on a global scale merit further exploration. But this is not the place for that. We move on to look at the evidence from our case studies about the ways in which elites perceive the various threats and promises that the poor represent to them.

The poor are no longer much feared as sources of contagion. Members of elites seem to agree that infectious diseases mostly belong to the past, and that the risk of infection is more effectively avoided by individual immunization than through public health measures. The nineteenth-century urban tradition of waterworks, sewers, pavements and public housing – which was echoed in the colonies by public health campaigns against malaria, cholera and yellow fever – has evaporated almost completely. Like their peers in the West, the elites in the countries discussed here primarily fear degenerative diseases such as cancer and coronary ailments, and try to protect themselves through personalized regimens and individual medical treatment. Medicine has been individualized medicine. In fact, however, a number of infectious diseases, such as tuberculosis, malaria and dengue fever, are making a comeback – if they ever entirely went away. The spectacular increase of HIV/AIDS is a case apart: the rich tend to believe that by avoiding risky habits such as intravenous drug use or venal promiscuity they may effectively protect themselves and their kin. They overlook the fact that a large reservoir of AIDS patients carrying all sorts of opportunistic infections, most ominously tuberculosis, may constitute an immediate threat to all citizens, no matter how carefully they may behave as individuals. These cavalier attitudes may soon change, when HIV infection, which is now spreading with alarming speed in many countries, turns into an epidemic of full-blown AIDS. Sadly, at that point it will be too late for the relatively cheap and effective public health measures that could have slowed down the spread of the primary infection in the first place: mass distribution of condoms and clean needles.

The elites of old were often troubled by the twin spectre of crime and rebellion. In the countries under study, organized collective violence, i.e. insurrection, is not a clear and present danger. It may have been in South Africa under apartheid, but it no longer is under the government of the African National Congress (ANC). In 2001 the poor flocked into the streets of Manila to protest against the deposition of President Estrada, a 'man of the people', in what many saw as a constitutional coup. They were unsuccessful. But on the whole, the poor, disorganized and ill equipped as they usually are, do not represent much of a violent threat to the elites. On the other hand, individual and incidental violence, i.e. petty crime, is much more of a concern. The standard argument is that poverty breeds crime. The crimes that are most feared by members of the elite, however, are not poor people's petty crimes such as burglary or shoplifting, but violent assault, kidnapping and gang warfare. Much criminal activity revolves around drugs – which often constitute an important but mostly invisible link between elite circles and criminal networks. Thus, the crimes most feared are only loosely associated with poverty, and much more with the organized underworld.

The townships of South Africa and the *favelas* of Brazil are vast no-go areas for all outsiders. At the same time, these war zones are quite effectively shielded from the residential areas where the rich live in heavily protected seclusion. Late-nineteenth-century cities were not so sharply segregated. On the contrary, it was held, especially by conservatives, that the elites and the poor should live in close proximity so that the former could serve as a moral example to the latter. In the West, the rich moved out of the squalid inner city towards the more spacious, greener neighbourhoods that were developed on the outskirts of the city, while the poor remained behind in the old inner city. In the contemporary cities of the South and the East, migrants recently arrived from the countryside squat in villages at the very edge of the city, while the downtown areas are reserved for offices and shops, and the wealthy live in quite remote suburbs. This rather strict segregation shields the rich from the impact of poverty, renders them less fearful and by the same token less concerned with poverty. They would much rather pay for private security guards than for single mothers on welfare. And, even though they are most reluctant to pay taxes, members of the Brazilian elite expect the state to combat crime and maximize their security.

It is spatial segregation which also offers the most effective protection against another age-old concern of the rich: migration, or rather invasion by hordes of desperate poor. But contemporary cities have grown in such a way that rural immigrants or refugees from distant wars remain isolated in their makeshift camps and squatter villages. The poor are limited to walking distances or the itineraries of public transport, while the rich drive their cars to the secluded suburbs where they live among their peers. In short, the individualization of medicine and the segregation of urban space have been most effective in reducing the threat of the poor to the rich.

But the poor do not appear only as potential criminals, rebels, germ carriers or vagrants; they may also be perceived in a more positive perspective, as possible recruits, workers, consumers and voters. In the late nineteenth century, anxiety about the ill health and scanty education of army recruits inspired major social and medical reforms, especially when war seemed imminent. In the cases discussed in this volume, war does not at present seem a pressing concern. Thus, military considerations do not carry much weight in the perception of the elites.

In most of the countries studied here, the miners, railroad workers and auto workers – the labourers in the 'spearhead industries' – were and still are quite well protected against the risks of disease, disability, unemployment, old age and death. So are the military, the teachers and the civil servants. In quite a few countries, which otherwise lack any social provision, a quite generous 'mini welfare state' operates for the benefit of these 'indispensable' employees. But the factories that have been established more recently in these countries usually come under the heading of 'light industries'. Skill and muscle count for little; patience, docility and nimble hands are more important. There is an inexhaustible reserve army of workers, idle young men and semi-skilled young women, who can be put to work in these factories and workshops. As a result, elites in general do not feel much pressure to undertake major reforms so as to ensure a steady supply of qualified labour. Yet if there is one positive measure that does get elite support, it is education to improve workers' skills, as all the case studies demonstrate.

Only a handful of interviewees in the countries studied make the point that, if the poor had more money to spend as consumers, retail business would expand and the economy as a whole would be strengthened. This insight in the 'generalized interdependence' of the economy hardly seems to play a role in the perceptions of the rich. Of course, in this instance too dilemmas of collective action loom in the background: a member of the elite who is willing to contribute to an income increase for the poor must accept that they will spend that increment in some store where the owner may well have shirked his obligations.

Most elite respondents put their faith in the forces of the market: free, open and competitive economies will result in the growth of the domestic economy. Economic growth directly profits the elites themselves, but it might also trickle down to benefit the poor. This perspective does not commit the rich to any kind of welfare measure; on the contrary, it relieves them of any obligation towards the poor. All wrongs will right themselves once the economy begins to expand. The trickle-down theory allows the rich to have their cake and share it too. No wonder that Filipino, Brazilian and South African elites (the ANC leadership excepted) strongly favour competitive markets with a strong growth potential.

This leaves one last perspective on the poor, in their role as voters in a democratic system. Indeed, the most promising avenue to increase the involvement of the elites with the conditions of the poor is through the mechanism of democratic elections. One Bangladeshi respondent suggests that the votes of the poor can be bought so cheaply that it is not even worth-while to take their political preferences into account. But the South African case especially shows that politicians must reckon with the opinions of the poor if they wish to be elected. Even if the poor cannot vote a government of their liking into power, they can bring down a government that has been especially unsympathetic to their interests. Thus, the perception of the poor as potential voters may prompt the elites to support policy proposals that benefit the neediest. In European history, there is a clear connection between the extension of the right to vote and the adoption of social policy measures. In the countries under study here, open and fair elections may very well be won by the party that promises the most generous policies on education, healthcare, housing and maybe even minimal old-age pensions. Electoral proposals that go farther in the direction of establishing a fully fledged welfare state are thought to be forbiddingly expensive given the vast dimensions of the problem of poverty, and would therefore provoke too much opposition to remain credible.

When writing about elite perceptions of the poor, it is tempting – in fact, almost irresistible – to also comment on elite misperceptions. Thus, the tendency to idealize the life of the rural poor, to ignore their hardship and evoke the abundance of food in the countryside, is one mode of denial of the harsh realities of poverty. There is a related mode of denial, in which the poor are represented as simply 'different', with other, lesser needs and a greater capacity to bear deprivation. This defence mechanism works even better when the poor are assigned to a different religious, racial or ethnic category, as is the case in Brazil and South Africa, in contrast to Bangladesh, where the population is much more homogeneous. (Compare, however, the Caribbean society of Haiti, where shades in skin colour are 'constructed' as existential distinctions.) Then there is the defence mechanism of 'blaming the victims' – their poverty is all of their own making (and conversely, the wealth of the elites is their own meritorious achievement).

One might well imagine a secondary analysis of the data collected here on elite perceptions, this time in terms of denial and distortion, projection and dis-identification. The methodological problem with such an analysis is that it presupposes a privileged position from where the facts may be perceived 'as they really are', as opposed to the distortions on the part of the elites. This approach assumes, moreover, that the elites must mobilize defence mechanisms in order to psychologically protect themselves against the stark facts of poverty which might prove too much for them to bear. In fact, many respondents may be more cynical than they appear, and during the interviews present views they hope will convince the researchers that things are not as bad as they might appear and they themselves not as mean as they might seem.

The evidence collected in this volume does not permit an overall explanation of the absence of strong welfare institutions in the countries studied. After all, none of these countries resembles anything remotely like a Western welfare state. Thus, differences in the perceptions of the elites cannot explain this absence of social policies. On the other hand, similar elite perceptions in all countries studied, which are different across the board from elite perceptions in all Western welfare states, might shed some light on the issue. Studies of elite perceptions in Western countries are very rare, and there are no data on the perceptions of elites during the founding period of the welfare state in Europe, the most relevant period for comparison. And even if a single difference between all historical, Western elite perceptions and all perceptions of contemporary elites in the South and the East were found, this may as well be the 'cause' as the 'consequence', or even both at the same time, of the institutional differences between Western welfare states and the countries studied in this volume. After all, elites in the welfare states of the West can afford to commiserate with the poor, since 'something is being done about it', in the passive mode, by the omnipresent, hidden subject: the efficacious, redistributive apparatus of the state. The same human identification with the poor is much more hazardous and costly for the elites in the countries discussed here and therefore much harder to afford.

Summing up, the nation-states of a century ago fostered a strong sense of national identification, bridging the gap even between the elites and the masses of the working poor. At the same time, strong, radical unions and the looming presence of the Soviet Union effectively conveyed a sense of menace to the elites. The urban health paradigm, also, conveyed a threat and a remedy. Moreover, it appeared worthwhile and feasible to invest in the education and health of the poor, who were during this period of rapid industrialization needed as workers, as military recruits and, increasingly, as consumers. Finally, the extension of adult suffrage, partly a result of the same conditions, much strengthened the impetus for social policy. It is most of all this last condition which seems to encourage acceptance of social reform among the elites in the East and the South.

Note

1 What follows is a paraphrase of the theoretical sections of de Swaan (1988), which served as one of the sources of inspiration for the present research project.

References

Bendix, R. (1964) *Nation-building and Citizenship: Studies of Our Changing Social Order*, New York: Wiley

de Swaan, A. (1988) *In Care of the State; Health Care, Education and Welfare in Europe and the USA in the Modern Era*, Cambridge /New York: Polity Press/ Oxford University Press

8 | Elites, poverty and public policy[1]

MICK MOORE AND NAOMI HOSSAIN

Elites, culture and poverty

Militant 'realists' among social scientists and social observers will believe three things about elites and poverty:

1 that elites are the beneficiaries – materially, culturally or psychologically – of poverty and inequality, and will therefore resist attempts to overcome them;

2 that ideas and culture have little or no independent influence on social outcomes, which are shaped mainly by material and institutional forces[2] – and therefore that elite perceptions of poverty have no consequences and are of little interest;

3 that even if ideas had some independent causal significance, it would not be practical to think of 'cultural engineering', i.e. consciously setting out to change the world by changing elite ideas.

Much of the time, the realists are probably right. The question of how often they are right cannot be settled through social science research. We simply do not have the analytic tools or the data to determine the answer. That does not prevent most of us having views on these issues. But those views reflect our ideologies, prejudices and passing intuitions. Suppose that the realists were actually wrong much of the time, on all counts? Suppose that elites did perceive reasons to try to reduce poverty and inequality;[3] that changes in ideas or political culture in some sense did help change their willingness to act; and that these changes in political culture could be achieved through conscious agency? We would want to know about it, and to see whether there were opportunities to influence public policy. We have one good case: a detailed account of political culture and public policy in late Victorian Britain, written by the distinguished historian Gertrude Himmelfarb (1991), which argues the anti-realist line on each of the three points. Using her words as far as possible, we will summarize her interpretation of the influence of Charles Booth.

In 1889, Charles Booth published the first of a seventeen-volume collection called *Life and Labour of the People in London*. Himmelfarb explains the radical differences between his explanation of poverty and the previous orthodoxy, as exemplified by Christopher Mayhew's *London Labour and London Poor* (1849):

Mayhew's 'poverty' was primarily that of the 'Street-Folk' and 'Those That Will Not Work' (as the subtitles of his work put it). His subjects – street sellers, street performers, street laborers, paupers, beggars, prostitutes – were, by his own account, a relatively small part of the population of London (2.5 percent). Yet his portraits of them were so striking, his representation of them as a distinctive 'race' with a distinctive 'moral physiognomy' so memorable, that they overshadowed the much larger class of workers who did not appear in his pages, workers who lived and worked indoors rather than on the streets and who led mundane and unsensational lives. Many readers and reviewers (and occasionally Mayhew himself) were so impressed by his dramatic 'revelations' that they assumed that the extreme and even exotic poverty he described was the condition of the working classes as a whole – that the 'street-folk' of the subtitle were equivalent to the 'London Labour and London Poor' of the title.

Booth tried to correct this mistaken identity by creating separate categories for the 'very poor', the 'poor', and the 'comfortable' working classes. The statistic commonly cited from his work has 30 percent of the population in 'poverty'. But that figure, as Booth made clear, included two distinct groups, the 'very poor' (7.5 percent), and the 'poor' (22.3 percent). The 'very poor' were in a state of 'chronic want', largely because of their aversion to regular work or their incapacity for it (caused by drunkenness or other debilitating habits). The 'poor', on the other hand, although not in 'want' (not ill nourished or ill clad), were in 'poverty', engaged in a constant struggle to make ends meet. His own 'clients', Booth candidly admitted – the poor he himself cared most about and whom he thought most worthy of society's concern – were those whose poverty was caused mainly by irregular employment; they might be 'shiftless and improvident', but they were also 'hardworking, struggling people, not worse morally than any other class'.

Where Mayhew, however unwittingly, had 'de-moralized' the laboring poor by confounding them with the lowest classes of the poor (the 'residuum', as they were called), Booth 're-moralized' the poor by separating them from the 'very poor' and freeing them from the stigma of pauperism and degradation. He thus redefined the idea of poverty and reinterpreted the social problem. The problem was no longer what it had been earlier in the century; the Malthusian poor (the 'excess' population who lived in a state of 'misery and vice'), or the pauperized poor (who were the subjects of the poor law reform of 1834) or the Mayhewian poor (the 'street-folk' and 'those that will not work'). The heart of the problem, as Booth saw it, was the large group of laboring poor whose poverty, while not catastrophic, was nonetheless problematic. Even when he offered a radical proposal for the very poor, he did so less out of solicitude for them than for the poor.

The poor who came to the center of the stage were not the old 'deserving poor'. That term became increasingly rare in the 1880s ... The 'deserving poor' of earlier times were judged deserving precisely because they did not qualify as a social problem. They were simply the laboring poor, existing in the natural condition of poverty that had been the fate of humanity since time immemorial, the condition of those who earned their living by the sweat of their brow. By the late-Victorian period, that 'condition' had become a 'problem'. It had become problematic not because it had become worse – on the contrary, the condition of most of the poor, as most contemporaries knew, was better than ever before – but because people had come to believe that it could and should be better than it was. The poor who now emerged as the social problem were deserving, not in the sense of being paragons of virtue, but in the sense of being deserving of society's attention and concern. And they were thought deserving because most of their difficulties (unemployment, sickness, old age) were recognized as not of their own making; because in spite of adversity and temptation most of them, most of the time, made a strenuous effort to provide for themselves and their families; and because for society's sake as much as their own they should be prevented from lapsing into the class of the very poor.

It was the poor, rather than the very poor, who were the beneficiaries of most of the reforms of the late-Victorian and Edwardian periods. (Himmelfarb 1991: 11–12)

The most economical summary of this story is that Booth helped to effect a change from a *behavioural* to a *structural* understanding of poverty. There are just two additional elements that we need to add to the account above. The first is the extent to which Booth was able to generate compassion in the minds of the elites of late-Victorian Britain by framing the ever present danger of the descent of the 'poor' to being 'very poor' in term of the 'loss of respectability' – a notion that resonated strongly with all classes (e.g. ibid.: 8–10, 118). The second is to emphasize that: 'Booth, like most of his contemporaries, persisted in thinking and speaking of the working classes in the plural; this, indeed, was the main point of his work. The differentiation of classes implied a differentiation of problems and thus of remedies – specific measures designed to alleviate specific forms of poverty' (ibid.: 167–8).

In presenting this interpretation of the influence of Booth's work, Himmelfarb recognizes the wider changes in the economy that made possible such a fruitful redefinition of the nature of poverty. Her views are not blindly culturalist. She does, however, make a convincing case against each of the three 'realist' positions summarized above. In this instance at least, elites were willing to do something about poverty; they were persuaded to act in part by changing understandings of the subject; and those changes were strongly pushed by an impressive propaganda exercise, backed by voluminous fact-gathering.[4] It is unlikely that this is an isolated case. For example, the relative success of post-1997 British governments in channelling resources to tackle spatial pockets of intense urban socio-economic deprivation appears to have been possible in part because this has been framed as an issue of *social exclusion*, which implies societal responsibility. This framing has displaced the highly stigmatizing concept of the *underclass*, which had been gaining currency under previous governments.

There are, then, reasons to think seriously about elite perceptions of poverty. We focus in the next section on some relatively concrete issues about contemporary poor countries. We choose not to go down the route of discussing in detail the connection between the arguments we put forward here and conceptual and methodological debates in social science about (political) culture and the political role of ideas. Let us simply note a few points on that topic. First, we do not view political culture as an independent variable, but as a set of orientations formed and re-formed in mutual interaction with institutional and material variables. Second, we are aware of the danger that cultural explanations can easily degenerate into various methodological pathologies, including reification, ethnocentrism and determinism. Third, we distinguish between *political ideologies* – 'formal, explicit, and relatively consistent definitions of political community' – and *political cultures* – 'the informal, implicit, and relatively inconsistent understandings of political community held by people within a given institutional setting' (Hanson 2003: 356). We are talking of the latter in this book. Finally, it is clear that an increasing number of contemporary political scientists are willing to make the case that culture – subjective orientations of social actors – is important in explaining political outcomes.[5]

Implications for the contemporary South

The story of Charles Booth illustrates, with the clarity normally only attainable with long historical hindsight, the *plasticity* of understandings of the character and causes of poverty. Those understandings changed within one country over a short period of time, as a result of efforts led by someone who might today be labelled a 'policy intellectual'. It seems obvious that the same trick might be pulled in contemporary developing countries: the poverty issue might be reframed in the minds of elites, to positive effect.

It would, however, be a mistake to end this book simply with the suggestion that what is possible in one place at one point in time is possible in others at other points. For public discourse about 'poverty' is constructed very differently in most countries of the contemporary South to how it was in Victorian Britain. In sum, and especially in the more aid-dependent countries, it is often more a global than an indigenist discourse. That may not be a good thing. John Toye summarized the situation as he saw it only a few years ago:

> The dominant conceptualisation of poverty thus remains the narrow economistic one of private consumption (or income poverty), albeit now with the headcount indices for the traditional upper and lower poverty lines supplemented by the calculation of the poverty gap and the index of poverty severity on Foster-Greer-Thorbecke lines ... The measures are *narrowly* economistic because they usually exclude even economic variables like the value of private assets, the use of common property resources, and the social dividend (public spending benefits minus taxes). They are economistic because they exclude social and political aspects of well being such as leisure, personal security, cultural goods, social recognition, and political rights. (Toye 1999: 7; emphasis in original)

Toye's concern was that the economistic, quantitative and morally and emotively neutral conceptions of poverty propagated by the international development community – aid agencies, NGOs, researchers – simply would not engage or resonate with national elites in the South. In one respect, his diagnosis is already to some degree outdated. As signalled especially by the high-profile publication *Voices of the Poor*, produced by the World Bank in 2000, some sections at least of the international development community are now insisting that poverty should not be viewed solely or principally as a material phenomenon. Instead, the world is urged to understand poverty in its full multi-dimensionality. Poverty is not only lack of income, lack of shelter, hunger and high mortality, but also insecurity, lack of dignity, exclusion, powerlessness and oppression.[6] We have moved towards aggregating under one term – poverty – a whole set of *deprivations*: the acute under-nutrition and persistent hunger of the millions who routinely fail to get enough to eat; the anxieties of many millions of others whose daily bread depends on the breadwinner not falling ill and on the opening of another construction site once the current job is completed; the destitution of people who are too old or sick to work and lack a family willing to support them; the dread of powerless women that they will be harassed or raped outside the relative security of their household; the burdens heaped on members of minority social and ethnic groups excluded from schools, places of worship and sources of clean drinking water; and the exploitation of illiterate bonded labourers by employers who know how to manipulate the police and judicial systems.

This broadening of the concept of poverty addresses one of Toye's concerns. It does not, however, address another: the fact that the dominant definitions of poverty, and therefore the implicit interpretations of what might be done to reduce it, are set globally – with something of a bias towards Washington, DC. We do not have to be rabid anti-globalizers to accept that there may be a real problem here. Can we really expect that elites in poor countries will be fully engaged or motivated by definitions of poverty that clearly bear the stamp 'made abroad', regardless of whether the definition is highly abstract and unemotive – such as an income of 'less than a dollar a day' – or more concrete and emotionally charged – such as the sexual exploitation of poor women by rich and powerful men? The answer must often be 'no'. Where in contemporary developing countries is the kind of discussion that was held in Victorian Britain, in which notions of *pauperism, destitution, very poor, poor, comfortable poor un/deserving poor* and *respectable poor* competed with one another, in a context in which there were some observable connections between specific terms and identifiable local situations? We certainly did not pick up many such nuances in our interviews. As we explain in Chapter 1, 'our' elites understood *poverty* much as people do in Britain, and were rarely able to talk with any fluency or conviction about differences within the mass of people they termed *the poor*. The fact that we did not tap that vein does not mean, however, that it has ceased to exist. It is surely worthwhile to explore the scope for more indigenist approaches to the framing of poverty which do resonate positively with national elites; and signal to them that this is an Afghan/Bolivian/Cameroon/Dominican problem, and not just something that has to be talked about to keep the aid donors happy. Because the thinking populations of many contemporary poor countries are exposed to strong global pressures to understand poverty in rather uniform ways, there is a case for greater local intellectual activism to reframe those understandings, in local languages, in ways that increase the likelihood of positive responses from elites.

Our research findings from five countries are in no way a substitute for this local intellectual activism. But some general discussion of what we found, placed in historical context, should help spark some ideas.

Fear and opportunity

It is evident that developing-country elites often lack the commitment to reducing poverty and inequality that aid donors now urge upon them. Elites typically enjoy a luxurious lifestyle yet surrender little of their income in taxes. With high walls, private schools, private medical care, private security and overseas university education, they can insulate themselves from the most direct adverse impacts of the poverty around them. We do not have to look far for stories of rural landlords paying police or private militias to intimidate the poor and landless, or urban elites condoning the brutalization or murder of street children. One can always find apparent winners in a situation of misery. For example, the fact that poverty enables elites to hire labour cheaply is often taken as evidence that they have an interest in the perpetuation of poverty. But none of these observations is evidence that elites are actually committed to the perpetuation of poverty.[7] Were this the case, they would be unusually irrational and, in a historical context, anomalous. Let us first look at the historical record.

There is plenty of evidence from past centuries that public action to spread the gains of economic growth and relieve poverty was stimulated or supported by perceptions among members of the elite that they too stood to benefit. We can loosely classify these perceptions into *negative* and *positive drivers*. A *negative driver* is defined by a sense of fear and a perception that the elite might actually be worse off if they fail to do something about poverty. By contrast, a *positive driver* – an understanding that there are potential gains from poverty reduction that can be shared and make most people better off – can be framed in terms of *opportunity*. The *fear* embodied in *negative drivers* may help stimulate urgent action but also justify repressive and coercive behaviour towards the poor (for example, harsh policing or sentencing, forcible clearance of urban squatter settlements). A sense of a potential *opportunity* does not have the same mobilizing power, but is much less likely to lead to repressive responses. Fear translates most easily into political arguments couched in terms of elite self-interests, and a sense of opportunity into more altruistic language. It should, however, be understood that motivations and emotions are likely to be mixed in all cases, and that 'naked' self-interest arguments were rarely deployed, in public at least. As in public policy-making generally, the more powerful arguments were those that simultaneously tapped into both perceptions of self-interest and beliefs about what is morally right.

Generally speaking, the farther we go back in history, the more the arguments deployed to stimulate European elites to support significant pro-poor policies fall into our negative category. It was the *threat* of disease in particular which stimulated major municipal and public health/sanitation reforms in western Europe from the early nineteenth century, and helped give momentum to continuing public health improvements (Evans 1987). As Abram de Swaan argues in Chapter 7, cholera was especially effective in inducing elites to do something about the living and sanitation conditions of the poor. 'Plagues' of communicable diseases continued to afflict even peacetime Europe into the twentieth century. Elites were not immune. The threats of crime and of social and political unrest were also continuous elements in elite responses to poverty. The first modern welfare state was established, in Germany under Bismarck in the late nineteenth century, in large part to undercut the appeal of the world's premier working-class organization, the German Social Democratic Party. There was, however, in addition a broader and less explicit motivation: to try to consolidate a coalition of national interests in support of *the* national project – industrial, commercial and military rivalry with Great Britain. In Britain, growing unease at German rivalry coincided with the emergence of the age of mass industrialized warfare. The likely outcome of European conflicts was increasingly seen to depend on the capacity of states to mobilize into the armed forces the large numbers of young men who could be shifted around by modern railroads and equipped by modern armaments industries. The physical fitness of ordinary working-class men became an important strategic concern. The Boer War in South Africa initiated in Britain something of a panic that the typical working-class male, reared in poverty and unhealthy urban conditions, was medically unfit to bear arms. It was more than coincidence that, in 1905, the same national budget that marked the introduction of the welfare state in Britain made provision for a big increase in military expenditure, directed against Germany (Searle 1971).

Nineteenth-century elites were not driven to take action against poverty only by invocations of self-interest. We have noted above the power of Charles Booth's arguments, which did not rely only on a notion of an elite interest in poverty reduction, but appealed also to something closer to altruism: an empathy with the poor arising from a common British concern with fear of loss of respectability. Even earlier, American governments had introduced more extensive 'welfare' programmes than is generally credited, and had been persuaded to do so by arguments that combined appeals to both altruism and common interest. Some proponents of welfare were able to exploit the traumatic Civil War of the 1860s. A substantial national pensions programme was later constructed around the idea of honouring the injured veterans (of the victorious army) – although the links between actual access to these pensions and war injuries or service were often tenuous. Also in the nineteenth century, many state governments in the USA were persuaded to fund substantial family welfare programmes on the grounds that a country such as the USA could not afford, ethically or materially, to allow its future citizens to grow up in poverty, ill health or ignorance (Skocpol 1992).

It makes sense that the *negative drivers* – narrow appeals to the self-interest of elites – should have been more prevalent in the earlier nineteenth century and in less democratic contexts, while *positive drivers* (appeals to common interests) and *national altruistic arguments* (invocations of obligation to others within the same *national* community) should be more prominent later and in democratic contexts. For more representative and democratic government changes the character of politically persuasive argument: there are strong selection pressures against arguments that do not credibly justify public policies in terms of broad and inclusive benefits. The case that public health needs to be improved to protect the rich against diseases carried by the poor is not very compelling in a democracy.

The limited usefulness of negative drivers in a relatively democratic environment helps both to explain and to offset potential concerns about the fact that elites in contemporary developing countries do not appear much motivated by these negative drivers. On the basis of our research at least, and in contrast to European history, elites in the contemporary South do not seem to fear that the prevalence of poverty will have very marked, direct, adverse effects on their own lives and lifestyles (see Chapter 1). Especially since the collapse of the Soviet bloc, the threat of organized class-based revolution has disappeared from most of the world; the elites we interviewed were unconcerned by this possibility. The nature of modern military technology is such that the poor are generally not needed in large numbers to fight inter-state wars. Cash to purchase arms, a strong national economy and a relatively small but educated and trained cadre of professionals are the immediate sources of military strength (Singer 2003: 60–3). Threat of crime does preoccupy some elites, especially those in highly unequal countries such as Brazil and South Africa; but they tend not to identify the poor as the major or sole culprits, and instead direct some of the blame at combinations of 'non-poor' urban criminals and thugs, and view politicians and the police as implicated, either by omission or commission. There is some element of mystery about why elites do not appear concerned that they are at risk from disease transmitted by the poor. This issue was never spontaneously mentioned during our interviews. One can certainly rationalize this in terms of: the partial 'conquest' of most infectious and contagious diseases; the fact that poor-country elites are vulnerable primarily to the lifestyle diseases of the rich; and their capacity to obtain expensive private curative medical care. Yet on objective grounds elites should perhaps be worried. The World Health Organization is concerned that old communicable diseases such as tuberculosis, polio and malaria are re-emerging, some in virulent drug-resistant forms. New communicable health threats such as Ebola and HIV/AIDS are also receiving increased publicity.

Contemporary elites appear irrationally unconcerned about threats to their own health from the prevalence of poverty. That may be regarded more as an opportunity than a problem: as the world in general becomes more concerned about the resistance of some major diseases, new and old, to drug treatment, there is likely to be scope to persuade elites that it is in their interest – as well as the interests of society generally – to tackle public health issues in a more comprehensive way, and to place less faith in specific curative interventions. Equally, there is little doubt that the re-emergence of something like an international communist movement, actively recruiting the poor, would on balance do a great deal to focus the attention of elites on poverty.[8] We need not, however, for three reasons, be too depressed by the apparent impotence in the modern world of some of the classic negative drivers of elite concern for the poor: perceived threats of disease, crime, revolution and military weakness. First, arguments couched in terms of negative drivers and threats to the elite from the persistence of poverty are not very consistent with democratic politics. Second, such arguments have ambiguous and contradictory political implications, and are sometimes associated with repressive practices towards the poor. Third, there is evidence of the potential influence of positive drivers: perceptions that there are synergies and mutual benefits from reducing poverty.

Let us begin with the observation that the most consistent element in the responses of different national elites to our questions was the idea that 'education' was the main solution to poverty.[9] Why this emphasis on education? There seem to be at least three contributory explanations.

First, there is probably an element of pragmatism here, based on the perception that, whatever else governments failed to do – and our interviewees were very sceptical about the capacities of their governments – they were relatively capable of putting up schools and appointing teachers. The quality of output may not have been very good,[10] but at least something positive appeared to emerge at the end of the process – more visibly in relation to education than, say, health services. This is not a point to be dismissed lightly: elites are unlikely to support public action against poverty if they do not perceive a feasible route through which governments can act and achieve results (Chapter 7). Similarly, one of the attractions of education as a solution is that it is not controversial. Opposition to the principle of expanding educational provision is rare. That too is important. More often than we tend to believe, proposals for policy change fail not because they lack support, but because they generate opposition (Ascher 1984: 34, 310–11).

Second, education was popular in part because it was implicitly viewed as a cure for a variety of ills, including: (a) the enmeshment of the poor in fatalistic, traditional, lazy, unenterprising or narrow-minded attitudes;

(b) their exclusion, through lack of access to the right languages and literatures, from the great world of ideas and civilizations; and (c) their lack of technical, scientific and vocational skills and aptitudes. These distinctions are made by us, not in most cases by our interviewees. While they almost universally talked of education in terms of its instrumental rather than its intrinsic value, they generally had broad and imprecise notions of the potential causal effects of education on poverty. Among the more precise were some of our Bangladeshi interviewees, who were aware that their country stands out internationally for the record of its non-government organizations in providing stable micro-credit services to large numbers of people in rural areas, especially women. Many linked education – as a means of equipping people to manage credit and become small-scale entrepreneurs – with an image of a successful boot-strap operation to lift the country out of poverty through widespread enterprise and market-led improvement in the productivity of scarce non-human and abundant human resources.

Third, and most important for present purposes, there appeared to be a substantial acceptance of what one might call the 'human resources' conception of development: the notion that development involves, both as cause and effect, the improvement in the general *quality of human resources*. This notion can be interpreted, variously, as a matter of people who are physically fit enough to work regularly, dextrously and efficiently; psychologically adapted to the routines and procedures of modern organizations; emotionally attuned to self-seeking enterprise; and intellectually skilled in terms of both basic literacy and numeracy and more demanding and creative abilities. However the notion is interpreted, formal education and training will play a central role.

This notion that 'high-quality human resources' are somehow central to economic prosperity has virtually been orthodoxy in international development circles in recent years. There are some evident reasons for this. One is that it provides a plausible interpretation of the East Asian economic miracles, especially those of South Korea and Taiwan, which have been widely scrutinized by developing-country elites. While there is continuing dispute about the relative contributions of markets and state guidance to these 'miracles', there is broad acceptance that widespread, high-quality education played a very important role (Hannum and Buchmann 2003). Another is that it fits squarely with 'new knowledge economy' notions that the key to prosperity lies in a skilled, educated workforce. A third lies in the loss of credibility of the alternative 'conspicuous construction' approach which has been so influential in many Southern countries over the last half-century: the idea that much of the essence and motor of development lay in the construction of massive buildings and other physical facilities, whether purely symbolic (palaces in the jungle); largely symbolic (giant sports stadiums; massive plazas-cum-parade grounds in capital cities); or instrumental with a large prestige dimension (mega-dams; major highways; large mechanized state farms in smallholder societies; uneconomic steel plants and paper mills). Few developing countries that pursued these strategies achieved sustained economic progress.

This general elite sympathy for the positive effects of education implies that there is considerable scope to construct persuasive narratives that justify policies that might reduce poverty in terms of the achievement of other, broadly accepted goals. For example, in Bangladesh recent elite support for mass primary education has translated into support for conditional cash transfers to poor households sending children to school. This is in a context in which other forms of 'handouts' or social safety nets for the poor receive little support from elites at the centre. If they are to be persuasive, these narratives will vary from context to context. They are, however, likely to contain a combination of two or more of the following generic elements:

- Relatively specific arguments linking policies that will be pro-poor in outcome – whether they concern education, health, sanitation, social insurance, vocational training, environment, crime, security, housing, etc. – to the advancement of this widely accepted (human resource-based) conception of development. One well-known example already in use is the argument that girls' education is the best means of fertility control. Immunization may be linked to development via, for example, its contribution to making female labour more reliable and efficient by alleviating the burden of caring for sick children, or protecting national investments already made in educating children. Improving housing for the urban poor can similarly be linked to development as a means of improving the health and reliability of workers; facilitating planned as opposed to unplanned urban expansion; or protecting the vulnerable poor from crime or 'infection' by criminal influences.
- More general assertions about the essential incompatibility of poverty, destitution, degradation and oppression with the achievement or condition of 'development' or some other urgent national goal. For example, the contemporary Indonesian elite – which has an impressive record of poverty reduction over the past two decades – is most likely to be engaged by an anti-poverty programme that is framed in a language that addresses its urgent concern of 'national unity'.
- Appeals, explicit or implicit, to a sense of rivalry with other similar countries, especially neighbouring countries, and to the sense of national pride that can be evoked through the belief that one is doing better

than one's neighbours. National pride matters a great deal. People like to show visitors that they are doing well in something, and especially doing better than what social scientists term their 'comparators'. The concept of 'development' provides many opportunities for displaying some kind of achievement.

- Arguments totally lacking visible instrumental content, which justify particular courses of action in terms of some variant of *national altruism*, i.e. doing what is right for the people of one's country. The most persuasive narratives have 'moral' as well as instrumental content.
- A plausible account of how particular objectives might in practice be achieved through public action. Persuasive narratives need to demonstrate not just that there is a problem that needs solving, but that there is a feasible solution.

The construction of persuasive narratives that link poverty reduction to broader national goals is not a job for economists, social scientists, aid donors or technocrats. Radio, print and TV journalists, writers and dramatists are more likely to have the requisite skills. This is, however, principally a job for politicians: devising and sustaining persuasive narratives is what good politicians do continually.

In summary

This book is self-evidently not a social engineering text. We undertook the research to try to satisfy some curiosity about the world. It is only in the course of interpreting our findings that we became optimistic about their practical value. We can see how a better understanding of how elites perceive poverty might contribute to public policies that will help reduce that poverty. As with any new type of knowledge – and especially with knowledge that is subjective, political and contested – the likely linkages to policy are difficult to predict. This chapter is not a forecast. We have rather painted a scenario, explaining why and how, in the circumstances typically prevailing in developing countries, the kind of knowledge that we have presented in this book might usefully inform public policy, by stimulating attempts to change either (a) elite understandings of the causes and character of poverty to make them more sympathetic to anti-poverty initiatives, or (b) the presentation of the role and purpose of those programmes, to better correspond with elite perceptions of poverty. There are seven elements to this scenario:

- Although the polities of the developing world are very diverse, one regularity is that power tends to be relatively concentrated in the hands of the kinds of people we have been interviewing – small national elites.

Compared with the historical experience of the now rich countries, these elites derive much of their power and influence from their roles as intermediaries in economic, political and cultural interactions between their countries and the external world.

- National elites have ambiguous attitudes towards, and interests in, the reduction of poverty and inequality. On the one hand, they might benefit from being powerful and wealthy in the midst of poverty, and fear the consequences of any significant change. On the other hand, they might often perceive poverty as a problem and a threat – a threat to the welfare of 'people like them', or to the prosperity, security or dignity of a larger (national) political and moral community with which they identify themselves.

- These concerns about the potential adverse effects of poverty and inequality are sufficiently salient, either actually or potentially, that they might often lead elites to support public action that reduces poverty.

- The concept of poverty is highly *plastic*: it not only means different things to different people, but understandings might in some circumstances be deliberately reframed to increase the receptivity of elites to anti-poverty concerns.

- This potential is likely to be realized mainly in national or even more local contexts: people are most likely to engage positively with interpretations of poverty that are formulated in their local languages and idioms, and framed in terms of local experience and culture.

- The international agencies and organizations concerned with economic development and poverty reduction not only pay no attention to these framing issues, but in practice behave in a contrary fashion, by promoting uniform, globalized concepts and definitions of poverty.

- More attention to locally appropriate framing of notions of poverty might pay dividends in terms of positive engagement of the attentions of local elites. 'As politicians know only too well but social scientists often forget, public policy is made of language' (Majone 1989).

Notes

1 Many people have contributed to the ideas presented here. We thank in particular: John Toye, for the initial inspiration; the fellow researchers with whom we have interacted over several years on this project – Gerard Clarke, Abram de Swaan, Anand Inbanathan, Jim Manor, Else Øyen, Elisa Reis, Marites Sison and Omar Thomaz; and Ben Dickinson, Sue Lane and Sue Unsworth for giving us their perceptions as aid practitioners.

2 The realist might believe that political culture either (a) is shaped and employed instrumentally by elites for purposes of social control or (b) simply has no significant independent consequences.

3 Mares (2003) has recently demonstrated the significant role that business interests sometimes played in constructing the welfare states of the contemporary rich countries.

4 In reality, there was a high degree of subjectivity in Booth's fact-gathering exercises. Although the notion of different classes among the poor was central to his analysis, the lines between them were defined in loose and impressionistic terms.

5 For some statements of the increasing influence of ideational variables in recent political science, see Berman (2001), Hanson (2003) and Lieberman (2002).

6 In the *Voices of the Poor* report, poverty is redefined as *ill-being*. In addition to references to various kinds of material poverty and ill health, the following dimensions of ill-being appear in the table of contents: *insecurity, (lack of) freedom of choice and action, exclusion, rejection, isolation, loneliness, vulnerability, worry, fear, powerlessness, helplessness, frustration, anger, humiliation, shame, anguish, grief, stigma, male frustration, anxiety, sense of inferiority, domestic abuse and violence, social exclusion, crime, persecution by police, lack of justice* and *lack of responsiveness*.

7 We were not, in this research, able to explore the hypothesis that the structural ties that link elites to the populations of their national territories might consistently be weaker in much of the contemporary South than in 'historical Europe'. In 'historical Europe', especially after industrialization, not only was the labour of the poor actually or potentially valuable, but the upper classes in general were engaged directly, albeit rarely face to face, with the poor in the process of production: the living conditions of the upper classes depended directly and visibly on the extraction of a surplus through the labour of the poor in the farms and factories owned by those upper classes. Did this direct material dependence on the poor significantly influence perceptions of poverty and beliefs about public policy? Are many of the perceptions and attitudes that we picked up in our interviews a reflection of the fact that many elites in the contemporary South are caught in a vice of cognitive dissonance? On the one hand, the dominant discourses of democracy and developmentalism, especially as aid donors shape them, impel elites to talk of poverty as if it were an important personal and national concern. On the other hand, because so many of their livelihoods are derived from political, bureaucratic, professional and trading activities, and from urban property ownership, they are not seriously engaged with the poor, directly or indirectly, as individuals or as members of a class. Differences within our five cases tend to support this hypothesis. Capitalist relations of production are more extensive in Brazil and South Africa than in our other three countries, and it was mainly in Brazil and South Africa that we found respondents who appeared to think of the poor in terms of their labour potential. These are big, important questions, difficult to research, but possibly crucial to the future of nation-states and the kind of social solidarity to which we still aspire.

8 We say 'on balance' because the cold war had some adverse effects in relation to poverty: while helping to mobilize some elites – as under the US-led Alliance for Progress in Latin America – it also helped (in Latin America

and elsewhere) to stimulate and legitimize the repression of political movements based among the working classes and the poor.

9 Family planning was also popular, probably for similar reasons.

10 Policies to widen access to education may be generally more politically feasible than those that aim to improve the quality of education (Corrales 1999).

References

Ascher, W. (1984) *Scheming for the Poor. The Politics of Redistribution in Latin America*, Cambridge, MA and London: Harvard University Press

Berman, S. (2001) 'Review Article: Ideas, Norms and Culture in Political Analysis', *Comparative Politics*, 33 (2): 231–50

Booth, C. (1892) *Life and Labour of the People in London*, London: Macmillan

Corrales, J. (1999) 'The Politics of Education Reform: Bolstering the Supply and Demand; Overcoming Institutional Blocks', *Education Reform and Management Series,* II (1), Washington, DC: World Bank

Evans, R. (1987) *Death in Hamburg: Society and Politics in the Cholera Years 1830–1910*, London: Penguin

Hannum, E. and C. Buchmann (2003) *The Consequences of Global Educational Expansion. Social Science Perspectives*, Cambridge, MA: American Academy of Arts and Sciences

Hansom, S. E. (2003) 'From Culture to Ideology in Comparative Politics', *Comparative Politics*, 35 (3): 355–76

Himmelfarb, G. (1991) *Poverty and Compassion: The Moral Imagination of the Late Victorians*, New York: Knopf

Lieberman, R. C. (2002) 'Ideas, Institutions, and Political Order: Explaining Political Change', *American Political Science Review*, 96 (4): 697–712

Majone, G. (1989) *Evidence, Argument and Persuasion in the Policy Process*, New Haven, CT and London: Yale University Press

Mares, I. (2003) *The Politics of Social Risk: Business and Welfare State Development*, Cambridge: Cambridge University Press

Mayhew, C. (1851–62) *London Labour and London Poor*, 4 vols, London

Searle, G. R. (1971) *The Quest for National Efficiency: A Study in British Politics and Political Thought, 1899–1914*, Oxford: Basil Blackwell

Singer, P. W. (2003) *Corporate Warriors: The Rise of the Privatized Military Industry*, Ithaca and London: Columbia University Press

Skocpol, T. (1992) *Protecting Soldiers and Mothers: The Political Origins of Social Policy in the United States*, Cambridge, MA: Belknap Press

Toye, J. (1999) 'Nationalising the Anti-poverty Agenda', *IDS Bulletin*, 30 (2): 6–12.

About the contributors

Gerard Clarke is a senior lecturer at the Centre for Development Studies, University of Wales, Swansea. Author of *The Politics of NGOs in South-East Asia: Participation and Protest in the Philippines* (Routledge: New York and London, 1998), his main research interests cluster around NGOs, civil society and development, especially in South-East Asia.

Naomi Hossain is a political sociologist currently based at the Research and Evaluation Division of BRAC in Bangladesh, where she is involved in research on village-level governance and the ultra-poor. Her book *Elite Perceptions of Poverty in Bangladesh* will be published by University Press Limited in Dhaka in 2005.

Noushin Kalati's work has focused on human rights, law and elites. She has studied at the Universities of Warwick, London and Westminster, and is currently a government analyst in London.

James Manor is a professorial fellow of the Institute of Development Studies, University of Sussex. He is the former director of the Institute of Commonwealth Studies, University of London, and has also taught at Yale, Harvard and Leicester Universities.

Mick Moore is a political scientist with over three decades of experience of researching, teaching and advising on issues of poverty and development in the South. He is currently professorial fellow at the Institute of Development Studies, University of Sussex, and director, Centre for the Future State. His most recent book, co-edited with Peter Houtzager, is *Changing Paths: International Development and the New Politics of Inclusion*, Michigan University Press, 2003.

Elisa Reis is professor of political sociology at the Federal University of Rio de Janeiro and a member of the Brazilian Academy of Sciences. She is current president of the Research Committee on Sociological Theory of the International Sociological Association, former president of the Brazilian National Association for the Social Sciences (ANPOCS) and former general secretary of the Brazilian Society of Sociology (SBS).

Omar Ribeiro Thomaz obtained his BA in art history from the University of Barcelona and his PhD in social anthropology from the University of São Paulo. Currently engaged as professor within the Anthropology Department at the State University of Campinas, he is also a research fellow at the Brazilian Center for Research and Planning (CEBRAP). His *Ecos do Atlântico Sul: representações sobre o Terceiro Império Português* was awarded as the best work of social sciences in Brazil in 2003 by the National Association of Social Scientists. He coordinates the work of researchers involved with the group 'Post-colonialism, nation and conflict', based at the University of Campinas and CEBRAP. His interests include Mozambique, Uganda and Haiti.

Marites N. Sison has been a journalist since 1986. She has worked as a correspondent for World Press Review and the wire agency Inter Press Service, and as a stringer for the *New York Times*. She has won awards in investigative journalism for articles published by the Philippine Center for Investigative Journalism, and, most recently, the New California Media Awards in the US. She has authored two books and has contributed to various journalism anthologies. She now writes from Toronto, Canada.

Abram De Swaan is research professor of social science at the University of Amsterdam and held the chair of sociology from 1973 until 2001. He was co-founder and dean of the Amsterdam School for Social Research (1987–97) and is presently its chairman. He has held visiting professorships at the New School, Columbia and Cornell, the Ecole des Hautes Etudes, the Ecole de Science Politique and the College de France. His major books are: *Coalition Theory and Cabinet Formations*, 1973; *In Care of the State: Health Care, Education and Welfare in Europe and the USA in the Modern Era*, 1988; *The Management of Normality; Critical Essays in Health and Welfare*, 1990; and *Words of the World: The Global Language System*, 2001. His most recent research is on the state, mass extermination and social identifications ('Murder and the state').

Index

labour, organized, 28 *see also* trade unions
land: *latifundia* ownership, 30; redistribution of, 47 (in Bangladesh, 48)
land reform, 167, 173
landless movements, 47
landowners, 28, 31, 93
languages: Creole (incorporation of, into educational system, 148; use of, 128, 131, 136, 137, 147, 148, 149, 188 (as cause of poverty, 147, 150)); French (as language of domination, 147; as symbolic good, 137; use of, 128, 136, 139, 140, 144, 148, 149, 150, 188)
Lavalas Family (Haiti), 149
Lavalasianisme, 142
Lebanese migrants to Haiti, 138
life expectancy, in Haiti, 127, 134
Lions Club, 75
literacy, 145, 199, 205; anti-illiteracy campaigns, 143; in Haiti, 134, 136
living standards, minimum, definition of, 8
local elites, contact with the poor, 117
L'Ouverture, Toussaint, 129

Macapagal-Arroyo, Gloria, 81–2
maids, domestic, 69, 70
malaria, 189; re-emergence of, 19, 162, 203
malnutrition, deaths from, 65–6
Malval, Robert, 138
Manigat, Leslie, 138, 144
Manor, James, 11
Marcos, Ferdinand, 61–2, 67, 81
market, faith in, 192
Maroons, 129, 131
Marx, Karl, 8
Marxism, immizeration theory of, 184
Mayhew, *London Labour and London Poor*, 195–6
Mbeki, Thabo, 161
Mendonça, R., 30
methodology of research, 1, 16, 32–4, 58–60

Metro Manila, 74, 80; squatters in, 73
micro-credit, 111; organizations in Bangladesh, 96; provision of, 114, 115–16, 205 (for poor women, 116)
migration: back to the land, 47; of Haitians, 131; of Lebanese to Haiti, 138; to cities, 28, 65, 97, 106, 108, 143, 162, 191
Mills, C. Wright, 2
Mindanao, 65, 67
misperceptions of poverty, 18
mobility, social, 47 (in Brazil, 33–4); spatial, of elites, 171
Moore, Mick, 21
mortality, infant, 109, 134
motivations of research project, 1, 3–4
Mozambique, as research subject, 9
mulattos, 129, 130, 140, 144–5, 188; survival strategies of, 137
multicultural societies, 10

nation states, 188; common institutional features of, 15
national altruism, 207
national unity, concern for, 206–7
négritude, 138
neo-liberalism, 183
noirisme, 131, 138, 142
non-governmental organizations (NGOs), 2, 14, 59, 96, 102, 116, 142; ambivalence towards, in Haiti, 146–7; effectiveness questioned, 116, 119; elite suspicions about, 45; in Bangladesh, 16, 20, 111, 115, 205; in Philippines, 16; involvement in social policy, 45; lifestyle of staff of, 146–7; pride in, 120; reservations about, 51; role in poverty reduction, 112 (in Philippines, 79–80)
norms about poverty, 3
nouveaux riches, 128
Le Nouvelliste, 128

oligarchy, national, in Philippines, 60–1

Index